Karoline Johanna Baumann

The Stage as Palimpsest

BIBLIOTHECA ACADEMICA

Reihe

Literaturwissenschaft

Band 6

ERGON VERLAG

Karoline Johanna Baumann

The Stage as Palimpsest

Conceptions of Time and Temporality in Shakespeare's *Troilus and Cressida* and *The Two Noble Kinsmen*

ERGON VERLAG

Zugl.: Berlin, Univ., Diss., 2013

Umschlagabbildung:
Salvator Rosa: *Studie für die Darstellung des Cadmus, der Drachenzähne sät.*
bpk / Kupferstichkabinett, Staatliche Museen zu Berlin / Dietmar Katz

Bibliografische Information der Deutschen Nationalbibliothek
Die Deutsche Nationalbibliothek verzeichnet diese Publikation in der Deutschen Nationalbibliografie; detaillierte bibliografische Daten sind im Internet über http://dnb.d-nb.de abrufbar.

Gedruckt auf alterungsbeständigem Papier.
Satz: Matthias Wies, Ergon-Verlag
Umschlaggestaltung: Jan von Hugo

www.ergon-verlag.de

ISBN 978-3-95650-465-5 (Print)
ISBN 978-3-95650-466-2 (ePDF)
ISSN 2198-2392

Contents

Introduction

This study examines how different notions of time and temporality are reflected in Shakespeare's *Troilus and Cressida* and Shakespeare and Fletcher's *The Two Noble Kinsmen*. I will read the plays with the help of the metaphor of the *palimpsest*, a term borrowed from palaeography to express the simultaneous existence of multiple temporal layers in a particular moment of time, an object or a literary text. Both plays derive ultimately from ancient sources (the *Iliad*, the *Thebaid*) that were rewritten many times throughout the Middle Ages. For both plays, the author(s) draw mostly on Chaucer's adaptations (*The Knight's Tale*, *Troilus and Criseyde*), although translations of the ancient classical sources existed, foregrounding the multi-layered, palimpsest-like nature of literary texts. Traces of different times are inscribed in plot, characters, motifs and conventions of works of literature, and the well-documented past of these plays facilitates the 'excavation' of these traces. The metaphor of the antisequential palimpsest is therefore not only particularly useful for reading these plays, but is also a helpful way to imagine time in general. It is much more productive than the idea of time as a unilinear sequence of events or of history as a series of clearly distinguishable periods that succeed and replace one another in chronological order.

The figure of the palimpsest has been used widely in poststructuralist and postcolonial discourse at least since Gérard Genette's influential *Palimpsests: Literature in the Second Degree*,[1] but it was already popular in the 19th century after Charles Baudelaire, influenced by Thomas de Quincey's *Confessions of an English Opium-Eater*, had compared human memory to a palimpsest in *Artificial Paradises*.[2] For the purpose of this study, however, I will mostly draw upon Jonathan Gil Harris's use of the term *palimpsest* in his book *Untimely Matter in the Time of Shakespeare*.[3] Harris does not regard the palimpsest merely as writing, as a specific kind of textuality, as was usually done in the wake of Genette's analysis.[4] Genette uses the palimpsest to describe a set of paratextual effects that alter and rewrite a past text. Harris reads *objects* as palimpsests as well, for example stage properties

1 Gérard Genette, *Palimpsests: Literature in the Second Degree* (Lincoln, Nebr.: University of Nebraska Press, 1997).

2 Charles Baudelaire, *Artificial Paradises*, trans. by Stacy Diamond (New York: Citadel Press, 1996), pp.147-149. Baudelaire briefly refers to the literary tradition as palimpsest-like as well: "The Grecian tragedy seemed to be displaced, but was *not* displaced, by the monkish legend; and the monkish legend seemed to be displaced, but was *not* displaced, by the knightly romance". *Ibid*, p.149.

3 Jonathan Gil Harris, *Untimely Matter in the Time of Shakespeare* (Philadelphia: University of Pennsylvania Press, 2009).

4 Harris (2009), pp. 16-17.

whose "cultural biography",[5] he argues, also needs to be taken into account. The "'new' new historicism of the object," as Patricia Fumerton calls it,[6] tends, like the "'old' new historicism of the subject",[7] to contextualise *syn*chronically, to focus, for the most part, on objects' cotemporal 'social life,' their present social and cultural significance.[8] In the practice of 'thick description'[9] made popular by Clifford Geertz, early modern feathers, for example, are discussed within the contexts of newly established global trade networks.[10] But objects' journey over time needs to be considered as well, because it forms and determines their cultural significance. To give an example, the religious past of early modern stage costumes, their former existence as ecclesiastical robes in churches and monasteries was still contained in them when they were used in theatres after the Reformation. Peter Stallybrass and Ann Rosalind Jones describe how the costume worn by the ghost of Hamlet's father, for instance, is still haunted by its past.[11] As Stallybrass argues, "clothes have a life of their own; they both *are* material presences and they *encode* other material and immaterial presences".[12] The sleeve which Troilus gives to Cressida as a token of love in *Troilus and Cressida*, and which Cressida then gives to Diomedes, incorporates its former owners, too: "Into the sleeve which passes from hand to hand, which has no secure owner or origin, are woven the identities of both Troilus and Cressida"[13] or, as Cressida puts it, "He that takes that [the sleeve] doth take my heart withal".[14]

---

5 Igor Kopytoff, "The Cultural Biography of Things: Commoditization as Process", in *The Social Life of Things: Commodities in Cultural Perspective*, ed. Arjun Appadurai (Cambridge: Cambridge University Press, 1986), pp.64-91. See also Harris (2009), pp.8-9.

6 Patricia Fumerton, "Introduction: A New New Historicism", in *Renaissance Culture and the Everyday*, eds. Patricia Fumerton and Simon Hunt (Philadelphia: University of Pennsylvania Press, 1999), pp.1-17.

7 Harris (2009), p.1.

8 Harris (2009), p.8.

9 See Clifford Geertz, *The Interpretation of Cultures* (New York: Basic Books, 1973), *passim.*

10 See Margaret W. Ferguson, "Feathers and Flies: Aphra Behn and the Seventeenth-Century Trade in Exotica", in *Subject and Object in Renaissance Culture*, eds. Margreta de Grazia, Maureen Quilligan and Peter Stallybrass (Cambridge: Cambridge University Press, 1996), pp. 235-259, and Harris (2009), p.8.

11 Ann Rosalind Jones and Peter Stallybrass, *Renaissance Clothing and the Materials of Memory* (Cambridge: Cambridge University Press, 2000), especially pp. 245-268. See also Harris (2009), pp.9-10.

12 Peter Stallybrass, "Worn Worlds: Clothes and Identity on the Renaissance Stage", in *Subject and Object in Renaissance Culture*, pp. 289-320, p.312.

13 Stallybrass, p.313.

14 *Troilus and Cressida*, ed. David Bevington, The Arden Shakespeare, Third Series (London: Thomson Learning, 1998, 2006), 5.2.88. All future quotations from *Troilus and Cressida* are taken from this edition and will be given in the body of the text.

But it is equally insufficient to 'read' objects *only* diachronically. Harris argues that Fredric Jameson's famous call to "always historicize!"[15] should not be understood as *either* "always synchronize" *or* "always diachronize", but should be taken to mean "always polychronize.[16] The palimpsest represents a *polychronic* temporality, a "temporality which is not one", as Kathleen Biddick puts it.[17] It means that the past, in fact multiple pasts (as well as futures), are contained in the present and that supposedly distinct, disparate moments of time are anachronistically conjoined, "compressed"[18] in a palimpsest-like manner.

Not only objects such as the stage clothes can be read as palimpsests. A theatre company's stage practices, acting styles or special effects constitute palimpsests as well.[19] It is important to note that the palimpsest is not an inert accumulation of inscriptions that just passively accrue over time. The different temporal layers each retain their ability to speak and to act. The palimpsest thus constitutes a "network of agency"[20] in which the traces of various times constantly rework and rewrite each other. Earlier inscriptions transform what has been written over them, while this, in turn, changes earlier writings. The inscriptions are not necessarily transparently legible, but even the most archaic or even obscure inscriptions are able to reorganise later ones and vice versa, so that they are constantly in a process of mutual transformation. Most importantly, there is no linear or hierarchical relationship between them. And just as the material writing surface, the vellum or parchment on which a text is written, enables the writing even as it is transformed by it, readers and writers from different times who work upon the palimpsest transform it, and are themselves transformed by it.[21]

The concept of the palimpsest-like, simultaneous and 'anachronistic' existence of various temporal layers in one moment of time contradicts notions of linear, hierarchical time and periodization systems that organise time into discrete temporal units of distinct, successive epochs. A past that resides in the present (or multiple pasts that reside in the present) is (are) never completely over or gone.

Nevertheless, as Michel de Certeau has pointed out, our image of the past tends to be pre-structured by the idea that the past, by necessity, constitutes an

---

15 Fredric Jameson, *The Political Unconscious: Narrative as a Socially Symbolic Act* (New York: Methuen, 1981), p.I.

16 Harris (2009), p.10.

17 Kathleen Biddick, *The Typological Imaginary: History, Technology, Circumcision* (Philadelphia: University of Pennsylvania Press, 2003), p.20.

18 Harris (2009), pp.16, 86.

19 Harris (2009), p.20.

20 Harris (2009), p.17.

21 Harris (2009), pp.16-17.

Other.[22] We encounter the past with the preconceived expectation of encountering cultural alterity, because we assume an *a priori* gap between the present and the past. Therefore discourse on the past is, in a very predictable way, informed by prevalent notions of alterity[23] and almost invariably takes the form of a *heterology*, as de Certeau calls it, a discourse on the *Other*.[24]

Of all past times this applies to the Middle Ages in a most particular way, because modernity usually defines itself in *opposition* to it. The Middle Ages or premodernity often gets assigned the role of the "all-purpose alternative",[25] our "all-purpose other".[26] A further theoretical concept I will draw upon is therefore the concept of Othering. Othering describes the mechanisms by which a Self constructs an Other, often in binary opposition, from those parts that it chooses not to acknowledge. This process is called Othering because those factors of the Self that are, for whatever reasons, perceived as negative, are externalised and projected elsewhere – on an Other created specifically for this purpose, which thus turns out as the Self's binary opposite. While the process of differentiation enables the Self to define itself, the (fictional) separation from negative qualities, their externalisation, creates an illusion of mastery.[27] The concept of a "self-consolidating other"[28] is derived from Jacques Lacan's description of the basic formation of identity[29] and the verb, "Othering", was coined for the process of collective identity formation by Gayatri Spivak in a conference on "Europe and its Others".[30] According to Lacan, a child that sees its own image in the mirror perceives enough resemblance in order to recognise itself but, at the same time, the reflection is sufficiently separate for the child to ground hopes of mastery. While the child had perceived itself, before this moment, as an incoherent and uncoordinated mass of limbs, this "anticipated mastery", albeit a fiction, from now on becomes the basis of its ego.[31] As Postcolonialists have shown in particular, collective identity construction can work

22 Michel de Certeau, *The Writing of History* (New York: Columbia University Press, 1988), pp.1-16.

23 de Certeau (1988), p.5.

24 Michel de Certeau, *Heterologies: Discourse on the Other* (Minneapolis: University of Minnesota Press, 1986, 1995), *passim.*

25 Lee Patterson, "On the Margin: Postmodernism, Ironic History, and Medieval Studies", *Speculum* 65 (1990), pp.87-108, p.93.

26 Lee Patterson, "The Return to Philology," in *The Past and Future of Medieval Studies*, ed. John Van Engen (Notre Dame: The University of Notre Dame Press, 1994), pp.231-244, p.237.

27 Bill Ashcroft, Gareth Griffiths and Helen Tiffin, *Key Concepts in Post-Colonial Studies* (New York, London: Routledge, 1998), p.170.

28 Gayatri Chakravorty Spivak, "The Rani of Sirmur", in *Europe and its Others, Vol. 1: Proceedings of the Essex Conference on the Sociology of Literature, July 1984*, ed. by Francis Barker *et al.* (Colchester: University of Essex, 1985), pp.128-151, p.131.

29 See Jacques Lacan, "Some Reflections on the Ego", *International Journal of Psychoanalysis*, 34:1 (1953), pp.11-17.

30 The *Essex Conference on the Sociology of Literature* in 1984. See *Europe and its Others* and *Key Concepts in Post-Colonial Studies*, p.171.

31 See Ashcroft, Griffiths and Tiffin, p.170.

in a similar way; the 'West', for example, has defined itself with the help of alterity by constructing the Orient as its dichotomic Other. But mechanisms of Othering are at work in many other binary pairs as well, for example in the opposition of man/woman, black/white, animal/human, animal/machine, culture/nature, and also modern/premodern. Like the invention of the Orient as its geographical Other by the Occident it has invented the Middle Ages as its temporal Other, a colonised past: time and space are interconvertible in this respect.[32] Othering occurs not only with geographically distinct areas, as Postcolonial Theory has pointed out, but also with areas of temporal distance. Premodernity arguably constitutes such a temporal Orient. It is no coincidence, therefore, that the first construction of the Middle Ages coincides with the beginnings of colonial expansion.[33] When Europe's imperialist project was beginning, it distanced itself from its own past, creating "Europe's Dark Continent of History, even as Africa is its Dark Ages of Geography".[34] The Middle Ages, like the child in the mirror, are "both a native past and an exotic otherness"[35] for modernity, an inverted mirror image. While this has contributed to the marginalisation of the Middle Ages, the Renaissance, on the other hand, is seen as the beginning of almost everything that is associated with the modern.[36] Whether subjectivity, nationalism or capitalism, it is readily supposed that its origins lie in the Renaissance, too readily supposed, as Margreta de Grazia argues: the link between the early modern and the latest modern is often taken for granted and parallels are too easily assumed and confirmed[37] when the Renaissance is made to appear as the beginning

> of every modern this-or-that: of subjectivity, the literary, literary subjectivity, pragmatism, technology, the world market, mercantile capitalism, commodity fetishism, slavery, contact with the East, urban sprawl, providentially driven fatality akin to terrorism, every manner of consciousness and the unconscious, including historical consciousness and more recently ecological consciousness.[38]

The Middle Ages, on the other hand, are condemned to be eternally Other, "obscure, difficult, strange, alien".[39] But premodernity's role as an area of undifferentiated Otherness[40] is as misleading as our taken-for-granted affinities with the

---

32 See John Dagenais and Margaret R. Greer, "Decolonizing the Middle Ages: Introduction", *Journal of Medieval and Early Modern Studies*, 30:3 (Fall 2000), pp.431-448, pp.434-435.

33 See Dagenais and Greer, p.431.

34 Dagenais and Greer, *ibid.*

35 John M. Ganim, *Medievalism and Orientalism: Three Essays on Literature, Architecture and Cultural Identity* (New York: Palgrave Macmillan, 2005), p.6.

36 Cf. Patterson (1990), p.92.

37 Margreta de Grazia, "The Modern Divide: From Either Side", *Journal of Medieval and Early Modern Studies* 37:3 (2007), pp.453-467, p.458.

38 de Grazia, p.458.

39 Patterson (1990), p.92.

40 Jeffrey Jerome Cohen,"Introduction: Midcolonial" in *The Postcolonial Middle Ages*, ed. Jeffrey Jerome Cohen (London: Macmillan Press, 2000), pp.1-17, p.4.

early modern age and, as David Aers argues, they probably result from the history of the subject, for example, being told as a linear, developmental story, which thus needs a clear beginning. So a transition from a field of complete Otherness is posited, an Otherness in which the subject, or whatever needs to be described, did not exist and against which it can be defined.[41]

But like other progress narratives and teleological histories, this offers no explanation for the uncanny presence of supposedly past violence and traumata within 'modern' societies,[42] just as the location of 'barbaric,' 'primitive,' cruel elements within foreign cultures does not explain their existence in one's own culture, or help deal with it, as the "fiction of mastery"[43] seems to promise.

Medievalists have therefore suggested the concepts of "Postcolonial Middle Ages"[44] and the Middle Ages' decolonisation as analogies to the decolonisation of geographical Otherness.[45] Constructed as a time of complementary Otherness, they argue, the Middle Ages are subject to the same colonised status as a colonised country, belonging to the nation of modernity, so to speak, but never able to achieve full citizenship in it.[46] The project of decolonisation, therefore, intends to disrupt linear time, like dichotomised space, and to excavate the "minus in the origin", in Homi Bhabha's words,[47] of Western progress narratives.[48] The notion of history's unidirectional movement through linear time[49] should be replaced by one of more hybrid temporalities[50] and, instead of constructing time's "linearisation as chronology",[51] our idea of time should allow for temporal interlacement and the coexistence of various temporalities. Instead of believing the simple master narrative of progress and total alterity,[52] we should conceive of the Middle Ages as an epoch that was different, but not the inverse of modernity.[53]

---

41 Cf. David Aers, "A Whisper in the Ear of Early Modernists; or, Reflections on Literary Critics Writing the 'History of the Subject,'" in *Culture and History 1350-1600: Essays on English Communities, Identities and Writing*, ed. by David Aers (New York: Harvester Wheatsheaf, 1992), pp.177-202, p.196.

42 Cf. Cohen (2000), pp.2-3.

43 Ashcroft, Griffiths and Tiffin, p.170.

44 See *The Postcolonial Middle Ages*, ed. Jeffrey Jerome Cohen (London: Macmillan Press, 2000), *passim*.

45 Dagenais and Greer, *passim*.

46 Dagenais and Greer, p.431.

47 Homi K. Bhabha, "DissemiNation: Time, Narrative, and the Margins of the Modern Nation", in *The Location of Culture* (New York, London: Routledge, 1994), pp.199-244, p.222.

48 See Kathleen Davis, "National Writing in the Ninth Century: A Reminder for Postcolonial Thinking about the Nation", *Journal of Medieval and Early Modern Studies*, 28:3 (1998), pp.611-637, p.630.

49 Cf. Dagenais and Greer, p.434.

50 Cohen (2000), p.1.

51 Cohen (2000), p.2.

52 Cf. Cohen (2000), p.6.

53 See Davis, *A Reminder for Postcolonial Thinking about the Nation*, p.629.

A Middle Ages that is present in the Renaissance and that 'acts' in the early modern collective consciousness resists the hierarchizing narrative of time as a chronological, teleological sequence of events. *Troilus and Cressida*, the topic of the first part of this study, is set in ancient Troy with protagonists from the Middle Ages. Shakespeare's adaptation of the Troy-material is not based on George Chapman's then recently published translation of the *Iliad*, but draws, for the most part, on a medieval source: Chaucer's *Troilus and Criseyde*. The characters Criseyde and Troilus are medieval additions to the Troy material that originate from the medieval romance tradition. If literature is to be seen as an especially dense repository of cultural memory,[54] then these 'medieval' antiquities put medieval lenses before our image of antiquity, or perhaps even stencils, creating a more complex image "of heterogeneity, overlap, sedimentation, and multiplicity"[55] than that of the Middle Ages as a simply 'inversed' modernity. The medieval characters acting in ancient Troy illustrate how recent history co-writes and re-writes more ancient history, how in a palimpsest recent layers rewrite and change earlier ones. The teichoscopy scene in *Troilus and Cressida* (Act I Scene 2) is also a good example of a polychronic network of multiple times, because it exists in so many variations since the 'original' scene of this kind in Book III of the *Iliad*, all of which have left traces in Shakespeare's. Not only does the 'original' text and do earlier inscriptions influence more recent ones, in the way we perceive the scene, but also the other way around. The behaviour of the protagonists is to a high degree influenced by their own literary fame, which precedes them and of which they are fully conscious. Their futures, especially the one Robert Henryson devised for them in his sequel to, or rather alternative ending of, *Troilus and Criseyde*, *The Testament of Cresseid*, influences their behaviour at earlier points in the plot: they display a certain resignation with regard to their 'fate'. This concerns not only the protagonists but also the larger frame, ancient Troy, where the story is set: the fall of Troy, although it does not occur in this play, appears to be a defining characteristic of the city of Troy even while it stands.

In the next chapter, I argue that *Troilus and Cressida* performatively recreates the period constellation of modernity and a Middle Ages constructed as its diametric opposite in the way the two opposed parties of Troy and Greece are arranged in binary opposition to each other, showing that indeed spatial concepts of alterity are applicable to fields of temporal distance. Troy and its Greek besiegers are drawn as complementary: while Troy appears as a medieval world that is committed to values like chivalry, honour, honesty and humility, connected with the literary genre of poetry, the Greeks are representatives of a Renaissance culture that is associated with cynicism, decadence, dissimulation, the lack of a

54 See Ania Loomba, "Periodization, Race, and Global Contact", *Journal of Medieval and Early Modern Studies* 37:3 (2007), pp.595-620, p.596.

55 Cohen (2000), pp.2-3.

reliable value system, haughtiness, overestimation and the literary form of drama.[56] Although the Middle Ages appear more positive here, while modernity gets assigned the negative attributes, this is in fact coherent with the concept of Othering. The Other can also be idealised as something to aspire to. In that case, the inversion is inversed, so to speak, and what is positive is located with the Other and what is negative with the Self, as when the Middle Ages were, for example, idealised by the Romantics. The Middle Ages are then, typically, perceived as a time of stability, while the present is in a (constant) state of crisis. But this remains within the same paradigm, because the past, the Middle Ages, still remains the Other, entirely different from the Self. *Troilus and Cressida*, nonetheless, shows that the two parts are merely two sides of the same coin and that the separation is a projection mostly with the help of the key characters, Hector and Achilles, who are drawn as the embodiments of their respective parties. This goes so far that the scene in which Achilles kills Hector indicates not only the fact that Troy is going to be destroyed, but also the exact way in which this is going to happen. The two archenemies also assimilate here to such a degree that they become almost indistinguishable: employing the same metre and rhyme, they speak their verses in harmony and one takes up the line of the other and finishes it. Almost paradoxically, but not quite, it is their very opposition that makes Achilles and Hector so similar. The binary pairs Hector/Achilles, or Troy/Greece, medieval, premodern/(early) modern merge. The lines of division that marked off the dichotomic opposites vanish and leave the parts as inseparable, showing that they are ultimately one and the same, that the Other really is a part of the Self. I mean "merge" quite literally here, because I also argue that the way Achilles kills Hector, how he takes advantage of Hector's defenceless situation and then repeatedly penetrates his body with swords, alludes to a rape. The violated (usually female) body often functions as a symbol for a nation under attack, either from without or within, as in *The Rape of Lucrece*. The killing and symbolic rape of Hector in *Troilus and Cressida* is still a little different, because it is also the culmination of an erotic attraction between him and Achilles that manifests early and increases throughout the play. So while Hector stands for 'violated' Troy here (the Greeks' intrusion into the city at night), there is at the same time a bizarre parallel to one of Shakespeare's most famous romantic scenes, namely the sonnet sequence that accompanies Romeo and Juliet's first encounter. Romeo and Juliet are also lovers from two opposing parties, whose first encounter that has them converge in a kiss is diametrically opposed to the absolutely final one between Hector and Achilles. I would argue that Hector and Achilles's dialogue from "Look, Hector, how the sun begins to set" to "'Achilles

[56] For this, I draw upon Eric Scott Mallin, "Emulous Factions and the Collapse of Chivalry: *Troilus and Cressida*" in Mallin, *Inscribing the Time: Shakespeare and the End of Elizabethan England* (Berkeley: University of California Press), pp.25-61, pp.38-39.

hath the mighty Hector slain'" (5.9.5-14) constitutes a sonnet as well, though a somewhat distorted one. It is not a complete sonnet, the rhyme scheme is a little different, but the sonnet tradition is definitely evoked and then dropped quickly, as if from shock at the parallel, or because an ugly, distorted sonnet fits such a horrible scene better. During the sonnet in *Romeo and Juliet*, the lovers approach each other, speak their lines together and then merge in a kiss, while Hector and Achilles merge for a killing and rape. If Achilles stands for '(early) modern' Greece and Hector for 'medieval' Troy, its dichotomic Other, Hector's end strongly emphasises the violence binary oppositions produce. For while the categories of identity and alterity are made and not given – Achilles and Hector, or Greece and Troy, turn out not to be so different after all – at the same time they produce very real effects, though not only for the Other: Hector is slaughtered brutally here, but his death also sets the clock ticking for Achilles, whose death, as we all know, is from this point on only a question of time.

The last chapter on *Troilus and Cressida* focuses on Cressida, the only character in the play who switches between the parties and belongs to both sides, Trojan and Greek. She is also associated with literature and text more than any other character in the play. According to Ulysses, "There's language in her eye, her cheek, her lip/ Nay, her foot speaks" (4.5.56-57). The main reproach against her, that of falsehood and dissimulation, is, interestingly, exactly what the Elizabethan theatre was accused of by its opponents. By the 'dissimulation' of acting, it was argued, 'natural' hierarchies get confused, for example when a common citizen dresses like a gentleman for the stage. In *Plays Confuted in Five Actions*, Stephen Gosson employs the same metaphor of sickness that Ulysses uses to describe the Greeks' major weakness.[57] But at the same time, Cressida is more confined by this role than any other character and she is fully aware of it. She knows her own future, her literary fame, and the limits it sets to her possibilities to act. In the speech in which she describes her reputation ("False, false, false!", 5.2.185) as fixed from the beginning to the end of time she establishes an analogy to the biblical history of creation, in which language gets assigned the ultimate performative power ("'Let there be light'; and there was light", etc.). According to Judith Butler, who quotes the same passage of the *Book of Genesis* in this context, the citationality of performative utterances is concealed ("masqueraded") by the installation of

57 Compare Stephen Gosson: "If privat men be suffered to forsake theire calling because they desire to walke gentlemen like in sattine & velvet [...] the whole body must be dismembred and the prince or the heade cannot chuse but sicken". Stephen Gosson, *Plays Confuted in Five Actions* (1582), facsimile edition (New York: Johnson Reprint Corporation, 1972), C5r, G6v-G7v; cited in Louis Montrose, *The Purpose of Playing: Shakespeare and the Cultural Politics of the Elizabethan Theatre* (Chicago: University of Chicago Press, 1996), pp.35-36. Compare Ulysses: "Degree being vizarded/Th'unworthiest shows as fairly in the mask"(1.3.83-84); "O, when degree is shaked,/ [...] The enterprise is sick" (1.3.101-103); "every step,/ Exampled by the first pace that is sick/ Of his superior, grows to an envious fever/ Of pale and bloodless emulation" (1.3.131-134).

a subject that appears as the origin of the utterance.[58] But Cressida is denied subjectivity here, the alleged new feature of modernity: this character, who has existed in various forms for centuries and who is fully conscious of her own 'literariness,' her past and future story, cannot liberate herself from what others want to see in her. She cannot change her own history, but is forced to repeat it. Discourse and repetition as the origins of social reality appear completely undisguised here, which is presumably why *Cressida* is reproached with dissimulation so much. But in the place that should show Cressida the subject, however much of a "masquerade" that (modern?) subject may be, a lacuna is exhibited.

The second part of this book is about Shakespeare and Fletcher's *The Two Noble Kinsmen*. I argue that, in this play, the stage itself becomes a palimpsest: a cross-sectional view of the stage would reveal a multi-layered palimpsest. In many other texts that deal with the Thebes material by Chaucer, Ovid, Statius and Sophocles, besides this play, the palimpsest is mapped upon a cross-section of the ground, as it were, as everywhere bodies are lying below the ground (Chaucer) or above it (the Argive kings) or almost above it like Polynices, who is covered only with dust, which is then removed and then put back again. The most important feature of all these bodies is the fact that they never are where they are supposed to be while moving up and down on the scale. In the prologue of *The Two Noble Kinsmen* Chaucer is evoked and pictured as crying out from the underground if the play does not meet his standards. The poet's attempts to direct the adaptation of his work (the play closely follows his *Knight's Tale*) from out of the grave demonstrates almost literally how the past retains its "power to speak, and hence to disrupt and transform its over-text".[59] In a similar way, the Gower character in *Pericles* directs Shakespeare and Wilkins's audience through the play, which is an adaptation of Gower's *Confessio Amantis*. The marriage of Hippolyta and Theseus with which *The Two Noble Kinsmen* begins turns into a funeral when the widows of Argive kings appear and have the celebration cancelled. A military campaign against Creon of Thebes is started instead, because Creon has forbidden the burial of the last war's victims. Again the past, the unburied bodies of the Argive warriors, intervenes in the present. This episode, along with other aspects of the play, evokes Sophocles's tragedy *Antigone*, in which Antigone refuses to obey Creon's prohibition of her brother Polynices's burial. *The Two Noble Kinsmen*'s protagonists Palamon and Arcite are revenants of Antigone's brothers Polynices and Eteocles and are, like Sophocles's Antigone, imprisoned for the rest of their lives. The unordered temporal layers of the palimpsest are represented by the bodies of the protagonists themselves, because it is impossible to assign Palamon or Arcite to either present or past. Instead, the play introduces us

[58] See Judith Butler, *Excitable Speech: A Politics of the Performative* (New York, London: Routledge, 1997), pp.50-51.

[59] Harris (2009), p.15.

to a whole company of revenants. It is impossible to keep the dead underground: past writers like Chaucer try to steer the course of the present from the grave, dead kings are lying unburied before the gates of Thebes and the marriage of the ruler of Athens turns into a funeral before it has even started. After the battle that Theseus leads against Thebes at the request of the Argives in order to establish chronological order, to separate the past from the present and enable the burial of the dead, the Theban princes Palamon and Arcite, far from it, find themselves "not dead/ Nor in a state of life" (1.4.24-25). Theseus does bring them back to life again, but with the intention of keeping them perpetually in prison. Their 'new' life under Theseus' rule thus begins with a symbolic re-birth that has them almost killed and then revived, but the initiation resembles more a vampire bite than a baptism, because it lends them a temporality that is even harder to determine. Of all the characters who belong neither definitely to the present nor entirely to the past, they are the most movable ones, which is also indicated by their physical move from Thebes to Athens.

In *Chaucer and the Subject of History*, Lee Patterson argues that Thebes and Athens represent two different understandings of time.[60] Thebes, the city that grew from dragon teeth, is forever under a curse of pointless repetition that survives all generations. This city stands for a recursive notion of time. Athens, on the other hand, the city whose patroness is Athene, the goddess of reason, is associated with ordered, linear, purposive history.[61] That is why the Argive warriors are lying unburied before Thebes and Theseus is fetched from Athens to sort out the dead to the dead and the living to the living. Thebes, which has recursiveness but also 'illegitimate' sexuality inscribed in its founding myth is drawn in opposition to Athens also in this respect, as Theseus' mission is not only to arrange time linearly but also to sort out his subjects into heterosexually married couples. The installation of heterosexual marriage is thus directly correlated with the installation of linear time. Both depend on oblivion for the sake of coherence: oblivion of the past, for example the victims of the war that enabled Theseus and Hippolyta's marriage, and oblivion of both Emilia and the kinsmen's homosexuality, the topic of chapter II.9.

The kinsmen, imprisoned forever, neither dead nor alive, are for some time in an in-between condition, between Athens and Thebes, linearity and circularity, sanctioned family and inheritance structures and 'illicit' sexuality. Then Theseus proceeds to allocate one of them to life and the other one to death, and here, at the finale, the cost of the definite classification of present and past becomes most obvious, as does the violence of the operation. Theseus' way of creating linear order not 'only' causes great personal pain for all protagonists, the kinsmen, Emilia

60 Lee Patterson, *Chaucer and the Subject of History* (Madison: University of Wisconsin Press, 1991), pp.75-78.

61 See Patterson (1991), pp.200-201.

and her sister Hippolyta, the former Amazon queen. It also appears as entirely arbitrary, because, after the tournament that Theseus had set up especially to decide between the kinsmen, victor and loser, the kinsman who is going to live and the kinsman who has to die are exchanged at the last possible moment.

Part I: *TROILUS AND CRESSIDA*: Inscribing Time[1]

When Troilus, in armour, walks by Cressida's window while Pandarus and Cressida watch, and Pandarus praises him, "Brave Troilus, the prince of chivalry!"[2], this short sequence evokes both the Homeric and Chaucerian tradition, combining them in a new way. The 'original' scene is in the *Iliad*, where Priam asks Helen to tell him about the Greek heroes that they both see on the plain from their location on the city walls. This constellation, known as teichoscopy ("viewing from the walls"), where one character describes events only she or he can see, has since become a common literary device. Chaucer creates such a scene in *Troilus and Criseyde*, but changes the characters: here, it is Pandarus who describes Troilus to Cressida. There are many examples in *Troilus and Cressida* where Shakespeare takes up the medieval version of the ancient source material (the *Iliad*), sometimes stressed by references to chivalry as in this case ("prince of chivalry"). I will argue that this proves that:

1.) Shakespeare consciously puts medieval adaptations in the foreground in this version of the Troy-material, using the Middle Ages as a stencil through which antiquity is seen. The characters of Troilus and Cressida, who are both medieval additions to the classical Troy material, are taken out of their medieval settings (from romances like *Le Roman de Troie* and others) and "transplanted" back to the classical world of Troy. The idea of the Renaissance's direct access to classical antiquity (its *re-naissance*) is thus shown to be illusory and (early) modernity's dependence on, and constitution out of the Middle Ages is emphasised. This also demonstrates the impossibility of direct access to antiquity, or to any other period of the past. Furthermore, it underlines the strong influence of the *writing* of history on our picture of the past, which also creates our image of ourselves.

2.) The way temporalities emerge in this play is not adequately described by notions of chronological progress, teleological linearity, or any concept that sees time as a successive sequence of (mutually exclusive) historical periods. Jonathan Gil Harris' concept of *Palimpsested Time*[3] is a more useful critical tool with which to read *Troilus and Cressida. Palimpsested time* means that the past resides in the now, that multiple temporalities are manifest and (re-)emerge in forms of cultural production, in matter (Harris' focus) but also in the literary text. In many

---

1 Phrasing from Eric Scott Mallin, *Inscribing the Time: Shakespeare and the End of Elizabethan England* (Berkeley: University of California Press, 1995).

2 *Troilus and Cressida*, ed. David Bevington, The Arden Shakespeare, Third Series (London: Thomson Learning, 1998, 2006), 1.2.220-1. Future citations to TC will be to this edition and given in the text.

3 Harris (2009), pp. 1-25.

scenes such as, for instance, the teichoscopy-variant in Act I.2, not only do we find palimpsest-like superimpositions of elements from each period of time since the "original" scene in Book III of the *Iliad*, but it can also be shown that more recent textual layers transform and rewrite the original text, since the characters seem to act in full awareness of their own literary fame.

3.) The way Trojans and Greeks are constructed in binary opposition to one another, most prominently in the two epitomes of their respective parties, Hector and Achilles, performatively retraces the configuration of modernity and the Middle Ages as its dichotomic Other. While the Trojans represent a medieval world of chivalry, honesty, humility and poetry, the Greeks appear to belong to a Renaissance world of cynicism, dissimulation, arrogance and drama. Hector and Achilles, in particular, form a complementary unit up to the point where they become indistinguishable, exchangeable, thus showing the mutual dependence of Self and Other and the degree to which the Other really is a part of the Self. Cressida, who more than any other character is connoted with literature and text, is also the one who switches between the camps and belongs to both sides.

I.1. Troilus and Cressida as a medieval in(ter)vention

Choosing the characters of Troilus and Cressida, both medieval inventions, as protagonists for a play about the Trojan War adds an interesting twist to the Trojan myth. The most obvious thing to do for an early modern author who was planning to write a play set in the besieged Troy would have been to consult George Chapman's new translation of the *Iliad*. But Shakespeare used Chaucer's *Troilus and Crisyede* as a source, although the main characters of Troilus and Cressida are a medieval attribution to the ancient source material, which was remodelled around these figures in the centuries between Homer and Shakespeare. With its combination of love and war, love as a motive for war, the legends of the siege of Troy were popular with medieval writers. Greeks and Trojans were easily turned into knights in shining armour, fighting for the honour of their lady.[4] The love story of Troilus and Cressida, set in besieged Troy, is a medieval invention. Chaucer's adaptation of Boccaccio's *Il Filostrato*, *Troilus and Criseyde*, became its most famous account and one of Chaucer's most popular pieces. But the story of Troilus and Criseyde was not invented by Boccaccio either. Its basic outlines were first told in the *Roman de Troie*, by French poet Benoît de Sainte-Maure, in the late 1150s (Criseyde/Cressida is named "Briseida"). The Sicilian Guido delle Colonne turned the *Roman de Troie* into *Historia destruc-*

4 A.M. Potter, '*Troilus and Cressida:* Deconstructing the Middle Ages?' *Theoria*, 72 (1988), pp.23-35, p.28.

tionis Troiae (1287), a Latin prose narrative. Since it is in Latin, it was later taken as the more authoritative source.

The story's background, the siege and destruction of the city of Troy by the Greeks, is of course older than that. The ultimate source is Homer's *Iliad*, but both Vergil and Ovid allude to the Trojan matter frequently and two other works of probably the first century CE, originally in Greek, purporting to be eyewitness accounts of the Trojan War were taken as such in the Middle Ages. Both these works claim that Homer could not have been able to tell the story accurately because he had lived too long after the events. The Trojan War, or the events that led to the legend of the siege and destruction of Troy, are now dated around 1250 BCE, while Homer probably lived around 850 BCE.[5] They profess to correct Homer's 'mistakes', even though they were written another one thousand years later. These were translated into Latin as *Ephemeris Belli Troiani* by Dictys the Cretan (4th century CE) and *De Excidio Troiae Historiae* by Dares Phrygius (6th century CE). Chaucer himself had probably read neither Dictys nor Dares, but did know a Latin poem written by Joseph of Exeter around 1190 called the *Iliad of Dares Phrygius*.[6]

Both John Lydgate, in his *Troy Book* (1412-1420), and William Caxton, in the first English book to be printed, *Recuyell of the Historyes of Troye* (1474) deal with the material. The *Troy Book* is an amplified translation of the aforementioned Guido delle Colonne's *Historia destructionis Troiae*, whereas Caxton translated Raoul Lefèvre's French translation of Guido's *Historia*. Since the focus in Chaucer's *Troilus and Criseyde* is more on the love story and the effects on the characters' interior lives, while the war serves more or less as a scenic background, Shakespeare took details about the war from Lydgate and, most of all, from Caxton.

Shakespeare's knowledge of Robert Henryson's narrative poem, *The Testament of Cressid* (published in Thynne's edition of Chaucer in 1532), a continuation of the story that has Cressida punished by the gods, become a leper and die, is indicated by references to Cressida and leprosy.[7] The connection between the Trojan War and the story of Troilus and Cressida was familiar by Shakespeare's time and there are references to various other dramatic adaptations that preceded Shakespeare's. There was, for example, an anonymous *Troilus and Pander*, a comedy in Latin called *Troilus ex Chaucero*, Henry Chettle and Thomas Dekker's *Troilus and Cressida*, of which a plot fragment survives, and plays about related

5 *The Iliad of Homer*, trans. Richmond Lattimore (Chicago: University of Chicago Press, 1951), p.18. All citations of the *Iliad* are to this edition and will be given in the text.

6 *Troilus and Criseyde*, ed. Stephen R. Barney (New York: Norton, 2006), p.xi. Future citations to TC will be to this edition and given, in parentheses, in the text.

7 As in "the lazar kite of Cressid's kind," *Henry V*, 2.1.74. Quoted from *William Shakespeare: The Complete Works*, ed. by Stanley Wells and others. The Oxford Shakespeare, 2nd edn (Oxford: Clarendon Press, 2005), pp.595-625.

topics like Nicholas Udall's *Thersites*, a Latin play called *Ajax and Ulysses* and a "tragedie of Agamemnon," also by Dekker and Chettle.[8] The high number of adaptations indicates the popularity of the motif in the early modern period.

So when Shakespeare turned to Troy as the setting for *Troilus and Cressida*,[9] he had more sources to refer to than the *Iliad* alone. The medieval Troy tradition is purposefully put in the foreground, I would argue, contrasted with the ancient 'original' in an occasionally parodying manner and with a special focus on the *making of* history. The *Troilus* story is very productive in this respect because of its particularly medieval genesis, as the adaptation history described above shows.

The name of Troilus is listed among the sons of Priam in the *Iliad* once, but he is mentioned only in passing at a late stage (Book XXIV l.257)[10] and when he is already dead. All we are told is that his "delight was in horses" and that he died in the war some time before Hector (whom he outlives in *Troilus and Cressida*). From this short reference, his role was expanded in the Middle Ages to full characterisation by the time that *Troilus and Cressida* was written.

Cressida does not occur in the *Iliad* at all and is a medieval creation to an even greater extent. The *Iliad* mentions a woman called Chryseis at the very beginning and says she is the daughter of a priest of Apollo, a captive Trojan who must be given back to her father in order to appease Apollo's anger (Book I ll. 111 ff.). When Agamemnon, who wants her as his mistress, agrees only on the condition that he can have Achilles' "prize," a woman called Briseïs (note the similarity to 'Chryseis'; Cressida's name is 'Briseida' in the *Roman de Troie*), Achilles gets into the famous rage that starts off the action of the *Iliad.* Calchas, who is Cressida's/Crisyede's father in both Shakespeare and Chaucer, a priest in Shakespeare and a "gret devyn" (= soothsayer) in Chaucer (I. 66), occurs as the seer Kalchas in the *Iliad*, where he interprets the punishment of Apollo and concludes that Chryseis must be given back to her father in Troy. He is a Greek here

---

8 See Bevington, p.375.

9 For the difficult generic classification of *Troilus and Cressida* see Paul Yachnin, 'Shakespeare's Problem Plays and the Drama of his Time', in *A Companion to Shakespeare's Works, Volume IV: The Poems, Problem Comedies, Late Plays*, eds. Richard Dutton and Jean E. Howard (Oxford: Blackwell Publishing, 2005), pp. 46-68: "The epistle attached to the 1609 Quarto edition of Troilus and Cressida tells us seven times that what we are holding is a comedy – it is 'passing full of the palm comical.' The title page, however, calls it a history. When the play was published in the 1623 Folio it was designated a tragedy" (Yachnin, p. 54). Heinrich Heine suggests that the decision should be left to the future because "we should need the help of that new aesthetics which has not yet been written" (cited in Yachnin, *ibid*). See also William R. Elton, *Shakespeare's* Troilus and Cressida *and the Inns of Court Revels* (Aldershot: Ashgate, 2000), p. 1: "In views often diametrically opposed, the play is claimed to be a tragedy (cf. Fl 1623); a history (cf. *Stationers' Register*, 28 January 1609); a comedy (cf. Epistle, Q 1609); a satire; or a combination of these. Coleridge considered 'no one of Shakespeare's plays harder to characterize'."

10 Richmond Lattimore, *The Iliad of Homer* (Chicago: University of Chicago Press, 1951). All citations of the *Iliad* are to this edition.

and not the Trojan Chryseis' father (*Iliad* Book I, ll. 1-205). "Chryseida" is the Greek accusative form of Chryseis (meaning "daughter of Chryses").

So the names and actions of the protagonists of *Troilus and Cressida* are present in the *Iliad*, but their positions and functions are different from those in the medieval adaptations and, later, Shakespeare's. Nevertheless, Shakespeare did make use of Chapman's translation of the *Iliad* in the scenes where the war situation is discussed, but for the love story, he relied on Caxton and Chaucer. There are several references to Homer/ Chapman: the commencement of the story *medias in res*, after the war has been going on for years, exactly like in the *Iliad*, for instance ("Beginning in the middle, starting thence away/ To what may be digested in a play", PROLOGUE 27-8). The debate in the Greek camp is another example (*Troilus and Cressida* 1.3.1-212, Book 1.1-356 of the *Iliad)*, as is the device of a lottery to choose the opponent for the duel (*Troilus and Cressida* 1.3.375-377, p. 51 of Chapman's *Seven Bookes* [11]) and others.[12]

I would suggest that the way a period creates a consciousness of itself in time, its relation to the past, how this past is created and perhaps even directions for the future, is enacted in the way that these early modern versions of ancient and medieval sources are used and interconnected. Shakespeare could have made a play out of ancient source material alone; the *Iliad* had, after all, been translated and he used this translation, as becomes clear from several details in the play. The focus on the literary tradition and, more specifically, the medieval literary tradition, highlights the fact that the antiquity that the Renaissance supposedly rediscovered (according to Jacob Burckhardt and others)[13] was not "authentic," due to its long tradition of reception and adaptations and was not re-discovered, because it had been there all along.

Medieval versions of the ancient source material are consciously put in the foreground in *Troilus and Cressida*, like a lens through which antiquity is filtered for the contemporary audience. This reflects the *making* of history, the perspectival standpoint from which any kind of knowledge of the past is created, *that* it is created – "produced, not discovered",[14] and the function of literature as an agent that constructs the past through the framework of the respective presence in an intertextual network.[15]

Since the *Iliad* had been translated in 1598 and Shakespeare had access to the translation, using it quite extensively for *Troilus and Cressida*, he would not have

---

11 George Chapman, *Seven Books of the Iliades* in *Chapman's Homer: The Iliad*, ed. Allardyce Nicoll (Princeton: Princeton University Press, 1998).

12 See Bevington, pp. 378-379.

13 Jacob Burckhardt, *The Civilization of the Renaissance in Italy* (New York: Harper, 1958).

14 Jean E. Howard, "The New Historicism in Renaissance Studies", *English Literary Renaissance*, 16:1 (1986), pp.13-43, p.24. See also White, "The Historical Text as Literary Artifact", *Tropics of Discourse: Essays in Cultural Criticism* (Baltimore: Johns Hopkins University Press, 1978), pp.81-100.

15 Cf. Howard, pp.23, 25.

had to use medieval authors for a play set in Troy. For his Roman plays, *Julius Caesar*, *Antony and Cleopatra* and *Coriolanus*, he relied on an ancient source alone, Plutarch's *Bioi Paralleloi.*[16] But for *Troilus and Cressida*, he deliberately combines medieval and ancient sources (ancient sources in a contemporary translation) in such a way that the embedment of history in stories becomes clear. The idea of a direct or privileged early modern access to ancient classical culture is thus shown to be a fiction. The fact that "any move into history is an *intervention*"[17] is illustrated by the story of Troilus and Cressida because these characters are medieval inventions that were added to the ancient story, although the authors of the stories set out to merely 'translate' the material they found. But a translation is always an interpretation, even if the translator does not (consciously) try to 'correct' the former authors' 'mistakes', as was the declared purpose of Dares and Dictys. They did what was understood as the task of a translator, but they also confused characters for others with similar names or mistook grammatical forms,[18] while the need to address contemporary issues and interests turned Troilus into a medieval knight, for instance, and so the story continued to change. An adaption of the love story of Troilus and Cressida is therefore also a comment on the reception of antiquity, because it highlights the history of notions of antiquity and how such notions change according to who looks at them. This, in turn, influences the viewer.

I.2. Polychronic text – the palimpsest

Troilus and Cressida creates a binary opposition between a Troy that is associated with notions of the medieval (chivalry, honour, humility and poetry) and a Renaissance world of cynicism, relative value, arrogance, and drama in which the Greek besiegers are stylistically situated.[19] The relationship of premodernity and modernity is thus represented as an effect of alterity, of what is known from postcolonial discourse as Othering, the construction of identity by differentiation from an Other that is set in binary opposition to the Self.

Cressida, however, crosses the dividing line and partakes in both worlds, as does her Chaucerian counterpart Criseyde. She is also a more specifically *literary*

---

16 See Gordon Braden, "Shakespeare's Roman Tragedies" in *A Companion to Shakespeare's Works, Volume I: The Tragedies*, eds. Richard Dutton and Jean E. Howard (Oxford: Blackwell, 2003, 2006), pp.199-218, pp.203-204. Shakespeare used Thomas North's 1579 translation, *The liues of the noble Grecians and Romanes.*

17 Howard, p.43.

18 As already mentioned, Cressida originates from an accusative mistaken for a nominative, while Calchas is a confusion of the Greek seer Kalchas with the father of Chryseis, who became Cressida. Homer's Kalchas "sees" that Chryseis must be sent back to the Trojans (*Iliad* I.68-100), instead of the other way around (back to the Greeks) as in the medieval versions and Shakespeare's.

19 Cf. Mallin, pp.38-39.

figure than any other character in this play. She is someone to be read and interpreted and is preceded by and perceived through her literary fame: "There's language in her eye, her cheek, her lip,/ Nay, her foot speaks"; (4.5.56-57) says Ulysses; "her wanton spirits [...] wide unclasp the tables of their thoughts/ To every tickling reader!" (4.5.57-62).

She has therefore been called "a creature of intertextuality",[20] a cipher,[21] a metaphor for the text and the literary tradition, which not only influences the way she sees herself and is seen by others, but predetermines her behaviour, because it limits the scope of her possibilities to (re)act.

The prologue introduces us to the two parties right away.

> In Troy there lies the scene. From isles of Greece
> The princes [...] to the port of Athens sent their ships
> Fraught with the ministers and instruments
> Of cruel war. (PROLOGUE 1-5)

It describes the intruding Greeks as "princes orgulous, their high blood chafed" (PROLOGUE 2). "Orgulous" was obsolete by Shakespeare's time, but common in Middle English and in Caxton.[22] The unusual expression helps to establish the elevated style of the prologue. At the same time, it connects the 'modern' Greeks with their medieval counterpart, Troy, from the very first moment.

Apart from presenting the Greeks as proud and overbearing ("orgulous," "high blood"), the first two sentences of the prologue already make some interesting assumptions about the scene they present. First, the geography of ancient Greece is slightly rearranged when the princes arrive "from isles of Greece:" while Ulysses is indeed from the isle of Ithaca, Menelaus' Sparta and Agamemnon's Mycenae are on the Peloponnesian mainland. Achilles and his Myrmidons are associated with Thessaly in the north of Greece.[23] The historical princes would have come from the Greek mainland, not from the isles. From the first line of the prologue, it becomes clear, then, that the world we are about to enter is a work of art that follows its own rules.[24]

The altered geography also alludes to the performativity of cultural identity, which works similarly to the performativity of gender in ways that Judith Butler described. Gender is not something that is naturally 'there'; it has to be performed. The long tradition that precedes them lends expressions of established gender stereotypes more impact than they would otherwise have, because all ear-

20 Carol Cook, "Unbodied Figures of Desire", *Theatre Journal*, 38:1(1986), pp.34-52, p.50.

21 Similar to Helen, cf. Cook, p.39.

22 Bevington, p.129.

23 Bevington, *ibid.*

24 *Some* of the 1186 ships listed in the *Catalogue of Ships*, the ultimate source for this, come from islands, though (*Iliad* Book II, ll. 494-759), but not those carrying the princes that appear in this play.

lier instances of citation are invoked. At the same time, the need for reiteration contains potential for subversion: copies are rarely, if ever, completely exact and slight alterations, consciously or unconsciously employed, can subvert what they supposedly enact. It is not just gender or cultural identity that are performed in this way but history too: literary texts, especially performed ones, establish a "social imaginary"[25] for a culture to preserve its past.[26] The little shifts that occur in each new version of a story, or in each performance, remind us of how history is created in the cultural memory: it has to be performed, but the performances vary and thus the way historical situations are perceived changes.

The word "orgulous" in the next line ("The princes orgulous, their high blood chafed") works in a similar way: it associates the Greeks with haughtiness and pride and alludes to literary 'fame' and the literary tradition, because the Greeks had a reputation of being hedonistic and boisterous in the Renaissance.[27] The play repeatedly refers to this image, as in "a merry Greek indeed" (1.2.105), "Ay, Greek, that is my name" (1.3.246), where "Greek" suggests cunning or wily person,[28] "Greekish girls" (3.3.213), "cogging Greeks" (5.6.12) or "a woeful Cressid 'mongst the merry Greeks!" (4.4.55). While this brings early modern England into Greek mythology, the word "orgulous" is at the same time a reference to Caxton, who used the word frequently and to Middle English. But interestingly, it is applied to the Greeks, the 'modern' part of the dichotomy and blurs the lines of demarcation right away.

There are other references to the medieval history of Troy in the prologue that remind us that it is not the *Iliad* that Shakespeare retells, but medieval accounts of that story. The ships that are mustered at Athens, for example ("The princes [...]/ Have to the port of Athens sent their ships"), are a detail to be found both in Lydgate's *Troy Book* (2.5066.3, 5096, 5155, 5208) and in Caxton's *Recuyell of the Historyes of Troye* (545-546). In ancient reports of the story, the *Iliad*, Aeschylus' *Agamemnon*, Euripides *Iphigenia at Aulis*, the assembling does not take place at Athens but at Aulis, in Boeotia in central Greece.[29] The prologue continues with several more details from Caxton: "Sixty and nine, that wore/ Their crownets regal, from th'Athenian bay/ Put forth toward Phrygia" (PROLOGUE 5-7). Caxton writes "The some of kynges and dukes" who "assemblid them to gyder at the porte of athenes were sixty and nyne" (*Recuyell of the Historyes of Troye* 545-6).[30] "Port of Athens" or "sixty and nine" are verbatim echoes of Caxton. The *Iliad* talks of forty-six

25 Jean E. Howard and Paul Strohm, "The Imaginary 'Commons'", *Journal of Medieval and Early Modern Studies* 37:3 (2007), pp.550-577, p.551.

26 Jennifer Summit and David Wallace, "Rethinking Periodization", *Journal of Medieval and Early Modern Studies*, 37:3 (2007), pp.447-451, p.448.

27 Bevington, pp.144, 173.

28 Bevington, p.173.

29 Bevington, p.129.

30 *The Recuyell of the Historyes of Troye* (1894), ed. by Sommer, cited in Bevington, p.129.

captains, not all of them princes or kings, in the "Catalogue of the shippes", which Shakespeare would have known from Chapman's translation.[31]

The prologue continues to describe the occasion for the war very laconically ("The ravished Helen, Menelaus' queen/ With wanton Paris sleeps; and that's the quarrel", PROLOGUE 9-10). The relatively short prologue does, however, take the time to list the six gates of Troy: "Dardan and Timbria, Helias, Chetas, Troien/ And Antenorides" (PROLOGUE 16-17), which are not in the *Iliad* but can be found in Caxton (507) and Lydgate (2.596-605), with spelling closer to Caxton.[32] Again, the topography of Troy is particular; it is almost as if a medieval stencil has been put between antiquity and the early modern view, as if to highlight the inevitably perspectival standpoint of historical knowledge.

The commencement of the story *medias in res*, however, after years of fighting, correlates with the beginning of the *Iliad*, which also starts "into the middle of things." The Trojan War is, in fact, the example Horace uses in his *Ars poetica* when he first defines this narrative technique. It is suitable to a narration of the Trojan War, Horace says and therefore the skilful poet will prefer it to a commencement *ab ovo*:

nec gemino bellum Troianum orditur ab ovo;
semper ad eventum festinat et in medias res
non secus ad notas auditorem rapit (147-149)

[Nor does he begin the Trojan War from the egg,
but always hurries to the action,
and snatches the listener into the middle of things.]

The prologue declares that

our play
Leaps o'er the vaunt and firstlings of those broils,
Beginning in the middle, starting thence away
To what may be digested in a play. (PROLOGUE 26-29)

This refers directly to a very prominent example of the classical art of rhetorics and, at the same time, to the tradition of Trojan War narratives: it points out that this event is, even at the time of Horace's writing, described by different authors in different ways. Virgil's *Aeneid* is another well-known example of this kind of beginning, "in the middle," where earlier events are narrated as past action. In this, therefore, we find a direct reference to classical literature. But the antiquity shown here is not heroic as it appears in the *Aeneid* at all, or, indeed, in any way appealing, because the reason for the Trojan War is described in such terse, almost cynical terms: "The ravished Helen [...]/ With wanton Paris sleeps; and that's the quarrel" (PROLOGUE 9-10).

31 See Bevington, p.129.
32 Bevington, p.387.

The prologue continues:

Now expectation, tickling skittish spirits
On one and other side, Trojan and Greek,
Sets all on hazard. (PROLOGUE 20-22)

"Expectation" was allegorised as wanton,[33] "tickling" is used in an erotic sense repeatedly in this play[34] and "[s]ets all on hazard" refers to a game of dice, or tennis.[35] The outcome of the war, its causes and the war itself are described with such nonchalance, indifference even, as if the subject were a game of chance or a sports event. The cynicism and arbitrariness with which the outcome of the war is expected in the prologue may be due to the fact that *Troilus and Cressida* was not intended for the public theatre: in the revised Quarto edition of 1609, the play is advertised by the publisher as never having been "staled with the stage, never clapper-clawed with the palms of the vulgar."[36] If it is true that the play was not performed in public, it was either not performed at all or it was intended for performance (perhaps only) in a more exclusionary frame, before an elite audience, possibly at one of the Inns of Court, where it would have been performed for an audience of law students and practitioners.[37] The preface's reference to "the best comedy in Terence or Plautus,"[38] the concluding lines, "And so I leave all such to be prayed for, for the states of their wits' healths, that will not praise it. *Vale*"[39] and the general tone suggest a learned, or even academic, audience, pointing further to the Inns of Court theory.

In any case, the publisher's preface distinguishes between the reader and the audience that the play would have found in public theatres. It refers to this audience in very disparaging terms ("staled with the stage"; "palms of the vulgar" etc.).

The way the prologue talks of the war ("expectation, tickling skittish spirits/ On one and other side," PROLOGUE 20-21) perhaps also aims at an elite audience with a slightly arrogant attitude, but in a more critical way, since it suggests that war, victory or defeat, means nothing more to them than gain or loss of money, just as if it was game of dice or sports ("Sets all on hazard," PROLOGUE 22).

33 Bevington, p.131.

34 E.g. "To think how she tickled his chin" (1.2.130-131); "The shaft confounds/ Not that it wounds/ But tickles still the sore" (3.1.112-114); "O, these encounterers, so glib of tongue,/ That give accosting welcome ere it comes,/ And wide unclasp the tables of their thoughts/ To every tickling reader" (4.5.59-62); "How the devil Luxury, with his fat rump and potato finger, tickles these together! Fry, lechery, fry" (5.2.57-59); "He'll tickle it for his concupy" (5.2.184).

35 Bevington, p.131.

36 *A Never Writer to an Ever Reader. News*, ll. 1-3. Bevington, p.120.

37 William Elton argues that *Troilus and Cressida* was designed specifically to be performed in the context of the Elizabethan law-revels tradition. William R. Elton, *Shakespeare's 'Troilus and Cressida' and the Inns of Court Revels* (Aldershot: Ashgate, 2000), *passim*.

38 *A Never Writer to an Ever Reader. News*, ll. 26-27. Bevington, p.121.

39 *A Never Writer to an Ever Reader. News*, ll. 35-37. Bevington, p.122.

The last lines of the prologue strike a similar note and liken the war situation to the theatrical situation, as if the war were also a form of entertainment:

Like or find fault; do as your pleasures are;
Now good or bad, 'tis but the chance of war. (PROLOGUE 30-31)

Although "like or find fault; do as your pleasures are" refers to the play on the first, most obvious level and addresses the audience as audience, it also refers to the war situation and invites the audience to like or dislike the war according to their personal taste, reducing it to a spectacle, a show to be watched for mere amusement.

Of course, this is just what the disillusioned tone of the prologue suggests. The learned impact of some of the discussions later in the play (the degree and order debate in Act I Scene 3, for instance, and many references to ancient or contemporary philosophical debates as well as numerous allusions to ancient mythology), a language that abounds with Latinisms and neologisms and the generally high level of abstraction demand a high degree of intellectual cooperation from the audience,[40] so that the play hardly passes as light entertainment. On the contrary, the suggested lightness makes the cruelty of the war just harder to bear.

Because Renaissance theatre in England made extensive use of the stage's possibility to function as a place where political and social issues could be debated,[41] even, or especially, those that were too delicate to be addressed openly, what at first sight seems to reduce the war to a show, an entertaining spectacle to "tickle" the nerves of the audience, at the same time points to the political implications of staging a play. So while the prologue alludes to the fact that monarchical political order and theatrical production are to some degree mutually constructive in the English Renaissance, its tone is so cynical that it suggests the emptiness or uselessness of both, theatre and politics.

"Expectation [...] sets all on hazard" (PROLOGUE 20-22), i.e. does not care who wins the war, still resonates when the prologue moves on "to what may be digested in a play" (PROLOGUE 29). This suggests a similar indifference as to whether or not the audience likes the play ("Like or find fault; do as your pleasures are," PROLOGUE: 30), before it returns to the war when it ends: "good or bad, t'is but the chance of war" (PROLOGUE: 31). The war is referred to as if it was an entertaining spectacle (while the "spectacle" is, in turn, connected with political practices, too) and it sounds as if it is irrelevant whether the audience likes it. The irreverence to the supposedly glorious deeds of the war heroes, the

40 Cf. *Kindlers Neues Literaturlexikon*, ed. by Walter Jens and others, 22 vols (Munich: Kindler, 1988-1998), 15 (1998), p. 316.

41 See Louis Montrose, *The Purpose of Playing. Shakespeare and the Cultural Politics of the Elizabethan Theatre* (Chicago: University of Chicago Press, 1996), pp.66-75; Stephen Orgel, *The Illusion of Power: Political Theater in the English Renaissance* (Berkeley: University of California Press, 1975, 1991), *passim.*

exact opposite of the epic celebration of martial heroism of Virgil or Statius, is extended to the audience of the war show/theatrical performance. And this is still quite harmless in comparison to the epilogue, spoken by Pandarus, in which Pandarus insults the audience, addressing them as bawds and pimps and bequeathing his own disease, syphilis, to them.

Just as the prologue starts rather unpleasantly and the epilogue ends worse, the play moves from cynicism in the beginning to sheer horror at the end. The butchery of the last scenes on the battlefield is not just a deflation of glorious heroic deeds, but also a merciless depiction of the horrors of war, especially since it forms such a stark contrast to the solemn, measured tone of the intellectual debates earlier in the play. But even these debates had their fallacies: when the question of whether the war should be continued is discussed, for example, the most rational and convincing arguments to end the war are thrown overboard within a moment by none other than Hector, the only character who had, so far, seemed to hold up what little sense of reason and justice was left in the world of the play.

In Act II Scene 2, Hector argues,

> Thus to persist
> In doing wrong extenuates not wrong,
> But makes it much more heavy. Hector's opinion
> Is this in way of truth; yet, ne'ertheless,
> My sprightly brethren, I propend to you
> In resolution to keep Helen still;
> For 'tis a cause that hath no mean dependence
> Upon our joint and several dignities. (2.2.186-193)

Hector, the personification of chivalry, who even more than the other Trojans embodies the virtues imagined to belong to a medieval past, such as honour, humbleness, loyalty, chastity (I will return to this in more detail), abandons all rational cause that would end the deaths and destruction of the war and resolves to continue it and to keep Helen, contrary to his own argument. The Trojan world is presented as being grounded on a medieval value system, the code of chivalry, which is, itself, shown to be inconsistent, because the principles of honour demand two mutually exclusive actions, namely to end the war *and* to continue it.

Similarly, Palamon and Arcite, the protagonists of *The Two Noble Kinsmen*, another play where codes of knightly conduct are discussed, have incorporated the codes of chivalry completely; nevertheless they find themselves in impossible situations time and again in the course of the play, from the exposition to the happy/tragic ending. While they take the ideals of chivalry so seriously that they are willing to adapt to them entirely, they fail to do so due to the contradictions inherent in these norms.[42] Hector, likewise, has come to the conclusion that it

42 See Peter Hadorn, "*The Two Noble Kinsmen* and the Problem of Chivalry", *Studies in Medievalism*, 4 (1992), pp.45-57.

was wrong to start the war in the first place and that to continue it does not make it better: "to persist/ In doing wrong extenuates not wrong,/ But makes it much more heavy" (2.2.186-188). At the same time, continuing the war is the only way to uphold the Trojans' reputation and be perceived as honourable, for the individual warrior as well as for the Trojans collectively: "'tis a cause that hath no mean dependence/ Upon our joint and several dignities" (2.2.192-193).

Hector claims to argue in the name of reason when he reproaches his younger brother,

> Now, youthful Troilus, [...] is your blood
> So madly hot that no discourse of reason,
> Nor fear of bad success in a bad cause,
> Can qualify the same? (2.2.113-118)

Paris and Troilus both argue for the continuance of the war for reasons that do concur with chivalric ideals:

> There's not the meanest spirit on our party
> Without a heart to dare, or sword to draw,
> When Helen is defended, nor none so noble
> Whose life were ill bestowed, or death unfamed,
> Where Helen is the subject. (2.2.156-160)

They use a whole catalogue of expressions from the register of courtly love and knightly honour: "our several honours all engaged" (2.2.124); "gracious" (2.2.125); "beauty" (2.2.147); "honourable" (2.2.149); "treason"; "queen" (2.2.150); "disgrace"; "your great worths"; "shame to me" (2.2.151); "generous bosoms" (2.2.155); "heart to dare"; "sword" (2.2.157); "noble" (2.2.158) and so on, to prove that Helen must be kept and the war must be continued:

> Well may we fight for her whom, we know well,
> The world's large spaces cannot parallel. (2.2.161-162)

Although this sounds like the prototypical medieval knight who has pledged himself to a lady, Hector objects to the argument, saying it offends both reason and morals:

> Paris and Troilus, you have both said well
> And [...] not much
> Unlike young men, whom Aristotle thought
> Unfit to hear moral philosophy. (2.2.163-167)

This is an interesting example of palimpsested time, time with "the traces of other times – past and future – legible within it:"[43] Aristotle lived from 384-322 BCE, long after the Trojan war, which is now dated to the early 12th century BCE and long after Homer, who probably lived in the 9th century BCE.[44] Never-

43 Harris (2009), p.24.
44 Bevington, p.362.

theless Aristotle has already formed the opinion of these characters that lived long before him.

The main problem for Hector is that Helen, the "beauty" (2.2.147) they "defend" (2.2.158), is married to someone else, to Menelaus, who has come from Sparta accompanied by half of Greece to get her back. The fact that she is married does not disqualify her as beloved lady in the courtly love tradition, ideally she *should* be unattainable, but Paris having an actual affair with her is another matter. Hector argues, therefore:

If Helen then be wife to Sparta's king,
As it is known she is, these moral laws
Of nature and of nations speak aloud
To have her back returned. (2.2.183-186)

So far his argument is consistent. But then he goes on to say,

Hector's opinion
Is this in way of truth; yet, ne'ertheless,
My sprightly brethren, I propend to you
In resolution to keep Helen still;
For 'tis a cause that hath no mean dependence
Upon our joint and several dignities. (2.2.188-193)

It becomes clear that the truth he believes in is not compatible with "dignity". What he believes to be true is not what would be advisable in practice, where an "honourable" reputation is more important, even if it involves dishonourable behaviour. His brothers, whom he formerly called "youthful" (2.2.113), "superficial" (2.2.165) and "unfit to hear moral philosophy" (2.2.167), whose reasons, he said, "more conduce/ To the hot passion of distempered blood/ Than to make up a free determination/ 'Twixt right and wrong" (2.2.168-171), he now addresses as "valiant offspring of great Priamus" (2.2.207): "I am yours" (2.2.205). And interestingly, he also does not seem to have changed his mind just now, switched sides from "a free determination/ 'Twixt right and wrong" to the "resolution to keep Helen still" spontaneously during the debate, persuaded by his brothers' arguments, but he had obviously made up his mind before, as becomes apparent when he continues,

I have a roisting challenge sent amongst
The dull and factious nobles of the Greeks
Will strike amazement to their drowsy spirits. (2.2.208-210)

He is referring to the challenge to a duel with which Aeneas was sent to the Greeks in Act I Scene 3 (which I will talk more about soon). If he has sent Aeneas on this embassy before the present debate, as he says, this means that he had already decided to continue fighting the Greeks in spite of what he argues "in way of truth". He must have thought about this before and was obviously unable to apply the "discourse of reason" and "these moral laws of nature and of nations" (2.2.184-185) to the present situation. His "youthful" and "superficial" brothers, "unfit to hear moral philosophy," who "for pleasure and revenge/ Have ears more deaf than adders to the voice/ Of any true decision" (2.2.171-173) are at the very same time the "valiant offspring of great Priamus" (2.2.207) and Hector agrees with them completely. The superficiality they are accused of, then, perhaps refers to the fact that they, unlike Hector, do not seem to be aware of the contradictions inherent in the code of chivalry.

The Trojans' adherence to the code of knightly conduct is suggested quite strongly in this dispute. Troilus quotes the whole canon of knightly ideals in his response: "glory" (twice in a few lines), "blood", "honour", "renown", "valiant", "magnanimous deeds", "courage," and "fame," and he calls Hector "worthy" and "brave" (2.2.195-204). He employs the word "canon" here himself: "may [...] fame in time to come canonize us" (2.2.201-202), "for the wide world's revenue" (2.2.203-206). He sees the potential in this war to lead to the Trojans "canonisation" (suggesting that he knows about the Trojan War's future literary fame), but he is unaware of the conflict Hector, who already *is* drawn as the embodiment of knightly virtues, describes, namely that precisely the application of the rules of the code violates it. Thereby Hector also calls attention to the fact that the code covers his brothers' "madly hot" (2.2.116) judgement, their inability to tell right from wrong (2.2.170-171), their deafness to the "discourse of reason" (2.2.116) and "raging appetites that are/ Most disobedient and refractory" (2.2.181-182). All these things directly oppose the demand of moderation, cool judgement and control of one's temper which their principles imply. When Troilus concludes his speech with the word "revenue" – "the wide world's revenue" (2.2.206) is the ultimate goal of their pursuit – he draws the link to the "Renaissance-Greeks" and their concern with monetary issues, which shows that their basic motivations are not that different after all.

Yet the Trojans are strongly connected with medieval chivalry, with honour and success in battle, as in the debate above and with the courtly love tradition as well. Paris combines both when he refers to the Trojan soldiers as "all the gallantry of Troy" (3.1.129-130) and Aeneas, too, when he delivers the challenge to the Greeks, employs the language of courtly love to entice them to military activity.[45] The Greeks' recognition of the style becomes apparent when Agamemnon calls "the men of Troy [...] ceremonious courtiers" (1.3.233-234), even though they are summoning the Greeks to a fight. Aeneas actually manages to do both, be a ceremonious courtier and at the same time disparage the Greeks, because he exaggerates the courtly idiom to such a degree that his ironic distance becomes apparent. He starts politely:

May one that is a herald and a prince
Do a fair message to his kingly ears? (1.3.218-219)

45 Cf. Mallin, pp.25-61, 46.

But then he pretends not to recognise the king. He uses the courtly idiom to ridicule his object by exaggerating the praise, but because the conventions allow for a high degree of exaggeration, it is hard for the Greeks to react to the provocation.

I ask, that I might waken reverence,
And bid the cheek be ready with a blush
Modest as morning when she coldly eyes
The youthful Phoebus.
Which is that god in office, guiding men? (1.3.227-231)

Agamemnon suspects that

This Trojan scourns us, or the men of Troy
Are ceremonious courtiers. (1.2.233-234)[46]

Aeneas immediately chimes in,

Courtiers as free, as debonair, unarmed,
As bending angels – that's their fame in peace.
But when they would seem soldiers, they have galls,
Good arms, strong joints, true swords, and – Jove's accord –
Nothing so full of heart. (1.3.235-239)

Courteous and gentle ("angels") in peace, courageous and resentful ("galls") in war – this is a summary of the ideal qualities of a knight. But Aeneas cites the chivalric convention only to mock Agamemnon and the Greeks with impunity and shows hereby that he, too, is capable of the more theatrical Greeks' performance and "ceremony", suggesting that medieval chivalry is something that needs to be enacted and performed.[47] Simultaneously, with his sonorous challenge to the Greeks, we are transferred entirely to the world of medieval romance, where knights fight in tiltyards for the favour of their lady:

He [Hector] bade me take a trumpet,
And to this purpose speak: 'Kings, princes, lords,
If there be one among the fair'st of Greece
That holds his honour higher than his ease,
That seeks his praise more than he fears his peril,
That knows his valour and knows not his fear,
That loves his mistress more than in confession
With truant vows to her own lips he loves,
And dare avow her beauty and her worth
In other arms than hers; to him this challenge:
Hector, in view of Trojans and of Greeks,
Shall make it good, or do his best to do it,
He hath a lady, wiser, fairer, truer,

---

46 In a parallel to this later in the play, Achilles finds Hector's politeness offensive: "I do disdain thy courtesy, proud Trojan" (5.6.16).

47 Cf. Andrew James Johnston, *Performing the Middle Ages from* Beowulf *to* Othello (Turnhout: Brepols, 2009), especially chapter 4: "*Othello* and the Chivalric Origins of 'Renaissance Man'", pp.225-312.

Than ever Greek did compass in his arms;
And will tomorrow with his trumpet call,
Midway between your tents and walls of Troy,
To rouse a Grecian that is true in love.
If any come, Hector shall honour him;
If none, he'll say in Troy where he retires,
The Grecian dames are sunburnt, and not worth
The splinter of a lance.' Even so much. (1.3.263-283)

While this is a reminder of the fact that the story of *Troilus and Cressida*, though set in Troy and ultimately derived from Homer, came to the Renaissance as a chivalric romance, or, rather, several chivalric romances (Benoît de Sainte-Maure, Guido delle Colonne, Raoul Lefèvre, Boccaccio), the homoerotic potential of the last line "To rouse a Grecian that is true in love" points to the ancient tradition again, where Achilles, at whom the challenge is ultimately directed, and Patroclus were depicted as lovers, which they ceased to be (at least so openly) in medieval stories. In Aeschylus, Sophocles, Plato, Theocritus, Martial, Lucian and other classical authors a sexual relationship between Achilles and Patroclus is assumed while in sixteenth century literature they were more likely to be characterised as intimate friends.[48] *Troilus and Cressida* is nearer to the ancient tradition in this, because several expressions used with regard to Patroclus hint at an erotic relationship between him and Achilles, for example "awkward" (1.3.149), meaning "turned the wrong way, back foremost,"[49] thus a potentially sodomitical suggestion and "preposterous" (5.1.23) later in the play: "preposterous" practices were also "sometimes associated with Rome and ancient classical practices of homosexuality."[50]

The term "preposterous," on another level, suggests a disruption of linear time, as Jonathan Gil Harris notes,[51] drawing on Patricia Parker's chapter on "Preposterous Estates, Preposterous Events:"[52] It connotes a reversal of "post" (from *posterus* = after, behind) for "pre" (from *prae* = before, in front), "behind for before, back for front, second for first, end or sequel for beginning," thus marking an inverse of orders claimed to be natural or necessary.[53]

Earlier metaphorical uses of the term "palimpsest" often refer to the palimpsest as to a specific kind of symbiosis between two hierarchically arranged textual layers, namely the well legible, authorised newer text and the earlier, "original" text which has been overwritten, but which remains visible in fragments within the later text. In his introduction to *Palimpsests*, Gérard Genette describes palimpsest-like intertextuality as such a dual disposition:

---

48 See Bevington, p.370.
49 The OED's oldest meaning of "awkward", now obsolete (Bevington, p.166).
50 Bevington, p.307.
51 Harris (2009), p.182.
52 Patricia Parker, *Shakespeare from the Margins: Language, Culture, Context* (Chicago: University of Chicago Press, 1996), pp.20-55.
53 Parker, p.21.

> By hypertextuality I mean any relationship uniting a text B (which I shall call the *hypertext*) to an earlier text A (I shall, of course, call it the *hypotext*), upon which it is grafted in a manner that is not that of commentary.[54]

Because the term *palimpsest* is often used in postcolonial studies,[55] it is perhaps tempting to imagine the palimpsest as defining the relation between the dominant, "official" coloniser's culture and the suppressed, marginalised culture of the colonised. "Preposterous" as a reversal of before for after or earlier for later, if we think of the relationship between the medieval and the modern (or, as here, Trojan and Greek) as a (post-)colonial one,[56] would then suggest that that order is simply inversed. But "preposterous" does not mean that past and present switch sides. In postcolonial studies the palimpsest is rather seen as an accretion of multiple inscriptions and layers that characterise any form of cultural experience in an on-going process;[57] instead, I propose the palimpsest as an unhierarchical network of *multiple* textual layers, not just two, as "a site of ongoing textual production that fails to erase the traces of earlier inscriptions", where "the present coexists with multiple pasts",[58] so that if order is inversed, this happens in more than one direction.

Back to the Trojan challenge: there is, throughout the play, also a strong erotic tension between Hector and *Achilles*. In the challenge to the fight, "Hector creates a homoerotic discourse. He calls on 'the fair'st of Greece,' but he means the men."[59] This is suggested by the pun on arms in "in other arms than hers" and other ambiguous expressions in the speech, such as "to <u>rouse</u> a Grecian that is true in love," "if any <u>come</u>, Hector shall honour him," or "The Grecian dames are sunburnt, and not worth/ The splinter of a lance" with a pun on '*son* [= man]-*burnt*' = infected with venereal disease[60] and "lance" = penis.[61] The challenge is proclaimed before all the Greek generals, but, as Ulysses points out,

> This challenge that the gallant Hector sends,
> However it is spread in general name,
> Relates in purpose only to Achilles. (1.3.322-324)

When Achilles hears of it, he acknowledges his "appetite" towards Hector, which he calls "a woman's longing," as he tells Patroclus:

> I have a woman's longing,
> An appetite that I am sick withal,

---

54 Genette, p.5.
55 See Ashcroft, Griffiths and Tiffin, pp.174-176.
56 See Dagenais and Greer, p.431.
57 Ashcroft, Griffiths and Tiffin, p.174.
58 Jonathan Gil Harris, "The Smell of Macbeth", *Shakespeare Quarterly*, 58:4 (2007), pp.465-486, p.472.
59 Mallin, p.46.
60 Eric Partridge, *Shakespeare's Bawdy* (New York, London: Routledge, 1947, 1968), p.253.
61 Partridge, p.169.

To see great Hector in his weeds of peace,
To talk with him, and to behold his visage
Even to my full of view. (3.3.239-243)[62]

Hector's challenge to the Greeks itself, however, even if it appears in medieval guise, is a detail Shakespeare would have found in the *Iliad.* While the challenge to the duel points to ancient sources, because the duel had disappeared in medieval adaptations, its rhetorical style is from the medieval courtly love tradition. The re-appearance of ancient story traits in medieval guise on the early modern stage is a good example of palimpsested time. The palimpsest is not only helpful for thinking about the multitemporal properties of *matter*, as is mostly the case in Jonathan Gil Harris' book *Untimely Matter in the Time of Shakespeare*, on which I draw. Harris, too, does not limit the usage of the term strictly to objects, but includes also "the onstage material practices of his [Shakespeare's] theater company [...] – their acting styles, special effects, and stage properties".[63] The stagecraft of the King's Men, i.e. something immaterial, "arguably constitutes English Renaissance culture's most sustained practical theory of untimely matter".[64] The idea of the palimpsest also works for the text itself, independent of the material surface on which it is written, whether animal hide or LCD screen: in the plot lines, motives, characters, conflicts, philosophical questions discussed, but also in particular expressions, stylistic and rhetorical devices, narrative techniques, etc., layers of multiple temporal origin overlap and interconnect. The fact that specific details from the classical tradition, like the challenge to the Greeks in Act I Scene 3, or the sexual relationship between Achilles and Patroclus,[65] can reappear in the early modern adapta-

---

62 This continues when they actually meet:

ACHILLES Now, Hector, I have fed mine eyes on thee [...]
HECTOR Is this Achilles?
ACHILLES I am Achilles.
HECTOR Stand fair, I pray thee. Let me look on thee.
ACHILLES Behold thy fill. [...]
ACHILLES Thou art too brief. I will the second time,
As I would buy thee, view thee limb by limb.
HECTOR O, like a book of sport thou'lt read me o'er;
But there's more in me than thou understand'st.
Why dost thou so oppress me with thine eye? (4.5.231-241)

Again, during the battle, Achilles cries, "Hector! Where's Hector? I will none but Hector" (5.6.49). I will return to this.

63 Harris (2009), p.20.

64 Harris (2009), *ibid.*

65 While erotic tension between Achilles and Hector is suggested, Achilles' real affair with Patroclus is referred to quite openly (if derogatorily) by the other characters: "with him Patroclus/ Upon a lazy bed, the livelong day/ Breaks scurril jests" (1.3.146-148); "Thou art thought to be Achilles' male varlet [...], his masculine whore" (5.1.15-17). Patroclus calls it "your great love to me" (3.3.223): "They think my little stomach to the war,/ And your great love to me, restrains you thus./ Sweet, rouse yourself, and the weak wanton Cupid/ Shall

tion implies that they were there all along, although they were less perceptible or even seemed to have disappeared. This is where the notion of the palimpsest is helpful, because it illustrates how earlier inscriptions cannot be erased from cultural memory: even if they are scraped or washed off, they can be made visible, readable again. The inseparable physical union of textual and temporal layers on the parchment contradicts the idea of historical periods as neatly distinguishable units that replace each other in a teleological progress.

The aforementioned teichoscopy scene (Act I Scene 2) is legible as such a palimpsest where the (medieval) past is clearly not past but resides in the (early modern) now. Its original is in the *Iliad* (Book 3, ll. 161-244), where Priam, king of Troy, asks Helen to tell him the names and give some information about the approaching Greek warriors while they are viewing them from the walls of the gates where they stand. From this episode, the narrative strategy of teichoscopy (teichos = city wall, skopein = watch) has been derived: the oral report of a character at a vantage point, who sees and describes things that are not displayed directly for artistic or, as on stage, practical reasons. Similarly to the *medias in res*-definition in Horace, this is not a random example of the employment of this dramaturgical device, but its first occurence from which it derives its definition and therefore a seminal moment in literary history, the origin of this element of the (Western) literary tradition. In *Troilus and Criseyde*, this scene occurs in a humorous variation, as one of Chaucer's many additions to Boccaccio: instead of Priam sending for Helen to come to the wall, it is Pandarus who lures Criseyde to a window under a false pretence, gives her a letter from Troilus to read and as if it was a coincidence,

> right as they declamed this matere,
> Lo, Troilus, right at the stretes ende,
> Com rydyng with his tenthe som yfere,[66]
> Al softely,[67] and thiderward gan bende
> Ther as they sete, [...]
> and Pandare hym aspide,
> And seyde, "Nece, ysee who comth here ride!" (II. 1247-1253)

Troilus parades past the window with his men: "God woot if he sat on his hors aright,/ Or goodly was biseyn, that ilke day!/ God woot wher[68] he was lik a manly knyght!" (II. 1261-1263). Of course, this has been carefully arranged. Pan-

---

from your neck unloose his amorous fold/ And, like a dew-drop from the lion's mane,/ Be shook to air" (3.3.223-227). Other references include "upon a lazy bed [...] with ridiculous and awkward action" (1.3.147-149) and "preposterous" (5.1.23) as discussed earlier. See also Alan Sinfield, "The Leather Men and the Lovely Boy: Reading Positions in *Troilus and Cressida*" in *Shakesqueer: A Queer Companion to the Complete Works of Shakespeare*, ed. Madhavi Menon (Durham, N.C. and London: Duke University Press, 2011), pp.376-384, p.379.

66 I.e. 'together with his party of ten' (Barney, p.131).

67 I.e. 'slowly' (Barney, *ibid*).

68 'Whether' (Barney, *ibid*).

darus, who has set himself the goal to assist his princely friend in gaining Criseyde's love, had instructed Troilus beforehand:

And whan thow woost that I am with hire there,
Worth[69] thow upon a courser right anon –
Ye, hardily, right in thi beste gere –
And ryd forth by the place, as nought ne were. (II. 1010-1013)

This is quite humorous compared to the pompous tone of this scene in the *Iliad*, where Helen describes the warriors: "That one is gigantic Aias, wall of the Achaians,/ and beyond him there is Idomeneus like a god standing/ among the Kretans" (Book III, ll. 229-231). Actually, there is comic potential in Homer's scene already, since Helen knows all the enemies so well because most of them had wooed her not long ago, but it remains unused. It is therefore not so far-fetched when Chaucer, who did not know the *Iliad* itself but was familiar with its sediments in the literary tradition, translates it into a comic scene, where Troilus tries to court Cressida by parading in front of her window. The tone Chaucer applies is certainly not heroic; to the contrary, it is almost burlesque: "To God hope I [says the narrator], she hath now kaught a thorn,/ She shal nat pulle it out this nexte wyke./ God sende mo swich thornes on to pike!" (II. 1272-1274). This sounds familiar: Shakespeare makes very similar erotic puns, in this play and others,[70] so that Shakespeare's text is already inscribed in Chaucer's and vice versa. Shakespeare takes up this scene, brings it a little more into line with its ancient original by reintegrating the other heroes, but at the same time underlines the reference to the Middle Ages by calling Troilus "the prince of chivalry" (1.2.220-221) and, more subtly, by letting Aeneas and Antenor enter first: they are the traitors in the medieval tradition, who open the gates to the enemy.[71] This construct of ancient and medieval components is transferred to the early modern stage in *Troilus and Cressida*, where it fits very well because it mirrors the theatrical situation with stage/scene and observers.[72] It could be said that the interconvertibility of space and time that is implied in the idea of the 'decolonisation' of the Middle Ages as modernity's temporal Orient[73] is illustrated here, be-

---

69 'Mount' (Barney, p.115).

70 For example in *All's Well That Ends Well*: "If ever we are nature's, these are ours; this thorn/ Doth to our rose of youth rightly belong" (1.3.125-126); in *Romeo and Juliet*: "It pricks like thorn" (1.4.24), where "thorn" alludes to "penis" (Partridge, pp.216, 260).

71 Bevington, pp.148-149. See Caxton, *The Recuyell of the Historyes of Troye*, ll.650-677 (cited in Bevington).

72 Even more so does a scene toward the end of the play where Troilus and Ulysses observe Cressida and Diomedes and are in turn watched by Thersites, while all five are of course watched by the audience (5.2.6-196). Cf. Julia Ruth Briggs, "'Chaucer … the Story Gives:' *Troilus and Cressida* and *The Two Noble Kinsmen*" in *Shakespeare and the Middle Ages: Essays on the Performance and Adaptation of the Plays with Medieval Sources or Settings*, eds. Martha W. Driver and Sid Ray (Jefferson, N.C.: McFarland, 2009), pp.161-177, p.165.

73 See Dagenais and Greer, p.431; Ganim, *passim*.

cause each period is assigned a certain space in the way people are grouped for this scene: those on show (the Trojan heroes) are of ancient origin; the observers (Pandarus and Cressida) are medieval inventions; the audience is contemporary, i.e. modern. The modern audience watches the ancient heroes cross the stage while simultaneously hearing medieval figures (Cressida and Pandarus) comment on the scene, thus seeing them through their eyes. Of course, most of the time they are not thus neatly arranged and this formation disintegrates after the scene.

Pandarus, who tries to aid Troilus in getting Criseyde's attention, has a name that, for Shakespeare's audience, already means "pander". His actions are also determined by his literary fame. Criseyde's infidelity to Troilus, the fact that she will leave him for Diomede, is already immanent in this constellation because she sits in the window while watching Troilus, assuming Helen's place who sat there in the original scene in the *Iliad*. She is thus paralleled to Helen, who has become the epitome of inconstancy in the literary tradition. Shakespeare uses this charged material for a persiflage of heroic narratives. The impatience with which Pandarus awaits Troilus' appearance ("Would I could see Troilus now. You shall see Troilus anon" (1.2.208-209)); "I marvel where Troilus is" (repeatedly; 1.2.211; 1.2.216)); his overeagerness ("Is not that a brave man?" "There's a brave man, niece"; "Look how he looks!" "There's a countenance! Is't not a brave man?" "Is 'a not? It does a man's heart good" (1.2.180-197), etc.) goes so far that when Cressida finally becomes interested and asks "Can Helenus fight, uncle?" he answers distractedly, "Helenus? No – yes, he'll fight indifferent well. I wonder where Troilus is" (1.2.214-6). This is a humorous dismissal of the elevated style in which the warriors are presented in Homer, not only in the teichoscopy scene but throughout the *Iliad*. When Troilus finally appears, Pandarus mistakes him for Deiphobus, while Cressida asks, "What sneaking fellow comes yonder?" (1.2.218). Pandarus, realising his mistake, quickly corrects himself, "'Tis Troilus! There's a man, niece! Hem! Brave Troilus, the prince of chivalry!" (1.2.220-221). He is obviously making too much noise because Cressida replies, "Peace, for shame, peace!" (1.2.222).

"The prince of chivalry" could hardly be introduced in a less heroic or more ironic way. *Troilus and Cressida*'s Trojan heroes belong to a medieval world based on a seemingly stable value system but, behind its façade, it appears *as* fragile, possibly empty, as the Greeks' world where order and rule are replaced by "many hollow factions" (1.3.80).[74] The Trojans' chivalry is portrayed as "pale and bloodless emulation" (1.3.134) as well, which is why Hector can say, "I am today i'th'vein of chivalry" (5.3.32), as if it was possible to put chivalry on or off like the costume of a knight. This becomes more painfully apparent on the battlefield later, when Hector slaughters a Greek because he wants his beautiful armour. When he says to the (dead) Greek "Most putrefied core, so fair without,/ Thy goodly armour thus hath cost thy life" (5.9.1-2), this can refer to the Greek as well

[74] I will look at the Greek camp more closely further below.

as to himself, because he is killed a moment later, defenceless because he has disarmed in order to put on the Greek's armour, which thus has indeed cost his life.

While the humanist ambition to restore ancient aesthetics and philosophy as 'authentically' as possible is shown to be doomed to fail because of the inevitable 'medievalness' that antiquity has adopted in the centuries in between, at the same time, it is questioned whether the ancient traditions are worthy to be emulated at all: "No – yes, he'll fight indifferent well" (1.2.215); the ancient heroes are not even that interesting. The antiquity presented here is unglamorous, unheroic. Pandarus judges the warriors, for example, by how "hacked" their helmets are: the more "hacks", the better.[75] The classical past is not only irretrievable, because there is no direct access to it, one that would not be transformed by the influence of what happened between then and the present, it is perhaps even irrelevant, if, that is, it is not connected to contemporary purposes. This purposeful interest in classical heroes is comically exaggerated in this scene: Pandarus praises the warriors to Cressida with the sole intention of arranging a match between her and Troilus. He draws her attention to the beauty of the men he describes while mentioning Troilus every time ("When comes Troilus? I'll show you Troilus" (1.2.187-188), etc.) until Troilus finally arrives.[76] Then he goes out of his way to present him in (what he thinks) the most favourable light:

> Mark him, note him. O brave Troilus! Look well upon him, niece, look how his sword is bloodied, and his helm more hacked than Hector's, and how he looks, and how he goes! O admirable youth! (1.2.223-226)

His attempts to point out how desirable Troilus is become more absurd: "Had I a sister were a grace, or a daughter a goddess, he should take his choice. O admirable man!" (1.2.228-231). It is supposed to convince Cressida that Pandarus would give any woman to Troilus if he could. This is an ironic exaggeration of a passage in Chaucer, where Pandarus assures Troilus that

> Were it for my suster, al thy sorwe,
> By my wil she sholde al be thyn to-morwe. (I. 860-1)

After Troilus has passed by, Pandarus loses interest in the warriors at once. When Cressida says, "Here comes more" (1.2.232) and we are waiting for more descriptions, he declines impatiently, "asses, fools, dolts; chaff and bran, chaff and bran; porridge after meat. I could live and die i'th' eyes of Troilus" (1.2.233-235). Even Achilles, the most famous and renowned Greek hero, is now only "a drayman, a porter, a very camel" (1.2.240).

---

75 "Look you what hacks are on his helmet, look you yonder, do you see?" (1.2.197-199); "his helm more hacked than Hector's" (1.2.225).

76 E.g. "A proper man of person" (1.2.186-187); "Look how he looks! There's a countenance!" (1.2.193-194); "Look ye yonder, niece, is't not a gallant man too, is't not?" (1.2.205-206).

Chaucer's Pandarus is closely linked to the narrator figure; one could posit that he is his alter ego. There are not as many signs that he has such a function for the author of the *play*, partly because his role is very much reduced here and because there are many other central figures (all the Greek and Trojan heroes) than in Chaucer's poem, which really concentrates upon the constellation of Troilus, Cressida and Pandarus. In this scene however, Pandarus does appear as a sort of director of a stage scene, a role he takes much more often in Chaucer (especially in the love scene in Book III, which he stage-manages). So, here at least, he is the one who presents the story to the audience. He does so in a way that highlights how the narrator's own interest controls what is being narrated (or how the historian's interest affects how the past is told), because the presentation of the Trojan heroes is comically distorted by Pandarus' trivial goal to make a match between Troilus and Cressida and the overambitious way in which he tries to achieve it. On the other hand, it becomes clear that the narrator is not free to create *any* story or history because the literary tradition has a life of its own. We don't believe Pandarus that Achilles is "a very camel", for example, because we know him from other texts to be formidable; without this background, the comical effect of the scene would not work in the same way.

I.3. The medieval/early modern dichotomy

The Trojans are associated with "medieval" ideals of chivalry and courtly love, but these are presented as contradictory ("Hector's opinion/ Is this in way of truth; yet, ne'ertheless..."), something rather performed than essential ("I am today in the vein of chivalry") and parodied by extreme exaggeration as, for example when Troilus is introduced at the very beginning of the play as a languishing Petrarchan lover. His unrequited love does not make him suffer nobly like it should, but makes him perfectly incapable of doing *anything*:

> I am weaker than a woman's tear,
> Tamer than sleep, fonder than ignorance,
> [...]
> And skilless as unpractised infancy. (1.1.9-12)

These are about the first lines Troilus speaks on stage. From the beginning, he is established not as a Petrarchan lover-hero but as the parody of one. Petrarchan love makes for a regress to early childhood rather than leading to noble refinement. When Troilus goes on to say to Pandarus, "Thou [...]/ Pour'st in the open ulcer of my heart/ Her eyes, her hair, her cheek" (1.1.49-51), the satirical exaggeration becomes grotesque. This tone is kept up in the play: many repugnant images of functions of the human body, like eating or getting eaten, digestion, excretion and decay, are to follow. It is a medieval trope that Troy had to fall because of its moral decay, an idea that derives mostly from how it is depicted in the last half of the *Metamorphoses*. The images of rottenness and decay allude to this trope, thus adding to the 'medievalness' of Troy as it is presented here. The (in this case) medieval future is already written upon the (ancient) past. The grotesqueness of the image ("pour'st her eyes in the ulcer of my heart") anticipates the butchery with which the play will end, when there is "nothing [...] but shapes and forms of slaughter" (5.3.12).

The Greeks, by contrast, are designed as the exact opposite of the Trojans, reflecting how alterity is constitutive of identity in a general sense and how premodernity generates modernity by constituting its dichotomic Other in a more specific sense. The Greeks represent a Renaissance world of dissimulation, arrogance, lack of a binding value system and drama, while the medieval Trojans, in binary opposition, are drawn as honest, humble, chivalrous and are associated with poetry. This begins right when they are mentioned for the first time, in the prologue, and the first scene in the Greek camp shows the Greek generals in a crisis. They discuss their failure in the siege and find the reason is not Troy's superior strength, but the fact that in the Greek army "the specialty of rule hath been neglected" (1.3.78), that there is "disorder" (1.3.95) and "chaos" (1.3.125). Most notably:

> The great Achilles, whom opinion crowns
> The sinew and the forehand of our host,
> Having his ear full of his airy fame,
> Grows dainty of his worth and in his tent
> Lies mocking our designs. (1.3.142-146)

Achilles, the mainstay and vanguard of the Greek army,[77] is the embodiment of the Greek hero, Hector's counterpart. Both of them are the personification, the essence of what 'Trojan' and 'Greek' stand for: what they say and do transcends these individual characters and says something more general about what is assumed about Greece and Troy. This goes so far that when Achilles kills Hector "in fellest manner" (5.7.6) in Act V, not only the fact *that* Troy is going to be destroyed is contained in this, but even *how* it is going to happen: Achilles lets his Myrmidons slaughter Hector when he is defenceless. Hector has taken off his armour to put on the armour of an unknown Greek soldier whom he killed for that reason: "I like thy armour well;/[...] I'll hunt thee for thy hide" (5.6.29-32). Here, he really abandons his code of chivalry and loses his chivalric integrity as he kills out of greed,[78] an allusion to Troy's moral decay that caused its downfall, according to the medieval literary tradition. More concretely, his greed makes him forget about the necessary caution when he takes off his armour in the middle of the bat-

77 "Sinew and forehand". See Bevington, p.166.

78 Eric S. Mallin sees the anonymous knight that is killed by Hector as the "figure of the Unknown Knight, who entered the lists anonymously, [...] an integral part of the tilts from medieval times"; "The *inconnu* hunted down and butchered represents a once glorious chivalry, now encumbered and made vulnerable by its own dazzling image. Hector, central chivalric force in Troy, kills the most recognizable Elizabethan image of chivalric privilege [...]. In so doing, he destroys the courtly ideal as it almost existed in the play" (Mallin, pp.57-58).

tle. Similarly, the Trojans will soon let greed prevail over carefulness when they decide to take the mysterious wooden horse into the city. Out of this, at night, Greeks hidden in the horse will come to open the gates to more Greek soldiers, who will kill the sleeping, defenceless Trojans and burn the city to the ground.[79] Achilles kills the defenceless Hector, who had also made the mistake to covet a beautiful but deceiving exterior. The dead body inside the shining armour – "most putrefied core, so fair without" (5.9.1) – again alludes to the medieval trope that it was Troy's excess and decadence, its 'rottenness', that led to its destruction. When Achilles addresses Hector before he attacks him, he likens Hector's end to the end of the day, as if Hector's life was a natural phenomenon:

> Look, Hector, how the sun begins to set,
> How ugly night comes breathing at his heels.
> Even with the vail and dark'ning of the sun
> To close the day up, Hector's life is done. (5.9.5-8)

Most obviously, this means that evening is coming and that fighting is done for the day, but not before Hector is killed. On a second level, it means that, for Hector, life ("the day", "the sun") is over, and death ("ugly night") will take over soon. But, at the same time, and on the *next* level, the metaphor works the other way round and makes Hector's life a larger temporal unit and his death a cut that concerns not just himself, but everyone. The sun darkens for everyone when the day or "Hector's life is done"; Troy's destruction, the end of an era will follow.

Hector, in turn, tries to appeal to Achilles' sense of honour and the rules of fair play:

> I am unarmed. Forgo this vantage, Greek. (5.9.9)

But Achilles has no mercy. Neither will his countrymen when they kill the sleeping Trojans in the night of Troy's destruction. Nonetheless, in his answer, Achilles takes up and continues Hector's rhythm and rhyme:

> Strike, fellows, strike! This is the man I seek. (5.9.10)

This signals how much Achilles and Hector are related to one another other. Here, in their final encounter, they literally complement one another: one completes the other's verse. Hector started speaking in rhymed verse while disarming:

> Now is my day's work done. I'll take good breath.
> Rest, sword; thou hast thy fill of blood and death. (5.9.3)

Looking back from Achilles' lines, we know that "day" also means "life" and that Hector's "rest" will be final. He rhymes "breath" with "death" in the next line, which is a good example of how the division between opposites can dissolve and

---

79 See Homer, *The Odyssey*, trans. Richmond Lattimore (New York: Harper, 1965), 4.271-274, 8.492-520 and Virgil, *The Aeneid*, trans. C. Day Lewis (Oxford: University Press, 2008), Book II.

let them conflate: "death" seems to be directly *opposed* to "breath". Yet when Hector says he will "take good breath", he means he is going to rest forever, as becomes clear when Achilles takes up this analogy and continues it, suiting the action to the word: he kills Hector. So, in fact, Hector is talking about his death when he talks about his breath, although the two words seem mutually exclusive, because "breath", in poetical language, usually connotes life, or soul,[80] terms in binary opposition to "death". Similarly, "blood" in the next line usually stands for 'life' and similar things, like love, strength, energy, temperament, passion (as in 'hot blood' etc.), but here it refers to bloodshed and thus death again. Things defined solely in relation to their opposites can assimilate to such a degree that they become indistinguishable: their meanings reverse and become their own opposite, like in the optical illusion of a reversible figure. To illustrate this even better, Hector and Achilles develop a slightly disordered sonnet together or, at least, a fourteen-line-poem that bears striking resemblance to a sonnet. Its rhyme scheme is a little unorthodox though. Hector starts with a quatrain in which the last two lines rhyme, then Achilles takes up his metre and rhyme scheme, continuing Hector's thoughts about the close of day. It goes as follows:

Act 5 Scene 9 *Enter* HECTOR [*dragging the Greek in armour*].

HECTOR	Most putrefied core, so fair without,	x[81]
	Thy goodly armour thus hath cost thy life.	x
	Now is my day's work done. I'll take good breath.	a
	Rest, sword; thou hast thy fill of blood and death.	a
	Enter ACHILLES *and his* Myrmidons.	
ACHILLES	Look, Hector, how the sun begins to set,	x
	How ugly night comes breathing at his heels.	x
	Even with the vail and dark'ning of the sun	b
	To close the day up, Hector's life is done.	b
HECTOR	I am unarmed. Forgo this vantage, Greek.	c
ACHILLES	Strike, fellows, strike! This is the man I seek.	c
	[*They fall upon Hector and kill him.*]	
ACHILLES	So, Ilium, fall thou! Now, Troy, sink down!	x
	Here lies thy heart, thy sinews and thy bone. –	x
	On, Myrmidons, and cry you all amain,	d
	'Achilles hath the mighty Hector slain'.	d[82]

Retreat [*sounded from both sides*] (5.9.1-14)

80 As in the Latin *anima* (or the Greek *pneuma*), which means both 'breath' and 'soul'.

81 This is to illustrate the rhyme scheme; "x" means "no rhyme".

82 If "down" and "bone" can be considered a rhyme, it is "d d e e". If it is an eye rhyme (i.e. a rhyme that the great vowel shift has made obsolete), then there is a reference to the temporal border between the Middle Ages and the Renaissance at the moment where Hector is being killed and Troy is dismissed ("Now, Troy, sink down").

The last four lines are spoken during and after the killing of Hector. Immediately afterwards, a retreat sounds "from both sides". These lines show great symmetry and reflect how the warriors approach each other, converge and separate again when Hector is dead. Their conjunction is not just linguistic: the sexual attraction behind the stated intention to kill had been established on their very first encounter and was continued to this last one. "Now, Hector, I have fed mine eyes on thee" (4.5.231), Achilles said when they first met but at the same time: "Tell me, you heavens, in which part of his body/ Shall I destroy him? Whether there, or there, or there?" (4.5.241-242). Achilles and Hector's aggression goes hand in hand with erotic attraction. When Achilles kills Hector, the physical union is consummated, first in the medium of language then in the flesh, albeit not that directly: it is not Achilles himself who kills Hector, he orders his Myrmidons to do so (which is also a prefiguration of the way the Greeks will swarm out at night and kill the Trojans in the night of Troy's destruction). The 'sonnet' that Achilles and Hector perform together perhaps links them to the most famous sonnet sequence in *Romeo and Juliet*, the one spoken by Romeo and Juliet together when they meet for the first time.[83] It has a similarly structured dialogue and has the speakers 'converge' in a kiss. The last four lines would be spoken by Romeo alone, if the parallel to Achilles was more complete. Juliet, however, has only one of the last four lines, so the balance is already leaning towards Romeo: she does not move, as she says ("saints do not move") and she is a "saint" (she'd been a "shrine" earlier) at the point where Hector is killed in his and Achilles' 'sonnet'. Romeo and Juliet are

---

83 It goes as follows:

ROMEO If I profane with my unworthiest hand
This holy shrine, the gentle sin is this,
My lips, two blushing pilgrims, ready stand
To smooth that rough touch with a tender kiss.

JULIET Good pilgrim, you do wrong your hand too much,
Which mannerly devotion shows in this,
For saints have hands that pilgrims' hands do touch,
And palm to palm is holy palmers' kiss.

ROMEO Have not saints lips, and holy palmers too?

JULIET Ay, pilgrim, lips that they must use in prayer.

ROMEO O then, dear saint, let lips do what hands do;
They pray, grant thou, lest faith turn to despair.

JULIET Saints do not move, though grant for prayer's sake.

ROMEO Then move not while my prayer's effect I take.

He kisses her

Romeo and Juliet, ed. Jill Levenson (Oxford: Oxford University Press, 2000), 1.4.206-219.

also lovers from two opposed parties and perform a sonnet together in perfect harmony but at their *first* encounter as opposed to this absolutely final one between Hector and Achilles. Romeo and Juliet see and approach each other, speak their sonnet together and kiss. It is all the more shocking that "the fearful passage" of Achilles and Hector's "death-marked love"[84] ends not 'only' in death as does Romeo and Juliet's eventually, but in rape and death: the way Hector dies, his body repeatedly penetrated by the weapons of Achilles' Myrmidons, very much resembles a rape. Afterwards Achilles says, "My half-supped sword, that frankly would have fed,/ Pleased with this dainty bait, thus goes to bed" (5.9.19-20).[85] Romeo and Juliet's sonnet leads to a *kiss*. While this parallel perhaps casts some shadow on the supposedly pure and romantic love of Romeo and Juliet, since there is some brutality in Romeo's "move not while my prayer's effect I take" (1.4.219), it confirms the idea of physical attraction and connection between the Greek and the Trojan archetypical heroes. With sonnet form of their exchange here evoking the harmonic first encounter between Romeo and Juliet, the encounter of Hector and Achilles seems all the more appalling by contrast. Their incomplete, only half-rhyming and rearranged (with the couplet *before* the last quatrain) sonnet seems a deliberate distortion of that shining sonnet in *Romeo and Juliet*. The incomplete rhymes also give the impression that the sonnet form is briefly quoted then almost immediately dropped as if at the horror of the scene. When Achilles says, "Look, Hector, how the sun begins to set,/ How ugly night comes breathing at his heels", conjuring up shadows ('breaths of night') from the corners, as it were, to darken the sky for this terrible scene, the visual "dark'ning of the sun" is accompanied by the cacophony of a distorted sonnet.

Fascinatingly, it is exactly their *opposition* that makes Achilles and Hector so similar. Their separation (the aggression between them that culminates in Hector's death) and unity (the attraction between them that culminates in the sexual act) coincide and this is not marked as a contradiction here.

Confirming the idea that Hector symbolises Troy, Achilles – still using Hector's metre and rhyme – addresses the dying Hector as "Ilium" and "Troy" ("So, Ilium, fall thou! Now, Troy, sink down!"). Thus the performance sets the course for the future: not only the past, or history, is performatively created but the future, too, because it is contained in this scene like in a nutshell, ready to become a reality soon. Therefore the end of Troy does occur in the play, although the events depicted stop before the city's destruction. It is contained in this scene and in some others. Cassandra, for example, screams, "Cry, cry! Troy burns!" (2.2.112), but she does so "with her hair about her ears" (2.2.97 *stage directions*), signalling to the audience that she is mad. The future occurs in prophecies and

---

84 This is how the prologue, also a sonnet, announces the story of Romeo and Juliet (*Romeo and Juliet*, prologue 9).

85 'Sword' often stands for 'penis' (Partridge, p.254).

symbols in the play, but the audience reads them in a particular way because this future has already happened for them. The play seems to be written for an audience that is able thus to read the signs and dialogues, so that the future (the fact that Troy is going to be destroyed) influences the image of the past (the way the play is read and interpreted), which gives the creation of history a somewhat circular character. It points to its auto-reference and illustrates how it is created by way of citations and (varied) repetitions.

As to the performative construction of a Greek/early modern counterpart of Troy/the Middle Ages, Achilles appears as the condensed image of 'Greek' in this play, the ultimate Greek hero, the "sinew and forehand of our host" (1.3.143), just as Hector is "Troy, [...] thy heart, thy sinews and thy bone" (5.9.11-12). When the reason why there has been no palpable success in the war so far is discussed among the Greek leaders, they find that the cause is "disorder" (1.3.95) and "chaos" (1.3.125) in the Greek army, which, in turn, is due to the fact that Achilles "having his ear full of his airy fame," has "dainty grown" (1.3.144-145) and has withdrawn from fighting. The Greek's "airy fame", that is reputation that is on everone's lips but insubstantial,[86] is associated with the early modern era and perceived in contrast to the binding value system of a supposedly stable medieval feudal society, whose loss has brought about a crisis of values. Achilles has become overbearing, refuses to fight and lies in his tent "mocking our designs" (1.3.146), as the Greek generals complain. His arrogance stands in striking contrast to Trojan 'medieval' humility, self-deprecation even, as in the scene where Aeneas submits the challenge to the Greeks – but it is ironically employed, self-consciously enacted: "I ask, that I might waken reverence,/ And bid the cheek be ready with a blush/ Modest as morning" (1.3.227-229), Aeneas says, but at the same time he pretends not to be able to tell "which is the high and mighty Agamemnon" (1.3.232), "that god in office" (1.3.231). He seems to be consciously performing his chivalric Trojan identity, which undermines the duality at the very moment when it is being established. Besides, the scene is happening on *stage*, as part of a performance and acted by an actor: actors act as Trojans *and* as Greeks, so that drama is in a way the basis for both, reflecting the early modern perspective from which the play is written, which sets limits to the Trojans' possibilities to employ 'their' medium, poetry. Even if a Trojan employs poetical language, like Aeneas in the above example, he does so as part of a performance. On the other hand, when Hector speaks in verse and rhyme, Achilles chimes in effortlessly (5.9.1-14). The play itself was probably not performed on public stages, as the preface of the 1609 edition to the "Ever" or "Eternal Reader" indicates,[87] so many people encountered both Trojan and Greek heroes in the form of a book.

---

86 See Bevington, p.166.

87 Bevington, p.120.

Nevertheless, the Greeks' proximity to drama and acting is proposed repeatedly. When Ulysses describes Achilles' misbehaviour, which, in his opinion, is the source of the Greeks' "weakness" (1.3.137), which he calls a "fever" (1.3.133), he describes a theatrical situation:

> With him Patroclus,
> Upon a lazy bed, the livelong day
> Breaks scurril jests,
> And with ridiculous and awkward action –
> Which, slanderer, he imitation calls –
> He pageants us. Sometime, great Agamemnon,
> Thy topless deputation he puts on,
> And, like a strutting player, whose conceit
> Lies in his hamstring, and doth think it rich
> To hear the wooden dialogue and sound
> 'Twixt his stretched footing and the scaffoldage,
> Such to-be-pitied and o'erwrested seeming
> He acts thy greatness in; and when he speaks,
> 'Tis like a chime a-mending, with terms unsquared,
> Which from the tongue of roaring Typhon dropped
> Would seem hyperboles. At this fusty stuff
> The large Achilles, on his pressed bed lolling,
> Cries 'Excellent! 'Tis Agamemnon just.
> Now play me Nestor.' (1.3.146-165)

The speech abounds with words taken from the semantic field of acting: "Imitation", "pageants", "puts on", "player", "dialogue", "acts", applause", "scaffoldage". But the description focuses on its artificiality: the player is "strutting", the dialogue "wooden", the footing "stretched", suggesting "strained, affected."[88] The reference to the means of representation, the frame ("scaffoldage") would be a classical alienation or distancing effect in a performance, because it destroys the illusion and, even if the play is not performed and there is no theatrical situation to which this could directly refer, the term draws attention to the unnaturalness, the inauthenticity of the action, its need to be supported by an artificial frame. "Wooden" implies clunky, hollow; "unsquared" not properly fitted;[89] "o'erwrested" overstrained.[90] This kind of acting calls to mind notions of (dis)simulation up to the point where the actor is called "slanderer" and it causes, according to Ulysses, the Greeks' "envious fever of pale and bloodless emulation" (1.3.133-134). To underline how far the performance is from the truth, Ulysses uses terms like "hyperboles," calls Achilles "large" (suggesting heavy, self-important, also prodigal)[91] and the performance "fusty" (stale, high-sounding).[92]

---

88 Bevington, p.360.
89 Bevington, p.166.
90 Bevington, *ibid.*
91 Bevington, p.167.
92 Bevington, *ibid.*

It is interesting how the performativity of "truth" is demonstrated across several levels of meaning and representation, because an actor miming Ulysses narrates on stage, within the fiction of the play, another performance that takes place constantly and that professes to be imitation, but is, according to this actor, slander. Why should we believe Ulysses or, rather, the actor *acting* as Ulysses, then at all? But the message to the audience, not the assembly of Greek leaders who listen to Ulysses, but *Troilus and Cressida*'s contemporary audience if it had one, or us the present-day watchers or readers of the play, is: the show *is* true, the imitation *is* lifelike, because the effect we know from Mark Antony's speech in *Julius Caesar*,[93] to take some other example from the Shakespeare canon, is working here too: the more Mark Antony points out that Brutus is "an honourable man", the more doubtful it becomes, because if it was indeed so obvious, of course, it would not have to be repeated and stressed so insistently. Likewise, the more that Ulysses denies that Patroclus' imitation bears the faintest resemblance to the real person, the more we start to believe that exactly this must be the case; if not, Ulysses would not have to disclaim it with so much effort: "as near as the extremest ends/ of parallels, as like as Vulcan and his wife" (1.3.167-168) or "from the tongue of roaring Typhon dropped" Patroclus' terms "would seem hyperboles" (1.2.160-161) and so on. It becomes even clearer when Ulysses first upbraids Achilles and Patroclus' impudence: "And then, forsooth, the faint defects of age/ must be the scene of mirth" (1.3.172-173), a moment later describing these effects in detail himself and with the same parodying exaggeration: "To cough and spit, and with a palsy fumbling on his gorget/ shake in and out the rivet" (1.3.173-175). "Gorget" and "rivet", terms from medieval warfare, help to demonstrate how incredibly old Nestor is, a relic from a distant past (also a kind of distancing effect). When Ulysses describes how Achilles laughs at this, it seems like a recommendation of the proper reaction, an invitation to his audience to do the same: "Sir Valour dies; cries, 'O, enough, Patroclus,/ or give me ribs of steel!" (1.3.176-177). It is hard to believe that sly Ulysses, the "man of many resources", as he is called in the *Odyssey*,[94] does not do this on purpose. One cannot really tell whose side he is on, the side of the Greek leaders or of Achilles and Patroclus, manipulating Agamemnon, Nestor and the rest, or somebody else's altogether. In this scene, he is presumably on the audience's side, constituting a kind of knowledge community with them. The Greeks themselves do not seem to notice the ridicule and criticism, which is part of the ridicule for the 'real', the theatrical (or reading) audience. Patroclus' performance is proven to be lifelike after all, paradoxically *because* Ulysses stresses its falsehood

93 *Julius Caesar*, ed. David Daniell, The Arden Shakespeare, Third Series (London: Methuen, 1998), 3.2.74-252.

94 *The Odyssey*, I.205.

so often. Thus his own (the actor who is acting as Ulysses) performance, along with the performance of *Troilus and Cressida* in general, appears more credible.

Achilles as the prototypical Greek and thus, as I argue, Renaissance person is the centre of his own theatre and stage-directs his own show ("play me Nestor" (1.3.165); he also stage-directs Thersites' railings: "Proceed, Thersites", he says later in the play, "Derive this. Come" (2.3.55-58)). Ulysses, too, is simulating when he professes to criticise Achilles and Patroclus while, in fact, he is confirming their criticism of the Greek princes. In doing so, he chooses words like "slanderer", "strutting", "stretched" and "hyperboles" which all allude to acting and, at the same time, to inflation, de-evaluation and over-estimation,[95] which is, according to Ulysses, the Greeks' "sickness" (1.3.140) and the reason why they are at a disadvantage with the Trojans ("Troy in our weakness lives, not in her strength" (1.3.137), as Ulysses points out). This confirms the idea that the Trojans are ascribed to a past world (the Middle Ages as a (relatively) recent past from an early modern perspective), because the present is usually perceived as a time of crisis, while the past is supposed to have consisted of stable values and reliable signifiers. This makes the Greeks contemporary (to the time the play was written). Along with Ulysses, the other Greek leaders too refer to a crisis of representation and to the insecurity brought about by the loss of traditional values and an effective status system.[96] For example, Nestor mentions: "imitation" (1.3.185), mere "opinion" (1.3.186), "infect" (1.3.187), "self-willed" (1.3.188), "proud" (1.3.189), "broad Achilles" (1.3.190), where "broad" suggests "puffed up" according to the OED,[97] "bold" (1.3.192) and "weaken and discredit" (1.3.195). These terms allude to acting and at the same time to the loss of "degree", a word that occurs eight times in the debate[98] (also "order" (1.3.88), "place" (1.3.86), "custom" (1.3.88) and "proportion" (1.3.87), all things that the Greeks are lacking). Troy, however, is "yet upon his basis" (1.3.75).

There are more examples for the Greeks being associated with drama, such as when Achilles simulates sickness in order not to have to talk to the Greek generals (2.3.66-74), which he obviously does not do for the first time, because Agamemnon replies, "We are too well acquainted with these answers" (2.3.111). The Greek princes, in turn, put on a show before Achilles when they pass by his tent pretending not to notice him, which is one of Ulysses' stratagems:

> Achilles stands i'th'entrance of his tent.
> Please it our general pass strangely by him,
> As if he were forgot; and, princes all,
> Lay negligent and loose regard upon him. (3.3.38-41)

[95] This was discussed in more detail in an unpublished seminar paper by Kathrin Bethke, "Nothings monstered": Economies of Pride in *Coriolanus* and *Troilus and Cressida*" held at the Shakespeare Association of America's 40th Annual Convention, 6 April 2012, Boston).

[96] Kathrin Bethke, *ibid.*

[97] Bevington, p.168.

[98] 1.3.83; 1.3.86; 1.3.101; 1.3.104; 1.3.108; 1.3.109; 1.3.125; 1.3.127.

This is one of the instances where the Greeks' connectedness with drama is used for some comedy and the heroism of the classical sources (*Iliad*, *Aeneid*) is deflated in a comical way, because the image of Greek elite parading in front of Achilles' tent, doing their best to pretend not notice him, does not leave much room for grandeur. This time it is Agamemnon who directs the action:

AGAMEMNON We'll execute your purpose, and put on
A form of strangeness as we pass along.
So do each lord, and either greet him not
Or else disdainfully, which shall shake him more
Than if not looked on. I will lead the way. (3.3.50-54)

The Greek princes' collective dissimulation on command provides a satiric image of the Greeks' association with drama. Their lack of a reliable system of reference and thus confused social order is likewise an issue that recurs throughout the play. Status insecurity is imagined as a kind of physical disorder in space, as in Ulysses' analogy of the planets roaming astray:

When the planets
In evil mixture to disorder wander,
What plagues and what portents, what mutiny,
What raging of the sea, shaking of earth,
Commotion in the winds, frights, changes, horrors,
Divert and crack, rend and deracinate
The unity and married calm of states
Quite from their fixure! (1.3.94-101)

The whole world falls apart in this picture, the universe reverses back to chaos, because the planets "to disorder wander". If the Greek leaders, particularly Achilles, do not follow "the specialty of rule" (1.3.78) and disobey Agamemnon, "the glorious planet Sol" (1.3.89), this will affect and harm society as a whole.

Their confusion and disorientation culminate in the scene where Agamemnon and his people helplessly err about in the dark, unable to find their way in their own camp: "We go wrong, we go wrong" (5.1.65) says Agamemnon, the leader, who earlier said, "I will lead the way" (3.3.54). "The glorious planet Sol" is off the track: not just his planets, but he himself "wanders to disorder". In this, the sovereign's lack of authority and incapacity to rule, they are similar to the Trojans, who are nevertheless chiasm-like diametrically positioned to the Greeks: Hector goes to the battlefield on the day of his death although Priam, his father, the king, tells him not to go (5.3.62-67 and 5.3.70). Priam is no great authority in this play; he is absent for most of the time. He appears only twice and has six speeches in total. Agamemnon, by contrast, has fifty-two speeches and appears in seven scenes.[99] And, when Priam appears, he is not very able to assert himself.

---

99 See *William Shakespeare: Complete Works*, eds. Jonathan Bate and Eric Rasmussen (Basingstoke: Macmillan, 2007), p.1459.

Even his son Hector, the noble and obedient knight, does not listen to him. This is the exact opposite, an inversion of the Agamemnon-Achilles situation: when Priam tells Hector *not* to go to battle, Hector refuses, saying he cannot go because of an oath:

PRIAM Ay, but thou shalt not go.
HECTOR I must not break my faith.[100] (5.3.70-71)

The disagreement between Agamemnon and Achilles, on the other hand, is because Agamemnon *wants* Achilles to fight, but Achilles refuses for the same reason as Hector, as it turns out:

to keep
An oath that I have sworn. I will not break it.
Fall, Greeks; fail, fame; honour, or go or stay;
My major vow lies here; this I'll obey. (5.1.40-43)

The idea of Trojan and Greek, or Hector and Achilles, as complementary parts of a unit is also expressed in the idea of "the blended knight": Ajax is "half made of Hector's blood" (4.5.84), another reference to Shakespeare's sources Lydgate and Caxton, according to whom Ajax is the son of Priam's sister and thus Hector's cousin.[101] This sister was abducted by the Greeks before Helen was abducted by the Trojans. As Troilus puts it, "for an old aunt whom the Greeks held captive/ He [Paris] brought a Grecian queen [...]/ Why keep we her? The Grecians keep our aunt" (2.2.77-80). It is Lydgate and Caxton's addition, which Shakespeare adopted, that Ajax is her son and thus related to Hector and that they treat each other with special kindness because of this (see 4.5.120-159). Out of the medieval source texts Shakespeare creates a "blended knight, half Trojan and half Greek" (4.5.87). This image can illustrate very well how, according to postcolonial theories of alterity, the Other really is part of the Self (but that part which the Self chooses not to acknowledge). This Other that is externalised, positioned elsewhere, is a projection. It is, of course, not really separable from the Self: as Hector himself makes clear, in this context, when he reflects upon how it is impossible to clearly distinguish between Trojan and Greek:

Were thy commixtion Greek and Trojan so
That thou couldst say, 'This hand is Grecian all,
And this is Trojan; the sinews of this leg
All Greek, and this all Troy; my mother's blood
Runs on the dexter cheek, and this sinister
Bounds in my father's', by Jove multipotent,
Thou shouldst not bear from me a Greekish member
Wherein my sword had not impressure made

[100] 'Faith' = 'assurance, pledge' (Bevington, p.332).

[101] *Troy Book* 3.2045-3.2048; *Recuyell of the Historyes of Troye* ll.589-590 (cited in Bevington, p.291).

> Of our rank feud. But the just gods gainsay
> That any drop thou borrowed'st from thy mother,
> My sacred aunt, should by my mortal sword
> Be drained. Let me embrace thee, Ajax! (4.5.125-136)

The union and inseparability is again put in erotic terms, as Hector continues, "Thou hast lusty arms!/ Hector would have them fall upon him thus" (4.5.137-138). But the image also reflects how people are treated as commodities in this play, like pieces of meat ("This hand", "the sinews of this leg". "the dexter cheek" etc.) and prefigures the subsequent encounter between Hector and Achilles, where Achilles insists upon treating Hector like a piece of cattle he wishes to purchase for slaughter but, strangely, again with erotic undertones. He begins,

> Now, Hector, I have fed mine eyes on thee;
> I have with exact view perused thee, Hector (4.5.231-232)

and makes it clear momentarily that he consciously treats Hector's warrior's as well as his erotic body like an article of commerce:

> I will the second time
> As I would buy thee, view thee limb by limb, (4.5.237-238)

(also: "joint by joint", 4.5.233), and then continues,

> Tell me, you heavens, in which part of his body
> Shall I destroy him? Whether there, or there, or there? (4.5.242-243)

The location of the Trojan/Greek, or friendship/enmity, love/hatred, Self/Other duality in the body of the "blended knight" is transferred to the temporal level by Achilles when he makes *time* the dividing factor, as opposed to the spatial separation that existed so far:

> Tomorrow do I meet the, fell as death;
> Tonight all friends. (4.5.269-270)

This reflects "the interconvertibility of space and time"[102] that informs the idea of the Middle Ages as temporary Orient or colonised past.[103]

I.4. Troilus true and Cressida false? The performative power of discourse

"Shall I not lie in publishing a truth?" (5.2.125)

Apart from Ajax, who is a "blended knight, half Trojan and half Greek" like the medieval Ajaxes of Lydgate and Caxton, it is Cressida, most prominently, who belongs to *both* worlds, because she switches between the camps. She is also the

102 Dagenais and Greer, p.435.
103 Ganim, p.12.

one who is very much associated with notions of reading and is herself seen as *text*, one could argue.[104]

There is one scene in which a *book* appears on stage. It is not the famous scene from Chaucer's *Troilus and Criseyde*, where Pandarus interrupts Criseyde's reading of either Statius' *Thebaid* or the *Roman de Thèbes* (II.78-112),[105] its 12th century French romance adaptation, which has spurred so many discussions about the question of genre and its implications, about vernacular chivalric romance versus Latin classical epic and the construction of 'male' and 'female' readings.[106] When Pandarus bursts in in the corresponding scene in *Troilus and Cressida* (1.2.36-170), Cressida has not been reading; nevertheless, the above scene, in which Pandarus attempts "to textualize her – to inscribe her in the romance he is writing for Troilus,"[107] influences Shakespeare's Cressida, as I will show in the remainder of this chapter.

If she were indeed reading the *Roman de Thèbes*, which her words seem to suggest ("This romaunce is of Thebes that we rede," *Troilus and Criseyde* II.100), she would be reading her own story soon, because the *Roman de Thèbes* is followed by the *Roman de Troie* in most manuscripts.[108] Pandarus interrupts her just in time before the situation becomes a "narrative impossibility."[109] But as Paul Strohm has pointed out, the Middle English term "romaunce" can refer to a Latin epic as well.[110]

Chaucer's Criseyde is a literarily-charged figure in many ways. The narrator constantly reflects on the conditions of writing, the literary tradition and his own position in it. The one scene where Shakespeare has someone read and be interrupted in *Troilus and Cressida*, is used for playing with generic distinctions, because here, Ulysses *pretends* to be reading. This is also a reference to Chaucer, because in *Troilus and Criseyde*, Pandarus, the narrator's alter ego, pretends to read after he has stage-directed the famous love scene (with potentially voyeuristic intentions),[111] a blurring of generic boundaries. Ulysses' reading, intentionally interrupted by Achilles,[112] is also part of a staged performance, part of the Greeks'

---

104 Although in the passage just quoted, Achilles turns Hector into text, too: "I have with exact view perused thee" (4.5.232).

105 See the discussion in Andrew James Johnston, "Geschlechter-Lektüren. Emotion und Intimität in Chaucers *Troilus and Criseyde*" in *Machtvolle Gefühle*, ed. Ingrid Kasten (Berlin: de Gruyter, 2010), pp.246-259, pp.247-251.

106 Carolyn Dinshaw, *Chaucer's Sexual Poetics* (Madison: University of Wisconsin Press, 1989), pp.28-64.

107 Gayle Margherita, "*Historicity, Femininity, and Chaucer's Troilus*", *Exemplaria* 6 (1995), pp.243-269, p.257.

108 Catherine Sanok, "Criseyde, Cassandre, and the *Thebaid*: Women and the Theban Subtext of Chaucer's *Troilus and Criseyde*", *Studies in the Age of Chaucer*, 20 (1998), pp.41-71, p.47.

109 Dinshaw, p.52.

110 Paul Strohm, "Storie, Spelle, Geste, Romaunce, Tragedie: Generic Distinctions in the Middle English Troy Narratives", *Speculum*, 46 (1971), pp.348-359, pp.354 ff.

111 See Johnston (2010a), p.257.

112 "I'll interrupt his reading" (3.3.93).

larger plan to trick Achilles into fighting again. So here is an actor playing someone who is reading in front of another actor and playing an actor who is *pretending* to be reading in front of an audience, perhaps an imagined audience because the play was printed to be read. The book that Ulysses is reading brings the reader into the story or onto the stage as well and opens a *Mise-en-abyme*-like scenario, with the question, "What are you reading?" (3.3.95) answered thus:

> A strange fellow here
> Writes me that man, how dearly ever parted,
> How much in having, or without or in,
> Cannot make boast to have that which he hath,
> Nor feels not what he owes, but by reflection;
> As when his virtues, shining upon others,
> Heat them, and they retort that heat again
> To the first givers. (3.3.96-103)

Here Shakespeare refers to his negotiation of the relativity of value in the play, of how worth is not inherent ("felt"), but ascribed ("reflected") by others, so that a person is defined by their social relations rather than their own (subject) consciousness; this makes Shakespeare, as author of this play, appear on stage, too, because the characters discuss his theses on stage, referring to him as a "the author". Ulysses continues,

> I do not strain at the position –
> It is familiar – but at the author's drift,
> Who in his circumstance expressly proves
> That no man is the lord of anything,
> Though in and of him there be much consisting,
> Till he communicate his parts to others;
> Nor doth he of himself know them for aught
> Till he behold them formed in th'applause
> Where they're extended – who, like an arch, reverb'rate
> The voice again, or, like a gate of steel
> Fronting the sun, receives and renders back
> His figure and his heat. I was much rapt in this. (3.3.113-124)

There are, once more, references to the theatrical situation, as in "his parts", "applause" etc., and, directly, to the situation of the writer in the moment when "he communicate[s] his parts to others" because the author seems to step out of the fiction to communicate without mediation to his theatre audience or readers. The last line, "I was much rapt in this", draws attention to how conventional genre distinctions are very cleverly mixed up in this 'multimedia performance' because, spoken aloud on stage, additional meaning is unwrapped: "rapt" means "deeply engaged in, transported by", but on stage, it is acoustically indistinguishable from "wrapped" = "absorbed".[113] "I was much wrapped in this" refers to the multiple

[113] Bevington, p.249.

roles the author plays in this scene: as the author of the book, in which these figures act in the minds of the readers and as the author who speaks out of the book that the figures read and discuss on stage. This links him to the many intradiegetic narrators Chaucer created in *The Canterbury Tales*, *The Legend of Good Women*, *House of Fame* etc. for which the concept of 'counter-authorship' has been created:

> Counter-authorship is an oblique literary form of self-presentation that allows the author to hide behind the veil of his fictions, while allowing us to follow him, through tracks he himself leaves – in his diction, images, myths, and so forth – some of them presumably 'conscious' but hardly all of them.[114]

Here, the author has invented the entire situation but, at the same time, appears out of a book that is being read as part of a drama within the drama, because Ulysses *pretends* to be reading it. And because this whole situation, in turn, is not acted out, but described in a book again, provided that *Troilus and Cressida* is being read, not performed on stage, the author appears at the outer and inner end of this pile of layers and references and is thus indeed "much wrapped". Since specific times in history are conventionally assigned to specific genres, Shakespeare could use the fact that drama is seen as Renaissance's, and epic (or romance) as the Middle Ages', prevalent means of literary expression to create another example of palimpsested time because, instead of distinct, successive periods along with their respective clearly assignable genres, this is an example of intermediality with interlacements too dense to be really distinguishable, like the blended knight.

The five acts of *Troilus and Cressida* correspond roughly to *Troilus and Criseyde*'s five books,[115] but the play has not simply replaced the epic poem. As the scene discussed above shows, the Renaissance drama did not supersede older forms but, rather, contains them. It may also contain genres that are to become popular in the future, because someone who is silently reading a book on stage could be seen as a harbinger of the later form of the novel. The 'sonnet' unrolling between Hector and Achilles at the time of death is also an example of intermediality: poetry, associated with the Middle Ages (and Troy, in this case) mingles with drama, identified as early modern, creating a multitemporal palimpsest. The other play that I mentioned in this context, *Romeo and Juliet*, contains many lyrical passages as well. It is filled with Petrarchan rhetoric, which is based on the courtly love tradition and the conventions of love poetry in general inform many of the play's situations.[116] Even *Romeo and Juliet*, widely considered to be a 'classical' work of dramatic art, contains multiple genres from multiple periods.

---

[114] Patrick Cheney, *Shakespeare's Literary Authorship* (Cambridge: Cambridge University Press, 2008), p.14.

[115] M.C. Bradbrook, "What Shakespeare Did to Chaucer's *Troilus and Criseyde*", *Shakespeare Quarterly*, 9:3 (1958), pp.311-319, p.313.

[116] See Levenson, pp.52 ff., for a more detailed description.

There is also a scene where the Greeks are reading and interpreting neither a book nor an author; instead their subject is Cressida herself. She is the centre of a 'bookish' discourse that is created around her. She is constantly referred to as someone to be read and interpreted, a "creature of intertextuality",[117] but also a woman of intr*a*textuality, because she is versed in Pandarus' and Troilus' idioms, too.[118] She is textually so fraught that her behaviour is very much predetermined by the literary fame that precedes her. She appears as "a woman who has read her own story and who recognizes the textuality of her existence".[119] This is, again, something that links her to Chaucer's Criseyde, who is often referred to in terms of reading and writing. This includes frequently the physical process of textual production, as for example when Troilus sees Criseyde for the very first time. He is so taken with her

> That in his herte botme gan to stiken
> Of hir his fixe and depe impressioun. (*Troilus and Criseyde*, I.297-298)

This evokes the practice of imprinting letters, or images, on wax tablets, a practice that is repeatedly mentioned in connection with Criseyde. She is, for example, referred to as a "ruby" in Book II (II. 585) and, shortly afterwards, Troilus uses a ruby to print his seal with it (II.1086-1088). A little later, Troilus' love is "engraved" in Criseyde's heart ("Hard was it youre herte for to grave," II.1241). In *Troilus and Cressida*, the connection between Cressida and writing is established before she even appears on stage when at the very beginning of the play, introducing her to the audience, Troilus says to Pandarus,

> Thou [...]
> Handlest in thy discourse, O, that her hand,
> In whose comparison all whites are ink
> Writing their own reproach. (1.1.49-54)

This contains her association with writing as well as the "discourse" that is created around her (by Troilus and Pandarus in this case but, in fact, by many more people, as will become obvious soon), a discourse that simultaneously enables and limits her actions, 'creating' a Cressida even before she has had a chance to present herself. In the scene where she is introduced to the Greek camp, Ulysses observes,

> There's language in her eye, her cheek, her lip,
> Nay, her foot speaks. (4.5.56-57)

117 Cook, p.50.

118 Wolfram Keller, "Passionate Authorial Performances: From Chaucer's Criseyde to Shakespeare's Cressida", unpublished paper from the conference *Performing the Poetics of Passion: Chaucer's* Troilus and Criseyde *and Shakespeare's* Troilus and Cressida, 13-15 May 2010, Free University of Berlin.

119 Cook, p.48.

If there is language even in her foot she is an excellent actor, too,[120] downright embodying the performativity of language. She might be adapting herself to the conditions of the Greek camp here already. Interestingly, the Elizabethan public theatre was, just like Cressida, frequently accused of guile, inconstancy and deceit by its opponents, who saw it as a threat to social order. In their view, natural, or even divine differences in hierarchy get confused when normal citizens dress and appear like gentlemen on stage.[121] What is more, the author of anti-theatrical tracts including *Plays Confuted in Five Actions* from 1582, Stephen Gosson, uses the same metaphor of sickness for the public theatre's effects as Ulysses in his analysis of what is amiss in the Greek army. He writes,

> In Stage Playes for a boy to put on the attyre, the gesture, the passions of a woman; for a meane person to take upon him the title of a Prince with counterfeit porte, and traine, is by outwarde signes to shewe them selves otherwise then they are, and so within the compasse of a lye... We are commanded by God to abide in the same calling wherein we were called, which is our ordinary vocation in a commonweale... If privat men be suffered to forsake theire calling because they desire to walke gentlemen like in sattine & velvet, with a buckler at theire heeles, proportion is so broken, unitie dissolved, harmony confounded, that the whole body must be dismembred and the prince or the heade cannot chuse but sicken.[122]

During the debate in the Greek camp, Ulysses argues in the same vein, "Degree being vizarded,/ Th'unworthiest shows as fairly in the mask" (1.3.83-84); "O, when degree is shaked,/ [...] The enterprise is sick" (1.3.101-103). He diagnoses that there is "an envious fever/ Of pale and bloodless emulation" (1.3.133-134), which leads to the question, "The nature of the sickness found, [...]/ What is the remedy?" (1.3.140-141). The Greeks suffer from the same disease that threatens early modern English society when degree and order are subverted by actors. Paradoxically, Cressida, who is seen as the epitome of falseness, inconstancy and deceit, is more bound to her role than is any other character and she knows it.

Ulysses also mentions the "tables of their thoughts" (4.5.61) ("their" refers to "these encounterers" = 'forward' women[123]) which they "wide unclasp [...]/ To every tickling reader" (4.5.61-62), a link to the ubiquitous writing table(t)s of *Troilus and Criseyde.* Cressida's textuality is not restricted to alphabetical text or acting; in 5.2.12-13, she is even a score of music: "Any man may sing her, if he can take her clef. She's noted" (again with sexual innuendo, like in the example before ("every tickling reader")). *Chaucer's* Criseyde, it can be argued, *becomes* text in Book V, the last book, in which she sets off for the Greek camp to become an

---

120 Keller, unpublished paper.

121 Montrose, pp.35 ff.

122 Stephen Gosson, *Plays Confuted in Five Actions*, facsimile edition (New York: Johnson Reprint Corporation 1972), C5r, G6v-G7v, cited in Montrose, pp.35-36.

123 Bevington, p.289.

absence from now on except for her letter and for one monologue in which she worries about her literary fame:

Allas, of me, unto the worldes ende,
Shal neyther ben ywriten nor ysonge
No good word, for thise bokes wol me shende. (*Troilus and Criseyde* V.1058-1060)

Criseyde has obviously come to see herself as a cipher by this point, one that is interpreted, appropriated by others. She seems to have internalised a hostile male (future) reading: she knows what she has to do, namely leave Troilus for Diomede and, although she regrets it, there is nothing she can do about it, because the story is already written out for her. Similarly, the narrator (another intradiegetic alter ego of the author, along with Criseyde and Pandarus), constantly worries about his own place in the literary tradition: he says to his work, "subgit be to alle poesye;/ and kis the steppes where as thow seest pace/ Virgile, Ovide, Omer, Lucan, and Stace" (*Troilus and Criseyde* V.1790-1792).[124] Furthermore, he apologizes time and again for having to write this sad story which he would love to tell differently if he could: but since the story is as it is, this is not possible. He says, to mention just one example,

And now my penne, allas, with which I write,
Quaketh for drede of that I moste endite.

For how Criseyde Troilus forsook –
Or at the leeste, how that she was unkynde –
Moot hennesforth ben matere of my book,
As written folk thorugh which it is in mynde.
Allas, that they sholde evere cause fynde
To speke hire harm! And if they on hire lye,
Iwis, hemself sholde han the vilanye. (*Troilus and Criseyde* IV.13-21)

In saying that he has nothing to do with what he just *has* to write, he reminds us of Pilate's gesture of washing his hands before the crowd: "See? I am innocent of Criseyde's ill fame. The pen writes it almost on its own". The narrator even admits the possibility that "they [his sources] lye" – but if they do, *they* "han the vilanye." On other occasions, he does not at all hesitate to deviate from his source (Boccaccio, mostly, although he never mentions him). Sometimes, he digresses silently; at other times, he openly states his disagreement and even refers his readers to other authors in case they want to know more about a particular issue or read a different story. He explains, for example,

if I hadde ytaken for to write
The armes of this ilke worthi man,

[124] The full quote is, "Go, litel bok, go, litel myn tragedye,/ Ther God thi makere yet, er that he dye,/ So sende myght to make in som comedye!/ But litel book, no makyng thow n'envie,/ But subgit be to alle poesye;/ And kis the steppes where as thow seest pace/ Virgile, Ovide, Omer, Lucan, and Stace" (V.1786-1792).

Than wolde ich of his batailles endite;
But for that I to written first bigan
Of his love, I have seyd as I kan–
His worthi dedes, whoso list hem heere,
Rede Dares, he kan telle hem alle ifeere. (*Troilus and Criseyde* V.1765-1770)

So, while Criseyde, with or without the narrator's approval, slowly disappears from Book V, Shakespeare's Cressida, on the other hand, does not cease to appear on stage in Act V. She does have conspicuously fewer lines, however. She seems to become increasingly silent towards the end of the play, paradoxically as she 'becomes' text the more. Her letter to Troilus from the Greek camp has forty-one lines in Chaucer. It has been assigned a prominent position in some manuscripts, with additional embellishments that make it look like a real letter[125] and an entire leaf to itself.[126] This letter is mentioned in *Troilus and Cressida* and even appears on stage, but its content is not made known: Pandarus hands it to Troilus but Troilus does not read it aloud, as is normally the case in scenes where letters are delivered. Instead, while he reads it, Pandarus makes one of his frequent and rather pointless laments about his physical diseases and how "the foolish fortune of this girl" (5.3.102) ruins him, so that it almost seems as if what Cressida has to say in the letter is deliberately 'cross-faded' with Pandarus' arbitrary rant. *Immediately* after Pandarus is done, he asks Troilus "What says she there?" (5.3.106). Troilus replies,

Words, words, mere words, no matter from the heart;[127]
Th'effect doth operate another way.
[*He tears the letter and tosses it away*] (5.3.107-108)

Arguably, Cressida, like Criseyde, comes to resemble a cipher, an empty signifier on which a collective fantasy is projected. In the passage described above, Ulysses, obviously still sullen because Cressida had refused to kiss him when she entered the Greek camp, 'explains' to Troilus before she has even said a word, "She will sing any man at first sight" (5.2.10-11). Thersites, observing Troilus and Ulysses who are observing Cressida and Diomedes, adds, "And any man may sing her, she's noted" (5.2.13). It is certain what she is going to do and everyone is familiar with it because, in this particular passage, as in others, her text seems to be written beforehand and is somehow read or heard even if she does not say a word. If Cressida is associated with the text itself, this is a text that seems to-

125 Martha Rust, "'Le Vostre C': Letters and Love in Bodleian Library MS Arch. Selden. B. 24" in *New Perspectives on Criseyde*, eds. Cindy L. Vitto and Marcia Smith Marzec (Asheville: Pegasus, 2004), pp.111-138, p.112.

126 Arch. Selden. B.24 presents the letter as an inserted legal document. Martha Rust, pp.131-132.

127 "Words" and "matter" are intertextual links to the scene where Hamlet (the famous modern subject) reads in *Hamlet* 2.2.194-198 (*The Oxford Shakespeare: The Complete Works*, eds. Stanley Wells, Gary Taylor and others (Oxford: Clarendon Press, 2005), pp.681-718).

tally powerless against its interpretation, on which, eerily, it does not have the slightest influence, because it is interpreted in ways that have little to do with anything it says: "th'effect doth operate another way". This becomes manifest in the scene described above, where the content of her letter is 'faded out' and Pandarus' blabber is inserted at the point where the audience could expect to be told what Cressida has to say. Instead, Pandarus' chatter, which is very repetitive in this play, obliterates Cressida's message.

It seems as if the reader, or interpreter, does not even need to see the text (or hear Cressida) to know what it will say, because they cling so firmly to preconceived opinions as to be blind towards what might be in it. But what is more, it seems as if Cressida herself – just like Criseyde – has internalised their reading. Long before she has to leave Troy, in fact before the actual affair with Troilus even starts, Cressida announces,

> When time is old and hath forgot itself,
> When waterdrops have worn the stones of Troy,
> And blind oblivion swallowed cities up,
> And mighty states characterless are grated
> To dusty nothing, yet let memory,
> From false to false, among false maids in love,
> Upbraid my falsehood! (3.2.180-186)

The emphasis and pathos make it sound almost ironic. Cressida seems tired of all the preconceptions and prejudices: the idea that, in an "old" future (future and past look similar here), when everything has dissolved "to dusty nothing" and the earth is without form and void like "in the beginning" (*Genesis* 1:1)[128] again people still won't have anything better to do than gossip about her is slightly absurd. The gossip is also completely discordant with the measured, slow, solemn tone of "When waterdrops have worn the stone", "and mighty states characterless are grated" and so forth.
This continues for some time:

> When they've said 'As false
> As air, as water, wind, or sandy earth,
> As fox to lamb, or wolf to heifer's calf,
> Pard to the hind, or stepdame to her son',
> Yea, let them say, to stick the heart of falsehood,
> 'As false as Cressid'. (3.2.186-191)

The enumeration of the elements continues the allusion to *Genesis* 1. When, after the void, everything that was created is listed, first the elements, then the animals and finally, to crown all, "God said, 'Let us make man in our image'" (*Genesis* 1:26), Cressida's falsehood comes up in this version of the story of crea-

[128] *The Holy Bible*, Revised Standard Edition (New York: Meridian, 1974). All Bible quotations are taken from this edition.

tion. This makes it very ironic, especially as Pandarus finishes the speech, "Go to, a bargain made" (3.2.192) and resorts to the language of business again. This is especially inappropriate because in the 'original' *Genesis*, God rests at this point, wherefore the seventh day is no business day. Even better, Pandarus now starts a (business-like) wedding ceremony (at the point where God creates a "wife" for "the man" (*Genesis* 2:18-23)):

> Seal it, seal it; I'll be the witness. Here I hold your hand, here my cousin's. If ever you prove false one to another, since I have taken such pains to bring you together, let all pitiful goers-between be called to the world's end after my name: call them all panders. Let all constant men be Troiluses, all false women Cressids, and all brokers-between panders! Say 'Amen'. (3.2.192-199)

The "Amen" is repeated no less than three times, once by each of them, Pandarus in the end and then Pandarus shows them "a chamber with a bed" (3.2.202-203). This is the unromantic beginning of the actual love affair, a mock wedding that does not even try to present itself as something other than a business deal. The only thing that is supposed to last is what is to be connected with their names. Troilus has a similar monologue that abounds not necessarily with biblical references, but with literary references in a more general sense, that all accord with the Trojans' general association with poetry:

> When their rhymes,
> Full of protest, of oath and big compare,
> Wants similes [...]
> As truth's authentic author to be cited,
> 'As true as Troilus' shall crown up the verse. (3.2.169-177)

His name stands for truth, Cressida's for falseness and Pandarus' for pander. Her association with the theatre and acting has been mentioned before. It could be argued that she appears as the embodiment of the performativity of history itself when she describes her reputation ("False, false, false!") as predetermined from the beginning of time to eternity and beyond, especially because she puts the history of her reputation in analogy to the history of creation, where language gets assigned the ultimate performative power: "'Let there be light'; and there was light", etc. (*Genesis* 1:3 ff.) According to Judith Butler, who quotes the same biblical passage in this context, the citationality of performative utterances is occluded by the instalment of a subject that appears as originator of the utterance.[129] But, to Cressida, the status of a subject is denied. This character, who has existed in various forms for centuries, who is conscious of her own literariness and who knows her character's future and past, cannot free herself from what others want to see in her. She cannot change the story written for her. Where Cressida's subjectivity should be, where she should stand as the author of

[129] Judith Butler, *Excitable Speech: A Politics of the Performative* (New York, London: Routledge, 1997), pp.50-51.

her performative speech – however fictive that authorship may be, if we believe Judith Butler, which I do – a lacuna is exhibited.

There are more allusions to the fact that the story is already written and the outcome determined and known to the characters who are unable to escape the narratives already written out for them. When Cressida learns that she is going to be exchanged for another prisoner and will have to leave Troy, she repeats,

> Make Cressid's name the very crown of falsehood
> If ever she leave Troilus! (4.2.101-102)

The communal exclamation "The Trojan's trumpet" (4.5.65), which would be heard as "Trojan strumpet",[130] at Cressida's exit strikes a similar note. Troilus fulminates,

> O Cressid! O false Cressid! False, false, false!
> Let all untruths stand by thy stained name. (5.2.185-186)

The 'fact' that Cressida is "false, false, false" is repeated like a mantra, so often that it is reminiscent of the concept of interpellation, the constative and performative effect of an exclamation and its need of iteration and thus the concept of performativity in Judith Butler's sense again. It is interesting that Cressida seems to have internalised her association with falseness and betrayal to such a degree that she is complicit in its perpetuation, such as when she calls herself, "O false wench!" (5.2.73) and then confirms the prejudices against her as if she is completely resigned to them: "I will not keep my word" (5.2.104) she says when she gives Troilus' sleeve, given to her as a love token, to Diomedes. Her words, a repetition of what has been said about her throughout the play (also about Helen, in a very similar way), are taken as "a proof of strength" (5.2.119) by Thersites.

In Chaucer, Criseyde is probably reading the *Thebaid* in Book II and thus, in a sense, her own story.[131] Although Pandarus interrupts her before she reaches the point where her future lover Diomedes enters the story, it cannot be inferred from the text that this is to be understood as her *first* reading of the *Thebaid*.[132] To the contrary, the way she refers to it seems to imply her familiarity with the epos.[133] *Cressida* certainly seems to have read her story before she appears in the play. It influences her behaviour, she acts according to what has so often been written about her, as Criseyde had prophesied, "Allas, for now is clene ago/ My name of trouthe in love, for everemo" (*Troilus and Criseyde* V.1054-1055) or "rolled shal I ben on many a tonge!/ Thorughout the world my belle shal be ronge!" (V. 1061-1062). Similarly, Troilus seems to know that his love for

130 Bevington, pp.368-369.

131 *Troilus and Criseyde*, II. 94-112. For the reasons why it is more likely that she is reading Statius' *Thebaid* than the 12th century French poem *Roman de Thèbes*, see Sanok, pp.45-48.

132 See Johnston (2010a), p.252.

133 Johnston (2010a), *ibid.*

Criseyde will kill him and that he will die at the end of the story; so when it finally happens at the end of Book V, one brief sentence suffices to describe the event: "Despitously hym slough the fierse Achille" (V.1806). But, in *Troilus and Criseyde*, this future that both protagonists seem to know (Criseyde will be unfaithful, Troilus will die from the pain) is bemoaned extensively,[134] while it is curtly, cynically commented in *Troilus and Cressida* ("Nothing but lechery!" (5.1.95), "War and lechery confound all!" (2.3.72)). Yet even in *Troilus and Criseyde*, the same circularity can be detected: Criseyde acts in this way because her literary fame prescribes her actions and then, in turn, this fame is given as proof of the veracity of the story, as the narrator explains:

> Hire name, allas, is publysshed so wide
> That for hire gilt it oughte ynough suffise. (V.1096-1097)

So, Cressida/Criseyde's name was indeed "rolled on many a tonge, thorughout the world", as Criseyde foresaw. At the time when *Troilus and Cressida* was written, she had already become a whore and died as a begging leper as a punishment by the gods in Henryson's sequel, *The Testament of Cresseid*, dated to around 1492. This circumstance influences the way she is seen by Shakespeare's contemporaries. It resonates from the repeated evocations of leprosy in *Troilus and Cressida* ("She never shrouded any but lazars" (2.3.30-31) or "I care not to be the louse of a lazar" (5.1.63)) and from sentences like "my mind is now turned whore" (5.2.120) where, again, the efficacy of rumours and fame is stressed in a way that accords with the concept of interpellation, because when Cressida 'deducts',

> Ah, poor our sex! This fault in us I find:
> The error of our eye directs our mind.
> What error leads must err. O, then conclude:
> Minds swayed by eyes are full of turpitude, (5.2.115-118)

Thersites takes this as "a proof of strength" that she has now "turned whore" (5.2.119-120). Henryson is also vague about whether or not she has indeed become a whore. He cites a rumour as his source:

> Than desolait scho walkit up and doun,
> And sum men sayis into the court commoun. (*The Testament of Cresseid*, 76-77)[135]

"Sum men sayis": Cressida's ill fame is a selfreferential endless loop. That Henryson's turn of the story was known to Shakespeare and his audience becomes even more clear in *Henry V*, written 1598-1599 and thus shortly before *Troilus and Cressida* (1601-1602), were she is explicitly associated with leprosy:

---

[134] He dies, in fact, because he intentionally fights so recklessly in the battle that he is killed before long.

[135] Quoted from the reprint of Robert L. Kindrick, *The Poems of Robert Henryson* (Kalamazoo, MI: TEAMS, Medieval Institute Publications, 1997) in Barney, pp.433-447.

To the spital go,
And from the powd'ring tub of infamy
Fetch forth the lazar kite of Cressid's kind. (*Henry V*, 2.1.72-74)[136]

She lives in "the spittaill hous" (391) in *The Testament of Cresseid.* Although the narrator presents himself as writing *after* the *Troilus*, which is a finished book at the beginning of the *Testament* ("I tuik ane quair[137] [...]/ Writtin be worthie Chaucer glorious/ Of fair Creisseid and worthie Troylus", 40-42), Troilus, dead at the end of Chaucer's *Troilus*, is alive again in *The Testament of Cresseid.* The *Testament* is no real sequel therefore, but rather an alternative version. Henryson's narrator does not seem to find Troilus' resurrection problematic. Except for wherever Cressida's fame is concerned, where everyone agreed so far, the narrator seems willing to accept the possibility of multiple, conflicting or even contradictory versions and, indeed, questions the idea of *one* authorised, reliable story: "Quha wait gif[138] all that Chauceir wrait was trew?" (64). Nevertheless, his Cressida exists in more than one version, too: when Troilus encounters her while she and other lepers are begging for alms, she has changed so much that he does not recognise her:

Than upon him scho kest up baith hir ene,
And with ane blenk it come into his thocht
That he sumtime hir face befoir had sene,
Bot scho was in sic plye he knew hir nocht;
Yit than hir luik into his mynd it brocht
The sweit visage and amorous blenking
Of fair Cresseid, sumtyme his awin darling. (*The Testament of Cresseid*, 498-504)

He is so moved by this remembrance of Cressida that he gives her gold and jewels, but he does not realize that this actually *is* Cressida. The idea here is that Troilus, the "trew knicht" (*The Testament of Cresseid*, 546), remembers Cressida as she looked when she was fair, before she betrayed him, but that her inward, moral ugliness has by now changed her outer appearance. The Cressida he sees is still able to stir a memory of the former, beautiful Cressida whom Troilus loved, but it is not strong enough to identify her. This situation occurs again, also a little changed, but still recognisable, when in Act V of *Troilus and Cressida* where he secretly watches Cressida, Troilus pretends not to be able to recognise her: "Was Cressid here?" (5.2.131); "This she? No, this is Diomed's Cressida./ If beauty have a soul, this is not she" (5.2.144-145); "This is not she" (5.2.149), "This is and is not Cressid" (5.2.153). In an inversion of Henryson's scene, where Troilus does not recognise the defaced Cressida because he still has the "fair" (504) picture of her "sweit visage" (503) in his mind, Shakespeare's Troilus mistrusts his

136 Quoted from *The Oxford Shakespeare*, pp.595-625.
137 = "Little book (quire)" (Barney, p.434).
138 "Who knows whether" (Barney, *ibid*).

eyes because what he sees *looks* like the Cressida he knew but does not behave like her. Therefore he says that still

> there is a credence in my heart,
> An esperance so obstinately strong,
> That doth invert th'attest of eyes and ears,
> As if those organs had deceptious functions,
> Created only to calumniate. (5.2.126-130)

He asks the paradoxical question, "Shall I not lie in publishing a truth?" (5.2.125). If 'truth' is what everyone takes for granted, like Cressida's falseness, which is proven by her ill fame which is proven by her ill fame and so on, one can indeed lie when publishing it. But the question of whether someone who has changed but looks the same is or is not the same person also leads to the negotiation of subjectivity again. "This is and is not Cressid" (5.2.153) prefigures Iago's "I am not what I am",[139] which has been seen as symptomatic of a (supposedly newly discovered) Renaissance subjectivity, [140] interiorised self-recognition and the ability to dissimulate it brings about. For her ability to dissimulate, Cressida does get assigned subject status here, at last, if only ironically. The fact that it is Troilus who notices her 'subjectivity' and puts it in words echoing Renaissance man's famous slogan (an echo from the future, once again) possibly reflects the fact that in this play identity is conferred to people by others, not intrinsic to anyone. It also concurs with Foucault's argument that it is the discourse that forms the subject instead of the other way round.

139 *Othello*, 1.1.65. Viola, cross-dressed as Cesario, has the same line in *Twelfth Night*, 3.1.139. Both quoted from *The Oxford Shakespeare*.

140 Cf. Johnston (2009a), p.302.

Part II: *THE TWO NOBLE KINSMEN:* The Stage as Palimpsest

As in *Troilus and Cressida*, Shakespeare drew extensively on Chaucer for *The Two Noble Kinsmen*, which was written in collaboration with John Fletcher in around 1612-1613 and first published in 1634. Some critics have doubted Shakespeare's participation in *The Two Noble Kinsmen*, while others have suggested alternative collaborators, such as the playwright and actor Nathan Field. Some claim the play is entirely Shakespeare's, but few scholars accept this.[1] Today, the play is included in all standard series of Shakespeare, but the precise shares of Fletcher and Shakespeare remain disputed.[2] It is impossible to tell with absolute certainty who wrote what exactly, but Jeffrey Masten argues that the question is irrelevant, since ascribing each particular scene to an individual author is an anachronistic approach that tries to install the concept of singular authorship into a period in which it did not yet exist. Concurring with Michel Foucault's argument that "the author is [...] the ideological figure by which one marks the manner in which we fear the proliferation of meaning"[3] and proposing that the author is a function, or "habit", of the text itself, "contemporaneous with (not prior to) [...] texts and their publication",[4] he shows that a more collaborative, less authoritative concept of authorship prevailed in the early modern period.[5] Arguing that what Foucault calls the "author-function"[6] emerged only later, as a process that drew upon already existing discourses ("classicism, author/ity, paternity"),[7] he advo-

---

1 See *The Two Noble Kinsmen*, ed. Lois Potter (London: Thomson Learning, 1997), pp.18 ff. All citations will be to this edition and will be given in the text. Cf. Julie Sanders, "Mixed Messages: The Aesthetics of *The Two Noble Kinsmen*", in *A Companion to Shakespeare's Works, Volume IV: The Poems, Problem Comedies, Late Plays*, eds. Richard Dutton and Jean Elizabeth Howard (Oxford: Blackwell, 2003), pp.445-461, p.445; Julia Ruth Briggs, "Chaucer ... the Story Gives": *Troilus and Cressida* and *The Two Noble Kinsmen*", in *Shakespeare and the Middle Ages: Essays on the Performance and Adaptation of the Plays with Medieval Sources or Settings*, eds. Martha W. Driver and Sid Ray (Jefferson, N.C.: McFarland & Company, 2009), pp.161-177, p.162.

2 The most common position is that Shakespeare wrote Act 1, the first two scenes of Act 3 and Act 5 (except for Scene 2, the first scene of Act 2 and Act 4 Scene 3), while Fletcher wrote, accordingly, Act 2 except for Scene 1, Act 3 scenes 3 to 6, the first two scenes of Act 4 and the second scene of Act 5. See Anne Thompson, *Shakespeare's Chaucer: A Study in Literary Origins* (Liverpool: Liverpool University Press, 1978), p.167. See *The Two Noble Kinsmen*, pp.16-34 for a more detailed discussion of the authorship question.

3 Foucault, "What Is an Author?" in *The Foucault Reader*, ed. Paul Rabinow (New York: Pantheon, 1984), p.119, cited in Jeffrey Masten, *Textual Intercourse: Collaboration, Authorship, and Sexualities in Renaissance Drama* (Cambridge: Cambridge University Press, 1997), pp.10, 169.

4 Masten, p.10.

5 Masten, pp.7, 12-27 and *passim*.

6 Foucault, "What Is an Author?" in *The Foucault Reader*, p.105, cited in Masten, pp.75, 188.

7 Masten, p.75.

cates a more collaborative concept of textual production that shifts the focus away from questions of authorial intention, essential textual properties and stable meaning to "discourses, figures, locations, and cultural practices",[8] where authors as subjects are inscribed in and constituted by these discourses and practices.[9] Since *The Two Noble Kinsmen* discusses the problems that occur when authority is located in one individual alone, as in the figure of Theseus, these observations are relevant for the analysis of the play, not only because it was not written by a single author. Theseus' rule, connected to the concept of linear chronology and progressive history, creates unsolvable dilemmas for the characters subjected to his authority.

I will first examine the prologue with its invocation of Chaucer and compare it to Gower's prologue in *Pericles*, finding examples of palimpsested time in the way that these two prologues refer to their respective sources and, perhaps, also to each other. I argue that, in *The Two Noble Kinsmen*, the palimpsest, with its different layers, is mapped upon the stage and that the dead, the half-dead and the living bodies of the characters, which frequently appear on the wrong side of the (stage) floor, symbolise the different levels of present and past times and their "tied, weaved, entangled" (1.3.42) position in the palimpsest. Drawing on Lee Patterson's notion of *Thebanness*, I argue, furthermore, that Theseus and Athens represent a linear and progressive understanding of time, while Creon and Thebes stand for a recursive temporality that has no aim. Theseus succeeds in imposing linear order upon Thebes' circular chaos, but at an inacceptable cost. His rule is, moreover, linked to compulsory heterosexuality, which is thus connected with linear temporal order, the production of legal heirs and family trees, while most of the protagonists are otherwise inclined.

II.1. The Prologue: "Constant to eternity"

The Two Noble Kinsmen is, as far as we know, Shakespeare's very last play. Unlike any other of his plays except for *Pericles*, its main source is openly acknowledged in the prologue. Like *A Midsummer Night's Dream*, it is based chiefly on *The Knight's Tale*, the first of the *Canterbury Tales*.[10] The prologue introduces it thus:

> We pray our play may be so [i.e. good], for I am sure
> It has a noble breeder and a pure,
> A learned, and a poet never went
> More famous yet 'twixt Po and silver Trent.
> Chaucer, of all admired, the story gives;

---

8 Masten, p.27.

9 Masten, pp.17-18.

10 For a detailed treatment of the play and its source, see Thompson, pp.166-215, and Ethelbert Talbot Donaldson, *The Swan at the Well: Shakespeare Reading Chaucer* (New Haven, London: Yale University Press, 1985), pp.50-73.

There, constant to eternity, it lives.
If we let fall the nobleness of this
And the first sound this child hear be a hiss,
How will it shake the bones of that good man
And make him cry from under ground, 'Oh, fan
From me the witless chaff of such a writer
That blasts my bays and my famed works makes lighter
Than Robin Hood!' (PROLOGUE 9-21)

The story's "noble breeder", Chaucer, is invoked and used to appeal for a benign reception of the play. While the fact that "Chaucer, of all admired, the story gives" is treated as an argument for the play's quality, the audience is, at the same time, asked to receive it well for the author's sake, since otherwise he might not be able to sleep peacefully. The prologue continues,

This is the fear we bring;
For, to say truth, it were an endless thing
And too ambitious to aspire to him,
Weak as we are, and, almost breathless, swim
In this deep water. Do but you hold out
Your helping hands and we shall tack about
And something do to save us. You shall hear
Scenes, though below his art, may yet appear
Worth two hours' travel. To his bones sweet sleep;
Content to you. (PROLOGUE 21-30)

It could seem that Chaucer is established as a fatherly authority here, installed as an author in the modern sense of the word and, as such, set in opposition to the collaborating dramatists, Fletcher and Shakespeare. But the prologue-speaker's "we" includes the theatrical company as well, not just the two playwrights,[11] and the audience's participation in the performance is also made clear: "Do but you hold out/ Your helping hands" is a request for applause,[12] which stresses the collaborative effort necessary for a stage performance.[13] Since the playwrights, the actors and the audience contribute to the success of the play, one can assume that Chaucer is included in the collaboration. In *The Three Noble Kinsmen: Chaucer, Shakespeare, Fletcher*, Kathryn Lynch argues that this play conceives of itself as "a collaboration between all three of these authors".[14] This does not mean that

---

[11] Masten, pp.56-57.

[12] Potter, p.139.

[13] "In some ways the theater is the most socially embedded of all the arts, depending as it does upon a direct process of exchange between performer and spectator and thus subordinating the contribution of the writer". Russ McDonald, *The Bedford Companion to Shakespeare* (Boston, New York: Bedford/St. Martin's, 2001), p.28.

[14] Kathryn L. Lynch, "The Three Noble Kinsmen: Chaucer, Shakespeare, Fletcher" in *Images of Matter: Essays on British Literature of the Middle Ages and Renaissance. Proceedings of the Eighth Citadel Conference on Literature, Charleston, South Carolina, 2002*, ed. Yvonne Bruce (Newark: University of Delaware Press), pp.72-91, p.72.

no poetic rivalry existed between the three of them; on the contrary, "Shakespeare's uneasy emulation of Chaucer" or "Fletcher's revisionary engagement with Shakespeare" generates, in her view, "productive friction."[15]

It is not just the prologue that makes the link to Chaucer's *Knight's Tale* so obvious: the epilogue, likewise, calls the play a "tale": "If the tale we have told/ (For 'tis no other) any way content ye..." (EPILOGUE 12-13).

A similar intermediality has been noted in *Troilus and Cressida*: different genres (drama, epic poetry) are interwoven in a palimpsest-like manner. They are no less inseparable than the historical epochs to which they are generally assigned. The categories get destabilised when, for instance, a play is called "the tale" ("for 'tis no other"). Unlike in the case of *Troilus and Cressida*, this does not happen within the play's body, but at prominent positions: the very beginning and end. Prologues and epilogues are characterised by the transition between two kinds of reality, when the theatrical fiction has not yet started or ended. Therefore, they are a great opportunity to address the theatrical situation directly, to address, for instance, the audience *as audience*, like here, but within the fiction of the play. Thus they point to the artificiality of the theatre, while simultaneously attesting to its power to generate a reality, as do our categories that create and form history.

II.2. "I carry winged time": The Gower figure in Pericles

For Matthews and McMullan, the prologue's invocation of Chaucer emphasises the agency of the Middle Ages in creating their own image:

> The medieval continues not just to be read and received in his [the author of the prologue's; they presume it is Fletcher] own day but also works to construct the ways in which it is read. [...] Medieval culture thus addresses attempts later made to adapt it [...]. At the same time as it gestures toward the sense of rupture between medieval and early modern, the prologue to *The Two Noble Kinsmen* shows an anxiety about the legacy of the one for the other and the possibility of *continuity* between them.[16]

The prologue may, in their view, be performing an act of historical mediation, but McMullan and Matthews are in fact reifing the periodising categories they set out to call into question, as Alex Davis laments: they never question the idea that the categories of medieval and early modern were created and articulated in the Renaissance itself, rather than being applied retrospectively. Thus the categories themselves remain.[17] Davis argues that Chaucer is not medievalised by the prologue in the same way that, for instance, Gower is in the prologue of *Pericles*.

---

[15] Lynch, *ibid.*

[16] *Reading the Medieval in Early Modern England*, eds. David Matthews and Gordon McMullan (Cambridge: Cambridge University Press, 2007), p.2.

[17] Alex Davis, "Living in the Past: Thebes, Periodization, and *The Two Noble Kinsmen*", *Journal of Medieval and Early Modern Studies*, 40:1 (2010), pp.173-195, pp.174-175.

According to Davis, Gower's "stiffly rhyming contribution is explicitly framed as 'a song that old was sung', addressed to 'these latter times/ When wit's more ripe'".[18] The author(s) of *The Two Noble Kinsmen*'s prologue could have done the same with Chaucer, but instead, they made him appear above all as noble, "a laureate poet, [...] in fact, as something like an English Petrarch".[19] Therefore, the line that is being drawn in the prologue is not so much one that distinguishes between early modern and medieval, he argues, but between popular and elite (a title like *The Three Noble Kinsmen: Chaucer, Shakespeare, Fletcher*, crossing temporal boundaries and creating an alliance based on nobility instead suggests the same). Instead of distancing Chaucer from the present, the prologue says that his writing "lives". In Davis' view, the question about which the prologue's prosopopoeia of Chaucer is anxious is, therefore, whether the play is going to be a "'famed work', worthy of posterity's approval, or [...] nothing more than a tale of Robin Hood, simplistic, vulgar, and foolish".[20]

While this sounds convincing, I do not think it is enough to claim that the authors do not address the Middle Ages as such or that they don't address questions of historical difference. The fact that, for instance, Shakespeare's work is "in many respects quite notoriously unmarked by signs of historical difference (clocks and doublets in ancient Rome, and so forth)"[21] does not necessarily mean that he, too, lacks historical awareness in a way that is often (unfairly) ascribed to the Middle Ages as, for example, in Peter Burke's famous dictum, "The Middle Ages never knew that they were the Middle Ages. [...] But the Renaissance was quite conscious of the fact that it was a Renaissance".[22] As has been shown for *Troilus and Cressida*, Shakespeare did reflect upon these categories and investigated how they are constructed. It is true, however, that the way that Chaucer is presented in the prologue of *The Two Noble Kinsmen* is different from how Gower appears in *Pericles*. The fact that Gower appears more antiquated is not the sole difference. Chaucer is in his grave, somewhere off-stage, not visible or audible to the audience. He is conjured up mentally and his bones shake in the audience's imagination, while Gower appears on stage as an actual person (John Gower's *Apollonius of Tyre* (1393) is the direct source of *Pericles*). He leads the audience through the play as *Chorus*, comments upon the events and speaks both the prologue and the epilogue. His prologue in *Pericles* starts,

---

18 Alex Davis, p.176.

19 Alex Davis, *ibid.*

20 Alex Davis, *ibid.*

21 Alex Davis, p.175.

22 Peter Burke, *The Renaissance* (London: Longmans, 1964), p.2, cited in Alex Davis, pp.173, 190. Cf. "The Middle Ages had left antiquity unburied and alternately galvanized and exorcised its corpse. The Renaissance stood weeping at its grave and tried to resurrect its soul" (Eric Panofsky, *Renaissance and Renascences in Western Art* (1960; repr. New York: Harper and Row, 1972), p.113, cited in Alex Davis, pp.174, pp.190 f.

To sing a song that old was sung
From ashes ancient Gower is come. (1.0.1-2)[23]

To "sing" a story is already an antiquated expression but, in addition, the song was "*old* sung" and an "ancient" Gower has come from "ashes". There are probably as many archaisms here as is possible in two lines; the metre was also obsolete by this time. He also speaks of himself in the third person, an old-fashioned way to refer to oneself which creates more distance from the speaker. Furthermore, he mentions that the story is not his own but that he, too, has heard it from someone else, just like "his" own author, who wrote *Pericles* (and him): "I tell you what mine authors say" (1.0.20). This hints at his function as Chorus and guide through the play, since "mine authors" can refer both to the historical Gower's sources and to the playwrights, because there is evidence that *Pericles*, too, was written in collaboration and that the first two acts specifically were written mostly by George Wilkins.[24] Gower's own narrator, in his *Apollonius of Tyre*,[25] also begins by emphasising the ancientness of the story:

Of a Cronique in daies gon,
The which is cleped Pantheon,
In loves cause I rede thus..."[26]

His source is a "Cronique" and the story took place "in daies gon". "Pantheon" refers to Geoffrey of Viterbo's rhymed Latin *Pantheon, or Universal Chronicle*.[27] Vernacular versions of the *Apollonius* material were popular throughout the Middle Ages in all over Europe. The ultimate source of the tale is a Latin novel from the 3rd century CE, which was most likely based on an even earlier Greek original.[28] Thus going back from beginning to beginning of the versions of *Pericles*, ever more levels of antiquity unfold. The ancient originals are now lost.[29] But even from the extant beginnings that all draw attention to the antiquity of their sources, a "hall of mirrors" opens, as Lynch calls this phenomenon with regard to *The Two Noble Kinsmen*: "Shakespeare and Fletcher reflect Chaucer,

---

23 William Shakespeare, *Pericles*, ed. Suzanne Gossett. The Arden Shakespeare, Third Series (London: Thomson Learning, 2004). All references to *Pericles* are to this edition.

24 Gossett, pp.62-70. For the purpose of this book, however, "the play will be treated as a unified meaningful whole that appeared on the Jacobean stage and was associated with Shakespeare's name" (Andrew James Johnston, "Sailing the Seas of Literary History: Gower, Chaucer, and the Problem of Incest in Shakespeare's *Pericles*", *Poetica* 41 (2009), pp.381-407, p.383).

25 The name change to "Pericles" may derive from Sidney's "Pyrocles" in the *Arcadia* or from the Athenian statesman Pericles whose biography is included in Petrarch's *Lives* (which Shakespeare used for *Coriolanus*, *Timon of Athens*, and *Antony and Cleopatra*). See Gossett, pp.72 f.

26 John Gower, *Confessio Amantis*, ed. Russell A. Peck (New York: Holt, Rinehart & Winston, 1968), Liber Octavus, ll. 271-273.

27 Gossett, p.71.

28 Gossett, pp.70-71.

29 For a detailed account of the *Apollonius* source material see Gossett, pp.70-76.

Chaucer reflects Petrarch, Petrarch reflects his source Boccaccio – truly 'an endless thing'".[30]

In view of all these very similar beginnings, being based on another story appears to be a standard quality of any story, to the degree where it is not possible to tell which version derives from which, just as one loses orientation in a hall of mirrors. The stories all appear to be arranged on the same level and reflect one another, mutually, simultaneously, creating an illusion of depth and distance, which could be another way to express the idea of a palimpsest-like structure of time, of the unhierarchical, simultaneous coexistence of multiple levels and layers of time.

Nevertheless, Gower's language is intentionally medievalised. It is mixed with Middle English phrases throughout the play ("iwis", 2.0.2, "speken", 2.0.12, etc.). In the prologue he uses octosyllabic couplets with four stresses, the same metre and rhyme scheme that (the historical) Gower employed in the *Confessio Armantis*. There are ironic rhymes that had been made obsolete by the Great Vowel Shift and were mere eye rhymes at the time of the play ("infirmities/eyes", "festivals/holy ales", "lives/restoratives").[31] In *The Two Noble Kinsmen*'s prologue, Chaucer does not appear on stage 'himself', embodied by an actor, but his name is invoked as a guarantee for a good, "worthy" play. The prologue tries to persuade the audience to approve of the present adaptation because the tale is by the venerable Chaucer. Gower, by contrast, precisely *because* he is allowed to speak for himself, has to employ the same modesty topos that the contemporary *Two Noble Kinsmen*'s prologue uses, but from the opposite direction, as it were: there, the noble poet is absent, in his grave, but he guarantees the play's quality from there and the danger of making the work "light" comes from the present. The author absent from the stage is seen as most venerable, no matter whether they are from present or past: this principle is applicable from both directions and thus indicates the multidirectionality of time, as opposed to unidirectional linear time.

Gower, because he has to stand before the audience himself, has to ask for forgiveness and benevolent reception. His apologetic remarks ("If you, born in these latter times/ When wit's more ripe, accept my rhymes", 1.0.11-12) say little about his time, but they are the equivalent to *The Two Noble Kinsmen*'s prologue's "Weak as we are", "almost breathless", "below his art", "lighter" etc. (PROLOGUE 24, 28, 20). In *The Two Noble Kinsmen*'s prologue, *Chaucer* is connected with "this deep water", "famed works", "nobleness" and the like (PROLOGUE 25, 20, 15). Both prologues employ comical images of the authors, such as Chaucer's blasted bays (20) or the playwrights and acting company drowning in Chaucer's deep water without the audience's saving hands (24-27). Gower, who sticks to his rhetorical modesty throughout the play, (metaphorically) gives his rhymes "lame feet":

---

30 Lynch, p.79.

31 Cf. Johnston (2009b), pp.386 ff.

I carry winged time
Post on the lame feet of my rhyme. (4.0.47-48)

But the opposition here is "winged time" and not, for example, contemporary more vivid rhymes, as Davis seems to imply when he sees Gower's "stiffly rhyming contribution" as a deliberately medievalised opposition to "these latter times/ When wit's more ripe".[32] It is not set in opposition to the theatre either, where there are visual, acoustic and even olfactory effects in addition to words (or rhymes).[33] "Rhyme" is opposed to "time", which has wings in this image, whereas rhyme only has "lame feet", as if it is constantly lagging behind a plot that flies by on wings.

The Gower of *Pericles* also stresses the need of the audience's imaginative participation: "Which never could I so convey/ Unless your thoughts went on my way" (4.0.49-50). "Imagine Pericles arrived at Tyre" (4.0.1) he says at another point, or "think you now are all in Mytilene" (4.4.51) or even "That he can hither come so soon/ Is by your fancies' thankful doom" (5.2.19-20). *The Two Noble Kinsmen*'s prologue, likewise, asks for the audience's collaboration. But what is more fascinating is that the Gower figure, while constantly pointing out how helpless he feels before his material and how much he depends upon the audience's willingness to cooperate, confidently directs and controls time, zooming in and out of the story at will. He very often briefly summarises what took a long time to happen: narrated time is frequently much longer than narrating time. Contrary to the image of carrying winged time on lame feet, as if time was constantly on the point of flying away, while the author is helplessly shuffling along, he massively interferes with the chronological progress of time, extends or abbreviates the plot, accelerates it with summaries or slows down when he 'zooms in' on particular scenes, as in the "lengthy"[34] scene where Pericles and Marina recognise each other after many years of separation, which is performed in a sort of slow motion. His rhymes are fast and time is also fast, on the other hand, when, for example, Marina, a baby at the end of Act 3, grows up in a few lines at the beginning of Act 4. While pretending to be adapting to the necessities imposed upon him by time and the given story, the narrator in fact uses time at his discretion. Time adapts to his purposes remarkably well, becomes slow in detailed scenes and fast in short summaries, so that instead of being "lame" and "winged", respectively, narrator and time move in congruence.

Pericles' Gower also interprets the story, as for example when he explains the dumb show in Act 3, a scene that would be hard to understand without his comments: "What's dumb in show I'll plain with speech" (3.0.14). Speaking prologue and epilogue, he leads the audience in and out of the play, but he also

---

32 Alex Davis, p.176.

33 For example malodorous special effects as described in Harris (2007), pp.465-486.

34 Masten, p.86.

"stands in the gaps" of the story, as he calls it,[35] perceptibly organising the material and directing the story.

Gower's presence as a narrator emphasises the medieval framing of supposedly classical matter.[36] His comments, summaries and explanations, articulated in sometimes fake Middle English and in an archaic metre, align him and his historical epoch with a particular aesthetics: "In as much as the undramatic is visibly associated with the medieval, Shakespeare identifies historical otherness as aesthetic otherness and vice versa."[37]

But even while aesthetic otherness is established as a marker of historical difference, there is little difference in the way that sources are treated and stories told on both sides of the divide. The Gower character pretends to stand helplessly before his material, the story he has to tell, suggesting that it happened *exactly* in this way, as he knows from his completely reliable sources, while he has only his rhymes' lame feet and the audience's willing cooperation as support. But then he proceeds to tell the story in such a way that the narrator's role, his influence upon the story is very much stressed. In a similar way the historical Gower's contemporary Chaucer denies all responsibility for his story when, in *Troilus and Criseyde*, he pretends to have no influence on it whatsoever, as I mentioned earlier:

> My penne, allas, with which I write,
> Quaketh for drede of that I moste endite. (IV.13-14)

Pericles' Gower's says, very similarly,

> Our scene must play
> His daughter's woe and heavy well-a-day
> In her unholy service. (4.4.48-50)

Interestingly, this refers to Marina's prostitution, while Chaucer's words refer to Cressida's unfaithfulness. "Disblameth me if any word be lame,/ For as myn auctour seyde, so sey I" (II.17-18), Chaucer's narrator writes. Shakespeare's Gower uses almost the exact same words: "lame rhyme" (4.0.48) and "I tell you what mine authors say" (1.0.20). Chaucer, like Gower, then proceeds to write a story of his own, deviating from his sources as he thinks suitable. So, when *The Two Noble Kinsmen*'s prologue in turn refers to its sources and says that Chaucer's story – the author who said one thing about his writing and then did another – lives "constant to eternity" (PROLOGUE 14), we already know to expect the same conscious manipulation of the material, including deviations, additions, etc., despite historical-aesthetic otherness. It is therefore unsurprising that the promise of eternal constancy introduces a story that consists mostly of very rapid and radical changes.

---

35 "Me, who stand i'th' gaps" (4.4.8).

36 Johnston (2009b), p.385.

37 Johnston (2009b), p.385.

At the same time, the phrase "constant to eternity" alludes to the "holy tie" of marriage; the prologue establishes an analogy that likens plays to brides:

> New plays and maidenheads are near akin:
> Much followed both, for both much money gi'en,
> If they stand sound and well. And a good play,
> Whose modest scenes blush on his marriage day
> And shake to lose his honour, is like her
> That after holy tie and first night's stir
> Yet still is Modesty and still retains
> More of the maid, to sight, than husband's pains. (PROLOGUE 1-8)

The focus on the cost of "new plays and maidenheads" draws another link to *Pericles*, where Marina's virginity is auctioned at the market: "He that will give most shall have her first. Such a maidenhead were no cheap thing, if men were as they have been" (4.2.53-55).

So, while new plays can be purchased like maidenheads, at the same time, poets breed their works like children ("our play [...] has a noble breeder and a pure", PROLOGUE 9-10). The play, which was just compared to a virgin, then becomes a child, bred by its writers: "If [...] the first sound this child hear be a hiss" (PROLOGUE 15-16). "This child" refers to this play. So while "the play" is just about to get married and will hopefully prove "constant to eternity" in the marriage, it is simultaneously a newly born baby, the product of its own marriage. The audience's response, applause or hisses, will be the very "first sound this child hear". The writers are the parents, or mothers, to be more precise, since they "breed" the child, but they are also the play's husbands, since the joke about "husband's pains" ("her/ That [...] retains/ More of the maid, to sight, than husband's pains", PROLOGUE 5-8) also refers to the pains that the writers have had in writing the play, suggesting labour pain. They also promise to be faithful to Chaucer's story ("constant to eternity"). The writers are therefore the maid's/play's husbands, but they are also the mothers. The unconventional chronology – the play is a young woman first and then becomes a newly born baby – already indicates that there are different modes of temporality at work in *The Two Noble Kinsmen*: aimless, disorderly Theban "recursiveness", as Lee Patterson calls it, is set off against Athenian "purposive linearity".[38] The curse that lays upon Thebes according to the mythology is closely connected to its non-linear temporality, because it condemns Thebes to endless, purposeless repetition, an endless series of tragic events, not the least momentous of which is Oedipus' incest with his mother. It also has a circular form: while Oedipus thinks he is escaping from the prophesy that told him he would kill his father and marry his mother, he makes it come true. He runs in the opposite direction of his home (as he believes it to be) and thus directly into his mother-and-wife's arms. It turns

38 Lee Patterson, *Chaucer and the Subject of History* (Madison: University of Wisconsin Press, 1991), p.201.

out, therefore, that his running from the curse to avoid the tragedy was already contained in the prophecy when it prompted his running away. The future was contained in the past which lead to the present, like a palimpsest which contains past, present and future in no chronological order and where, instead of simple, linear, "developmental" sequences of cause and effect, there are heterogeneity, overlap, sedimentation, multiplicity,[39] in short "a polychronic compression of diverse moments in time".[40]

So, when *The Two Noble Kinsmen*'s prologue describes the play as the writer's child and bride at the same time and the writer, in turn, as the play's husband and father, or rather mother ("breeder"), it draws a link to the famous Theban incest and the particular understanding of time connected with it. At the same time, it is another cross-reference to *Pericles* and the incest between Antiochus and his daughter, which the Gower figure talks about in the prologue (1.0.21-30) and which Antiochus' riddle describes in similar terms:

He's father, son, and husband mild;
I mother, wife, and yet his child. (1.1.69-70)

Oedipus and Iocaste have four children (who are at the same time Iocaste's grandchildren and Oedipus' siblings): Antigone, Ismene, Polyneikes and Eteocles. Palamon and Arcite are reincarnations of these brothers, Polyneikes and Eteocles, their *Doppelgänger*,[41] on whom the curse continues to work while they are torn between Theban circularity and Athenian linearity.

II.3. The funeral-marriage

"Constant to eternity", the metaphor of constancy in marriage, refers among other things to the playwrights' faithfulness to their source: Chaucer's text. Yet alterations were made: the added subplot of the Jailer's Daughter, the changed rules of the tournament and changes to Theseus' character, among other things. The invoked constancy also stands in marked contrast to the abrupt changes that characterise the play. Palamon and Arcite, the protagonists, swear love to each other in a language that refers to marriage very clearly: "We are one another's wife, ever begetting/ New births of love". And, like the works that are simultaneously married to, and bred by, the poets in the prologue, at the same time, "we are father, friends, acquaintance,/ [...] I am your heir and you are mine" (2.2.80-83). But, a few moments later, they both fall in love with Emilia, within seconds of catching sight of her and become mortal enemies upon the spot ("Friendship, blood,/ And all the ties between us, I disclaim", 2.2.174-175; "I shall live/ To

39 Cohen, pp.2 f.

40 Harris (2007), p.471.

41 Jody Greene, "*The Two Noble Kinsmen*: Philadelphia, or, War" in Menon, pp. 404-413, p.406.

knock thy brains out with my shackles", 2.2.221-222). The winner of the combat that is set up to decide the argument dies from a sudden accident and loses not only his future wife, whom he had just won, but also his life, while the loser who was about to be killed, wins both.

The queens, foreboding birds

After the prologue is over, a wedding procession enters the stage. Immediately, the first of the sudden changes that refute the prologue's promise of constancy occurs; the procession turns into a military expedition and then into a funeral. The wedding itself is the result of a war: Theseus is marrying the defeated Amazon queen Hippolyta. Therefore the right to bury and the right to marry are paralleled: both are achieved by victory in war. The way that the wedding is interrupted also suggests an analogy between marriage and funerals. The wedding procession is led by a boy strewing flowers while singing a song that lists different kinds of flowers, playing on their symbolic meaning. As "thyme" in "sweet thyme true" (1.1.6) sounds like "time",[42] it strikes a similar note as the prologue's "constant to eternity", while the juxtaposition of "Oxlips in their cradles growing" and "Marigolds on deathbeds blowing" (1.1.10 f.) again underlines the ambiguity of this death-marked love. And, after briefly stating that no "Bird melodious, or bird fair" (1.1.17) is absent, without naming them in particular, the song then enumerates all the birds that are not invited, "the birds of death and sorrow, of discord and ill omen":[43]

> The crow, the sland'rous cuckoo, nor
> The boding raven, nor chough hoar,
> Nor chatt'ring pie,
> May on our bride-house perch or sing,
> Or with them any discord bring,
> But from it fly. (1.1.19-24)

As if to demonstrate the performative power of language, immediately after these birds are mentioned three queens "*in black, with veils*" (1.1.24 SD) flutter on stage. They instantly start to beg Theseus to help them bury their husbands and ask Hippolyta and her sister Emilia to help them to persuade Theseus. The husbands died in the war against Creon, who is now ruler of Thebes and who has forbidden their burial.

The dead husbands, crying widows and the wedding ceremony turned into a funeral point to Hippolyta's fate now that she is married: even though it is only in some versions of the legend that she dies before Theseus falls in love with another woman (in others, she is deserted), the former Amazonian queen ceases to

42 Potter, p.141.
43 Greene, p.405.

have a literary life of her own after the marriage and disappears from mythological stories. There is a sense, therefore, in which the birds that feed on carcasses, symbolised by the three queens, have come to announce the death of the legendary Amazonian queen and her fall from being a famous warrior to the nameless wife of Theseus. The fact that she is soon either dead or deserted, depending on the version of the myth, shows that she is no longer needed after the marriage. Furthermore, the fact that a military campaign leads to a wedding and from there to another campaign that leads to a funeral (Theseus achieves the right to bury the dead kings) and that marriage and funeral are then paralleled suggests circularity and recursiveness even here, at the beginning of the play, while, for Theseus, they present a linear sequence of successes, one victory after the next.

The unburied kings

Theseus going to war against Creon for the right of the widows to bury their husbands is where Statius' *Thebaid* ends after twelve books and where *The Two Noble Kinsmen*, like *The Knight's Tale*, begins. The medieval and early modern versions, starting with Boccaccio's *Teseida*, continue or, perhaps, intervene in the ancient story, as the abrupt beginning with the intervening widows suggests, who interrupt the ceremony like a bad weather front and turn the marriage into a funeral, prompting Theseus to change his mind and go to war instead. But, as it turns out, the interruption is not as sudden, and the transformation from nuptials to funeral not as radical, as it might at first seem: the queens appear as the foreboding birds that have been listed among the birds that should stay away. These 'negative' birds are listed right after the birds that are welcome, without any real transition. Similarly, the preceding description of beautiful flowers that decorate the celebration is ambiguous, too, since the danger of a sudden inversion into the opposite seems immanent from the couplet where "cradles" and "deathbeds" are paralleled in the sentences' grammatical structure:

> Oxlips in their cradles growing,
> Marigolds on deathbeds blowing.[44] (1.1.10-11)

This shows that the appearance of the widows has been built into the scene from the beginning. The way they break onto the scene – not from without but from within – likens the scene to a palimpsest where the past, represented by the widows, is not concluded yet and continues to work on the present. The unexpected guests, who show up at the marriage and insist on drawing attention to their dead but unburied husbands, stand for a returning past that disrupts linear order. They also represent the future contained in this scene, since they are widows

[44] Oxlips on their leaves might look a little as if they were lodged in a cradle, but marigolds are not associated with death in Gerard's *Herbal* (Potter, p.141). In *The Winter's Tale*, it is one of the "flowers of middle summer" (4.4.105-107, *Oxford Shakespeare*). Potter, *ibid.*

and, as such, stand for the end of marriage as opposed to its beginning, the wedding, which is about to be celebrated here and as symbolic announcers of Hippolyta's end. Therefore they "bring discord" like the birds with which they are aligned and, as the negative attributes of these birds indicate ("sland'rous cuckoo," "chatt'ring 'pie; "discord"), evidence of other existing times is not very welcome.

In *The Knight's Tale*, the widows act more aggressively than in Shakespeare and Fletcher's version: they throw themselves onto the train and take the reins of Theseus' horse.[45] *The Knight's Tale*'s Theseus, although he usually is gentler than *The Two Noble Kinsmen*'s, therefore reacts more angrily at this point:

"What folk been ye, that at myn homcomynge
Perturben so my feste with criynge?"
Quod Theseus. "Have ye so greet envye
Of myn honour, that thus compleyne and crye?" (905-908)

In *The Two Noble Kinsmen* the widows are more submissive: they fall upon their knees before Theseus, Hippolyta and Emily immediately, so that Theseus says only, "Sad lady, rise" (1.1.35). If the scene is a palimpsest then, in *The Knight's Tale*, the past erupts violently while, in *The Two Noble Kinsmen*, it emerges so naturally and self-evidently that there is an even stronger focus on the presence of the past in the present, surfacing at times to become *more* visible.

Encouraged to deliver their request, the widows start to complain about "cruel Creon" (1.1.40) thus:

He will not suffer us to burn their bones,
To urn their ashes, nor to take th'offence
Of mortal loathsomeness from the blest eye
Of holy Phoebus, but infects the winds
With stench of our slain lords. Oh pity, Duke;
Thou purger of the earth, draw thy feared sword
That does good turns to th'world; give us the bones
Of our dead kings that we may chapel them. (1.1.43-50)

Again the same birds appear, "the crow," "the boding raven" (1.1.19-20) from the song, now as symbols of decay, birds that dissect the dead:

[our] sovereigns [...] endure
The beaks of ravens, talons of the kites
And pecks of crows, in the foul fields of Thebes. (1.1.39-42)

45 "But swich a cry and swich a wo they make/ That in this world nys creature lyvynge/ That herde swich another waymentynge;/ And of this cry they nolde nevere stenten/ Til they the reynes of his brydel henten". Chaucer, *The Canterbury Tales*, Fragment I, ll. 900-904, in *The Riverside Chaucer*, ed. Larry D. Benson (Oxford: Oxford University Press, 1987), pp.37-66. All subsequent references to *The Knight's Tale* will be to this edition. See also Patterson (1991), p.199.

The number of references to people and things 'undead' that have occurred in the short time since the beginning of this play is remarkable. First Chaucer cried out from his grave in the prologue, then flowers grew on graves, dead kings were rotting away on the ground and birds fed on carcasses. More often than not, the living and the dead are on the 'wrong' side of the ground: they fail to fall into the usual categories. As if the palimpsest were mapped upon what is below and above the ground, life and death are interwoven and the past is not easily got rid of: not yet concluded, it refuses to stay at the bottom, like Chaucer and the unburied kings, and sometimes breaks out and flings itself upon the present, like the three queens.

II.4. "I am your heir and you are mine": Figurations of Palamon and Arcite

Chaucer and the dead kings whose bodies cannot be removed are dead but also undead; likewise, Palamon and Arcite themselves appear exactly in this way. Alive and well at Thebes at the beginning of the play, they are soon brought to the brink of death, transported to Athens and restored to health there, only to be imprisoned forever: they are kept in a shadowy, zombielike condition halfway between death and life. From then on, even after their release from jail, they jump at any chance to proclaim their readiness to die: "'tis to me/ A thing as soon to die as thee to say it" (3.6.158 f.); taking up the marriage/death analogy from the wedding procession: "Then take my life; I'll woo thee to't" (3.6.156); "Let's die together, at one instant" (3.6.177); "never trifle,/ But take our lives" (3.6.260-261); there are many more examples. Although, in general, Shakespeare and Fletcher's Palamon and Arcite are more distinguishable than Chaucer's,[46] in their affinity to death, they are so much alike that they, quite extraordinarily, start to speak their lines together, forming a chorus of their own:

THESEUS	Say, Emilia,	
	If one of them were dead, as one must, are you	
	Content to take the other as your husband?	
	[...]	
	Are you content too, princes?	
PALAMON and ARCITE	With all our hearts.	
THESEUS	He that she refuses	
	Must die then.	
PALAMON and ARCITE	Any death thou canst invent, Duke.	(3.6.272-281)

46 Andrew James Johnston, "Subjectivity and the Ekphrastic Prerogative: Emilia's Soliloquy in *The Two Noble Kinsmen*" in *Solo Performances: Staging the Early Modern Self in England*, ed. Ute Berns (Amsterdam: Rodopi, 2010), pp.49-65, p.58.

If they really are indistinguishable, twins,[47] or two incarnations of the same idea, they switch between life and death at the end of the play when Palamon, consigned to death, is exchanged for Arcite, who dies instead. It seems that, for some reason, Theseus cannot stand them being alive at the same time. He insists that only one of them can live; "If one of them were dead, as one must" (3.6.273), he says, for example. As long as both of them are alive, they are kept in a vampire-like half-existence, entombed. Order is restored as soon as they are separated and one can be sorted out to life, the other one to death, or one to the present (and future, because Palamon is given to marriage and procreation) and the other one to the past. This, though, brings about tears and suffering and the sorting appears very arbitrary and cruel. It is striking how unanimously Palamon and Arcite nevertheless consent to Theseus' authority over their lives. They tried to kill each other just moments ago, but they agree so much that one of them must die that they merge more than at any other point in the play, becoming more indistinguishable than ever when they speak their lines in unison. This distinguishes them from *their* twins, the Theban brothers Polynices and Eteocles, the flames of whose funeral fires continued to fight after their death – perhaps because, in that case, *both* had died, and they had not been separated like Palamon and Arcite at the end of *The Two Noble Kinsmen*, where one is clearly assigned to death and the past and the other to life and the present.

Both Palamon and Arcite romanticise their future as dead people. Palamon imagines his ashes (another link to Polynices and Eteocles' funeral pyres) and future lovers who will bless them:

> I fall with favour
> And lovers yet unborn shall bless my ashes. (3.6.282-83)

At first, this sounds like a fantasy about an impressive reputation that extends so far into the future that Palamon will still be praised when he has long been turned to dust. But it could also mean that he is so little at home in the present that his admirers' life spans must not even coincide with his. Distancing himself twice from them, he pictures a) them as yet unborn and b) himself as long gone ("my ashes").

Arcite, too, continues the conflation of marriage and burial established in the play's opening procession. He does it even more straightforwardly by simply marrying his grave or, rather, letting his grave marry him:

> My grave will wed me
> And soldiers sing my epitaph. (3.6.284 -285)

47 Kenneth Muir calls them "Tweedledum and Tweedledee" for their lack of distinguishing characteristics. Kenneth Muir, *Shakespeare as Collaborator* (London: Methuen, 1960), p.127, cited in Jo Eldridge Carney, "The Ambiguities of Love and War in *The Two Noble Kinsmen*" in *Sexuality and Politics in Renaissance Drama*, eds. Carole Levin and Karen Robertson (Lewiston, NY: Edwin Mellen Press, 1991), pp.95-111, p.96.

Palamon imagines his ashes, blessed by lovers and Arcite sees himself as an epitaph, sung by soldiers. This echoes *The Knight's Tale*'s ascription of the kinsmen to Venus and Mars respectively. It is not, though, kept up as strictly as in the source and the way it is done suggests that they are two sides of the same coin rather than individual persons: they appeared a moment ago as *one*, of one heart and soul (and voice); now they are split into Venus ("lovers") and Mars ("soldiers"). But "lovers" and "soldiers" are paralleled in the sentence structure in the same way that "cradles" and "graves" were in the song with which the play started.

Perhaps as a result of the zombielike state to which Theseus reduced them when he locked them up, forever, according to his initial plan, they cannot imagine any direct connection to people alive in their present. They constantly try to establish relationships to people either dead or unborn and, in addition, place those people in a future when they themselves are dead. They claim to love Emilia, who does not even want ever to marry. Emilia seems, in fact, like a pretext over which the cousins fight and declare their intention to either kill or be killed.

It is precisely their willingness to kill and die which appeases Theseus when he finds them duelling in the woods. His first reaction was to proclaim: "Both shall die!" (3.6.136). After they have made clear that they will rather die than leave the dukedom and travel separately, "ever strangers/ To one another" (3.6.255-56), and although especially Palamon does not sound very penitent when he says, "I [...] must and dare kill this cousin/ On any piece the earth has" (3.6.261-63), Theseus is assuaged: "Now I feel compassion" (3.6.271).

He also ordered "Both shall die!" before having recognised them. In reality, he does not want these particular cousins to die, as he had explained earlier:

Rather than have 'em
Freed of this plight and in their morning state,
Sound and at liberty, I would 'em dead;
But forty-thousandfold we had rather have 'em
Prisoners to us than death. (1.4.33-37)

He wants to compete with death about the right to keep them. This confession is unusual for Theseus, who most of the time masquerades his agency in what happens to his subjects, calls it fate and refers to the gods' will when, in fact, it is him exerting absolute power over them, [48] ordering them to leave the country, to die or to get married as he thinks fit. This will be discussed in more detail further below.

Palamon and Arcite usually accept his orders and do not question his authority. They almost appear like robots controlled by Theseus. Perhaps it is a result

48 See Laurie Shannon, "Professing Friendship: Erotic Prerogatives and 'Human Title' in *The Two Noble Kinsmen*" in *Sovereign Amity: Figures of Friendship in Shakespearean Contexts* (Chicago: University of Chicago Press, 2002), pp.90-122, p.108. Theseus' absolutist rule is Shakespeare and Fletcher's invention; "Chaucer's Duke is much more constitutional", Johnston (2010b), p.57.

of their near-death followed by a resurrection as his prisoners that they resign to their fate so willingly, as in this quote from relatively early in the play:

PALAMON We are prisoners,
I fear, forever, cousin.
ARCITE I believe it
And to that destiny have patiently
Laid up my hour to come. (2.2.3-6)

When Arcite, demeaning himself before Theseus, says, "I am a villain fit to lie unburied" (3.6.171), this is an allusion to the unburied Argives once again, but it is also a resonance of the story of Antigone's brothers, Polynices and Eteocles.

II.4.1. Eteocles and Polynices in Statius' Thebaid

As mentioned before, Palamon and Arcite are introduced as "*Doppelgänger*" of Eteocles and Polynices,[49] Oedipus and Jocasta's sons who killed each other in the battle about Thebes. Although Palamon and Arcite are officially cousins, "kinsmen", they also refer to each other as "twins" (2.2.18). They seem to be Creon's nephews:[50] Creon is a brother of Jocasta, Polynices and Eteocles' mother. They display very similar behaviour to their predecessors, especially in their quarrelling. Polynices and Eteocles are famous for the fact that their hatred outlived them so that after their death their funeral pyres continued to fight, as described in Statius's *Thebaid*. Fletcher and Shakespeare probably knew the *Thebaid* from Lydgate's *Siege of Thebes*, a retelling of the *Thebaid* that was included in the 1561 edition of Chaucer's *Works*.[51] Polynices, leading the Argive warriors, fought against Thebes and was therefore declared a traitor. It was forbidden to bury him and his body lay unprotected outside the city walls. His sister Antigone, joined by Polynices' wife Argia, nonetheless performs the funeral rites, ignoring Creon's order and is sentenced to death.[52] Antigone and Argia had met accidentally while they were both looking for the corpse secretly at night. They mourn together and wash the body but, when they want to burn it, they realise they don't have any fire. "By chance or godly intervention" (Book XII l. 420), Eteocles' body is lying nearby on a pyre that is still smoking. The women are able to revive the fire from a spark and lay Polynices next to his brother. As soon as the flame rises again it splits into two, each part menaces the other and strives to be the higher (XII 429-435). Argia and Antigone now realise that they have laid Polynices next to his brother, because they recognise remnants of Eteocles'

49 Greene, p.406.
50 "Our uncle Creon" (1.2.62).
51 Potter, p.44.
52 Statius, *The Thebaid*, Book XII in *The Thebaid. Seven Against Thebes*, ed. Charles Stanley Ross (Baltimore: The Johns Hopkins University Press, 2004). All quotations from the *Thebaid* are from this edition.

sword and belt on the corpse. The fight becomes so violent that "the discordant pyre formed a chasm" and "a tremor shook the field and towers of Thebes" (XII 448-49). The watchmen wake up, Antigone and Argia are discovered, "confessed/ their misdeeds openly, and they were fearless,/ for they could see the corpses were consumed" (XII 451-53). Their own death matters less to them than the proper performance of the funeral rites. The line between death and life thus becomes fluid here and the border is more of a busy intersection than a one-way street. People linger on the intersection for quite some time and Antigone in particular seems to believe that it matters little which side of the road you are on. The ground outside Thebes thus becomes a place of palimpsested time, of "temporal indeterminacy",[53] where multiple temporal realities coexist, whose various lines touch and cross each other in many ways and get entangled like the flames fighting over their struggle to consume the (not so) dead bodies of the brothers.

The behaviour of fires, flames and smoke is closely observed in *The Two Noble Kinsmen* and *The Knight's Tale*, too. When Palamon, Arcite and Emilia offer sacrifices on the altars of their respective godheads, Venus, Mars and Diana before the tournament starts, they observe anxiously how the fire gets brighter after the prayer or, as in Emelye's case in *The Knight's Tale*, they die down (she lights two), then rekindle, before one of them is extinguished. This supposedly predicts how the tournament is going to turn out for them, albeit somewhat cryptically. In *The Two Noble Kinsmen*, Emilia is the only one who lights a fire on the altar, but there are several echoes of the altar fires in Palamon's address to Venus, which begins, "Our stars must glister with new fire or be/ Today extinct" (5.1.69-70).[54]

But whereas Palamon and Arcite start quarrelling as soon as they are out of Thebes and never stop until one of them is sorted to the living and the other to the dead, including a quick swap at the last minute, Polynices and Eteocles killed each other. Palamon and Arcite often stress that it is necessary that one, but only one of them is dead; Polynices and Eteocles set off to the underworld together. There is some delay when Polynices is not buried right away, but Eteocles obviously waits for his brother, keeping his funeral pyre alive long enough to be able to give the vital spark to Polynices' body. Then they can leave together – and continue fighting. It is the fight that survives but, in fighting, the brothers are united, first in this world, then in Hades. Palamon and Arcite, on the other hand, must not both be alive: one has to be below, and the other above, the ground, but it does not seem to matter which one of the two is on which side.

There is, nevertheless, a link to the rapid exchange of Arcite and Palamon, living and dead noble kinsman at the end of *The Knight's Tale* and *The Two Noble*

53 Harris (2007), p.477.

54 Other references include: "boys through bonfires,/ Have skipped thy flame" (5.1.86-87); "To Phoebus thou/ Add'st flames hotter than his: the heavenly fires/ Did scorch his mortal son" (5.1.90-92). The reference to the "all moist and cold" (5.1.93) moon goddess, Diana, also belongs in this category, because it is an opposition to (dry and hot) fire/the sun.

Kinsmen in the *Thebaid* as well: at its end, Antigone and Argia are about to get killed for opposing Creon's law. They are already at the point of being executed when an urgent messenger arrives:

> Meanwhile the ruffian Creon had commanded
> the widowed daughter of Adrastus and
> Antigone to die. He chained their hands
> behind their backs, but both of them rejoiced.
> Proud, and in love with death, they stretched their necks
> for execution, just as Phegeus brought
> an embassy from Theseus. (XII. 677-683)

At the end of *The Two Noble Kinsmen*, Palamon's head is already on the block, his knights proclaim, "We'll follow cheerfully" (5.4.39), but then a messenger enters "*in haste*":

> Hold, hold! Oh, hold, hold, hold! (5.4.40)

At this point in the *Thebaid* the message is brought that Theseus has come from Athens to wage war against Creon to bury the soldiers, the precise point where *The Two Noble Kinsmen* starts.

II.4.2. Sophocles' Antigone

Sophocles' tragedy, *Antigone*, likewise tells the story of Antigone's clandestine burial of her brother Polynices. As in the *Thebaid*, Polynices had fought against Thebes on the side of the Argives, Creon declared him a traitor and forbade his burial. Therefore his body is lying unburied outside the city walls, a situation that reverberates in Arcite's "If she say 'traitor',/ I am a villain fit to lie unburied" (3.6.170-71). The presence of the dead body left unburied creates some confusion here, too. The marriage of Antigone and Creon's son, Haemon, is connected to death in a similar way to Theseus and Hippolyta's wedding in *The Two Noble Kinsmen*, but the images are grotesque on a level that *The Two Noble Kinsmen* reaches only when the Argive Queens describe the rotting unburied warriors. Antigone and Haemon's wedding is not 'only' interrupted to become a funeral as Theseus and Hippolyta's is, but takes place *after* their death. Just as Polynices and Eteocles' quarrel could continue after their death in the *Thebaid*, so a marriage can take place after the couple's death in *Antigone*: things of this sort are possible in the temporality of Thebes. In a grotesquely ironic interpretation of a wedding kiss, Haemon, winning "the pitiful fulfillment of his marriage/ within death's house"[55] takes [the already dead] Antigone in his arms and "gasping poured a sharp stream of bloody drops/ on her white cheeks" (1238-39).

[55] Sophocles, *Antigone*, ll. 1241-1242 in *Sophocles I*, eds. David Grene and Richmond Lattimore (Chicago: University of Chicago Press, 1991), pp.159-212. All references are to this edition.

"Death's house" refers to Antigone's residence: Creon has sentenced her to live in a cave for the rest of her life:

> I will bring her where the path is loneliest,
> and hide her alive in a rocky cavern there.
> I'll give just enough of food as shall suffice
> for a bare expiation, that the city may avoid pollution.
> In that place she shall call on Hades, god of death,
> in her prayers. (774-779)

This is not so different from Palamon and Arcite's perpetual imprisonment in Theseus' realm, "not dead/ Nor in a state of life" (1.4.24-25). Like Theseus, Creon seems to see himself as a competitor with death, because after Antigone has repeatedly refused to obey him, he orders her imprisonment as if he is offended by her preferring death's rule to his and as if to prove to her that she has made a bad choice:

> In that place she shall call on Hades, god of death,
> in her prayers. That god only she reveres.
> Perhaps she will win from him escape. (776-778)

Compare Theseus' words, "I would [...] rather have 'em/ Prisoners to us than death" (1.4.35-37). But where Theseus orders, "our richest balms,/ Rather than niggard, waste" for their treatment and adds, mysteriously, "their lives concern us/ Much more than Thebes is worth" (1.4.31-33), Creon declares, "I'll give just enough of food as shall suffice". This is symptomatic for the behaviour of the two rulers in most of their different incarnations and it becomes ever clearer in the course of *The Two Noble Kinsmen*. Creon usually orders cruel things bluntly and has the reputation of a cruel and despotic tyrant, while Theseus, who does the same things with a nicer veneer (as when he restores the cousins' health regardless of the costs but to the same effect: to imprison them for the rest of their lives, like Antigone), is seen as a righteous ruler.

Since she is in prison, guards play an important role in *Antigone*, too, just like the Jailer and especially the Jailer's Daughter in *The Two Noble Kinsmen*. The Jailer is in danger because the Daughter has freed Palamon[56] and, likewise, Antigone's guards are held accountable by Creon: "Then for this her guards,/ who are so slow, will find themselves in trouble" (931-32). But, in *Antigone*, they do not only guard prisoners, they also have to watch corpses. They watch Polynices' body as carefully as if it were alive:

> We sat on the brow of the hill, to windward,
> That we might shun the smell of the corpse upon us.
> Each of us wakefully urged his fellow

[56] Compare "Now, my father/ Twenty to one is trussed up in a trice" (3.4.16-17) or the Jailer's anxious questions: "Heard you no more? Was nothing said of me/ Concerning the escape of Palamon?/ Good sir, remember!" (4.1.1-3).

With torrents of abuse, not to be careless
In this work of ours. So it went on. (411-415)

The efforts invested in preventing the corpse from being buried are amazing. It is also fascinating, on the other hand, how Antigone spares no effort and even risks her life trying to bury it. Since she is unable to do so in the dry and hard ground without any tools, she only puts a little dust on it. The guards are shocked when they discover it, brush the dust off and inform Creon, who gets very angry and threatens to put the guards into the same liminal state between life and death in which he has been trying to keep Polynices:

If you and your fellows do not find this man
Who with his own hand did the burial
And bring him here before me face to face,
Your death alone will not be enough for me.
You will hang alive. (304-309)

Antigone, for her part, is equally appalled when she sees that someone has *removed* the dust:

She was crying out with the shrill cry
of an embittered bird
that sees its nest robbed of its nestlings
and the bed empty. So, too, when she saw
the body stripped of its cover, she burst out in groans,
calling terrible curses on those that had done that deed;
and with her hands immediately
brought thirsty dust to the body. (423-430)

This brings us to the wedding ceremony from the beginning of *The Two Noble Kinsmen* again: when Creon sentences Antigone to live in a cave for the rest of her life, *The Two Noble Kinsmen*'s Janus-faced marriage-funeral shines through in Antigone's lament, "Tomb, bridal chamber, prison forever/ dug in rock" (891-892). Weddings are not only seen as funerals, but also as eternal incarceration, to "live a buried life in such a home", (888) as Creon puts it. This could also refer to Palamon and Arcite's imprisonment by Theseus. Marriage is treated like a funeral, while on the other hand "a buried life" is imagined like a happy marriage. When Palamon and Arcite are entombed together, they fantasise about their happy life together and the family they are going to have:

We are one another's wife, ever begetting
New births of love; we are father, friends, acquaintance,
We are, in one another, families;
I am your heir and you are mine." (2.2.80-83)

Antigone, too, envisages an encounter with her family in her "rocky tomb". The above quote goes on,

Tomb, bridal chamber, prison forever
dug in rock, it is to you I am going

to join my people [...]
When I come
to that other world my hope is strong
that my coming will be welcome to my father,
and dear to you, my mother, and dear to you,
my brother deeply loved. (891-900)

Antigone's love and family life are even more macabre than Palamon and Arcite's. The relations to her family seem to exist more in death than in the world of the living at all. Her most precious memories of family members concern the funeral rites she performed for them: "For when you died,/ with my own hands I washed and dressed you all" (900-901).

In the course of the play, Creon is, therefore, accused of not keeping up the necessary order, not properly distinguishing between life and death or present and past. Tiresias, the blind but clairvoyant prophet reproaches him,

You have thrust one that belongs above
below the earth, and bitterly dishonored
a living soul by lodging her in the grave;
while one that belonged indeed to the underworld
gods you have kept on this earth without due share
of rites of burial, of due funeral offerings,
a corpse unhallowed. (1066-1072)

Interestingly, the first part of the accusation could also be addressed to *The Two Noble Kinsmen*'s Theseus, not only for his imprisonment of Palamon and Arcite, who, like Antigone, have to "go to the vault of death while still alive" (920-921): he also uses the tournament to place "a living soul in the grave", since he orders that the loser be put to death along with his whole retinue. In *The Knight's Tale*'s version, there is no execution of the losers, which is a considerable deviation from the source, contradicting the prologue's alleged fear of making Chaucer's work "lighter". Chaucer's Theseus mitigates the consequences of the tournament, saying that 'it were destruccioun/ To gentil blood to fighten in the gyse/ Of mortal bataille' (1.2538-40).[57] He arranges the tournament in order to prevent the cousins from killing each other. Shakespeare and Fletcher's Theseus decides that the loser of the competition must die, plus the knights that supported him: "Th'other lose his head,/ And all his friends" (3.6.296-297). So not only Creon, but Theseus, too, tries and sometimes succeeds to "thrust one that belongs above/ below the earth". The proposed death extends to several people: both Palamon and Arcite, temporarily; Palamon's retinue almost, who are saved at the last minute; finally Arcite permanently. One could add the symbolic death of the Amazonian queen to this list.

Nonetheless, Theseus is fetched from Athens to sort out Thebes' temporal disorder. He does, but only as concerns the last part of what Creon is reproached

57 See Lynch, p.81.

with, the denied funeral rites ("One that belonged indeed to the underworld gods you have kept on this earth without due share of rites of burial"). The linear order he tries to impose upon the events (I will return to this) brings about a lot of suffering for his subjects, while not changing anything for the better.

Throughout *Antigone*, Creon insists on the non-separation of death and life, past and present. He repeatedly confirms it, even at the end when he has come to regret the injustice done to Antigone. By the end of the play, he has gone through a learning process and regrets his mistakes: "Oh, the awful blindness of those plans of mine" (1264-65); "Yes, I have learned it" (1271). But, as concerns polychronicity, the simultaneous existence of present and past, he keeps up what he has practiced before. He in fact applies it to himself when he says at the end of the play, "It is a dead man that you kill again" (1288), making even himself *unzeitgemäss*,[58] "untimely". He says this when ordering his servants to remove himself from the scene: "Servants, lead me away, quickly, quickly" (1321). Theseus, at the end of *The Two Noble Kinsmen*, orders servants to remove *Arcite* from "the stage of death" (5.4.123), in words that distance himself from the body as much as possible: "Bear this hence" (5.4.109).

In this light, Creon and Theseus look quite similar. Although they are set up as opposites in *The Two Noble Kinsmen*, the good, responsible ruler and the bad, despotic one, the differences are only on the surface, in the appearance of their commands and in their reputation. Both rule despotically but, while Theseus likes to refer to the gods and cites their will as the origin of his verdicts, Creon does no such thing. Creon attributes all his deeds to himself, not to the gods: he "makes heaven unfeared" (1.2.64), as Palamon puts it. But this way, it is possible for him to undergo a learning process in the course of the play and to arrive at new insights at the end of *Antigone*, unlike Theseus, who at the end of *The Two Noble Kinsmen* does not seem to reflect upon, let alone question or regret anything he has done. All he has to say about Arcite's death is, "A day or two let us look sad" (5.4.124-125). Yet, although Creon regrets the suffering he inflicted upon his subjects, what he comes to realise is *not* that life and death have to be strictly separated and linearly arranged. He maintains his practice of interweaving present and past, of retaining the past in the present. He also blames himself for the deaths in the play, again in a clear, but this time chiastically opposed, parallel to Theseus: "It was I that killed her. Poor wretch that I am, I say it is true!" (1319-20); "Lead me away, a vain silly man who killed you, son, and you, too, lady. I did not mean to, but I did" (1339-41). Theseus, who writes linear progress history and neatly distinguishes between past and present, says in an unconcerned fashion,

58 Harris uses this term from Nietzsche's *Unzeitgemäße Betrachtungen* to denote "the anachronistic apparition of a supposedly superseded past in the present" and a "temporality that is not one" (Harris (2009), pp. 11, 13).

> The gods my justice
> Take from my hand and they themselves become
> The executioners. (5.4.120-122)

In both *The Two Noble Kinsmen* and *Antigone*, Creon is generally reproached with regarding himself, rather than the gods, as responsible for events, as Palamon and Arcite's dialogue at Thebes shows (1.2.62-83).[59] But this contains the possibility of critical reflection, new insight and change. Theseus does not achieve any insights whatsoever. Where even Chaucer's Theseus has a long speech at the end of the play, *The Two Noble Kinsmen*'s Theseus merely refers to the "heavenly charmers", as he calls the gods. He suggests to "with you leave dispute/ That are above our question" and concludes nothing but "Let's go off" (5.4.135-136). Addressing the gods as "charmers" gives the impression that they are tricksters who employ magic tricks to delude people. But perhaps it is Theseus who attempts to do just that.

II.5. 'Thebanness' and 'Athenness'

Obviously it works to a certain degree; people come to Athens to ask Theseus for help. It is no coincidence that the dead bodies that Theseus is asked to remove lie outside of *Thebes* and that it is *Creon* who forbids their interment. Creon personifies what Lee Patterson has termed *Thebanness*: "a fatal recursiveness that undermines all progressivity upon which the ideals of secular history are based".[60] As mythology has it, there is a curse on Thebes from which it can never be redeemed. It is passed on from generation to generation *ad infinitum*, truly "an endless thing":

> The Theban story is itself about disordered memory and fatal repetition, about the tyranny of a past that is both forgotten and obsessively remembered, and about the recursive patterns into which history falls. [...] Thebanness is a fatal doubling [...] that issues in a replicating history that preempts a linear or developmental progress.[61]

The city of Thebes was cursed before it even existed. According to Ovid's *Metamorphoses*, Cadmus, exiled from his home because he was unable to find and bring back his sister Europa (who had been abducted by Zeus), killed a snake that happened to be sacred to Mars. Thereupon, the goddess Athene appeared and told him to sow the snakes' teeth into the ground. Immediately warriors grew out of the teeth and killed each other presently.[62] Lee Patterson calls this incident the "central, recursive act of Theban history, the first instance of a chthonic return that

---

59 Creon even ascribes things others have done to himself: "[He] attributes/ The faculties of other instruments/ To his own nerves and act" (1.2.67-69).

60 Patterson (1991), p.200.

61 Patterson (1991), pp.75, 77.

62 Ovid, *Metamorphoses*, Book III ll. 1-162, in *Metamorphoses*, ed. and trans. Charles Martin (New York, London: W.W. Norton & Company, 2010). Quotations from the *Metamorphoses* are from this edition unless otherwise indicated.

is then endlessly repeated".[63] The soldiers are born and immediately grown-up, confusing chronological order from the first moment of their existence, start to fight each other as hastily as Palamon and Arcite and return to the earth instantaneously. This remarkable birth-death signifies to Patterson "the profound circularity of Thebanness, its inability ever to diverge from the reversionary shape ordained in and by its beginning".[64] Only five of the warriors survive and proceed to build the city, obviously also in an instant: in the next sentence, Thebes stands already.[65] The story continues in fast-forward mode, Cadmus marries the daughter of Mars and Venus and gets children and grandchildren, who are also grown-ups at once: "You might seem fortunate/ in having Mars and Venus as your in-laws/ Cadmus; nor is this all, for in addition/ are offspring worthy of your noble wife,/ your sons and daughters, the pledges of your love,/ and grandsons too, already grown to manhood".[66] Venus and Mars are the two godheads that Arcite and Palamon, respectively, are associated with, although not as consistently in *The Two Noble Kinsmen* as in *The Knight's Tale*. Their child with the fitting name Harmonia thus in a way represents the unification of the kinsmen and Cadmus is granted what Emilia could not do: marry both. Emilia's wish, "Were they metamorphosed/ Both into one!" (5.3.84-85), thus has a correlation in the *Metamorphoses*. It underlines the indistinguishability of the kinsmen to an even greater extent. They are hardly differentiated for most of the time and call themselves "twins" (2.2.18). So, even at the point where Emilia tries hardest to distinguish between them, any differences dissolve by the reference to their unification in the *Metamorphoses*. The fact that the founding myth of Thebes, from where all repetition takes its course, is referred to here suggests the futility of laying one or the other of the kinsmen to rest, supposing that they stand for those parts of the present that are arbitrarily sorted out and denied (i.e. the cousin that has to die) or chosen and promoted for the present and future (his surviving twin).

II. 6. Polychronicity and Multitemporality

The way themes and motifs recur, the way the past never ceases to work on the present in *The Two Noble Kinsmen* does suggest circularity but it is, perhaps, even more accurately described as an instance of palimpsested time. Arguably, people's bodies and their relative positions on different levels below or above the ground stand for the different levels of the palimpsest and the tangled layers of past, present and future times. In *Untimely Matter*, Harris, drawing on Michel

---

63 Patterson (1991), p.75.

64 Patterson (1991), p.76.

65 "Iam stabant Thebae". *Metamorphoses*, Book III l. 131, *Metamorphoseon libri quindecim*, Lateinisch/ Deutsch, ed. and transl. Michael von Albrecht (Stuttgart: Philipp Reclam, 1994, 2003).

66 *Metamorphoses*, Book III ll. 164-169.

Serres, differentiates between two slightly different concepts of "polytemporality" that are both contained in untimely matter: *polychronicity* and *multitemporality*.[67] Polychronicity refers to the meaning of time as a moment or a period in a chronology and therefore means the collation of many different moments in one. I argue that this existence of past moments in the present is symbolised in *The Two Noble Kinsmen* and, more generally, in the stories that evolve around Thebes or deal with *Thebanness*, by the dead bodies that continue to influence the present and refuse to be buried in the ground, dismissed to the past or 'superseded' by the present. Multitemporality, by contrast, refers to another meaning of time: time as a *conception* of temporality, an *understanding* of the temporal relations between past, future and present. Multitemporality therefore means different understandings and experiences of temporality. This kind of multitemporality can be found, for example, in the different approaches to time that Thebes and Athens, or Creon and Theseus, represent in *The Two Noble Kinsmen*, namely non-directional, unchronological time and linear progress history.

But there are more variations of temporality than those two opposed concepts. Multitemporality can also be found in the flexible, bendable idea of time that shines through in the way the foundation myth of Thebes is told in the *Metamorphoses*, the story of the soldiers born out of the snakes' teeth, which Lee Patterson calls the "chthonic return that is then endlessly repeated"[68] and which inscribes the unescapability, the recurrence of the past into Theban history from its beginning. From the moment Athene appears and tells Cadmus to sow the teeth, the story is suddenly told in fast-forward: the warriors are born from the earth, grow up, fight, die and return to the earth in one instant,[69] which strongly suggests circularity. The few that survive build and inhabit Thebes where Cadmus has grown-up grandchildren within a moment. The fact that he marries Harmonia, who is herself the offspring of the union of Mars and Venus, perhaps includes a link to the future here as well: an answer to Emilia's dilemma with the two indistinguishable/irreconcilable Venus-and-Mars-cousins ("Were they metamorphosed/ Both into one!", 5.3.84-85) is built into the *Metamorphoses* at this point. And then it is *Athene*, of course, who tells Cadmus to sow the teeth. She is the goddess of wisdom and strategy and patron of Athens and thus also stands for the linear understanding of time that is associated with Athens and juxtaposed to Theban non-linearity in *The Two Noble Kinsmen*.

Multitemporality relates here to this relativity and flexibility of notions of time. It indicates the multitemporal dimensions of the palimpsest described by

67 See Harris (2009), pp.3-4.

68 Patterson (1991), p.75.

69 "Iamque brevis vitae spatium sortita iuventus/ sanguineam tepido plangebant pectore matrem". *Metamorphoseon libri quindecim* (ed. von Albrecht), Book III ll. 124-125: "The dying youth of Thebes beats with warm breast on its bloody mother", trans. in Lee Patterson (1991), p.75.

Harris. The palimpsest "compresses different times within one surface"[70] and shows that there are multiple temporal relations possible between present, past and future.[71] Therefore a city, especially one like Thebes, can be "sown", built and stand almost simultaneously. Cadmus, who has just been exiled by his father, has grown-up grandchildren shortly afterwards: the past "explodes" upon the present,[72] like the warriors that spring up from underground.

Thebes appears as a polychronic assemblage and Creon does not try to master or 'purify' the past, overwrite it with the present or separate a living *after* from a dead *before*.[73] The past is not 'superseded' by the present in Thebes.[74] Like in a palimpsest, the 'under-text' of the dead bodies (Polynices, the Argives, Chaucer in his grave) is not a dead letter, or body, buried beneath or by the living (word). It "retains its legibility".[75] "Even as it is temporally distanced [...], it retains a power to speak, and hence to disrupt and transform its over-text",[76] as Harris writes about the palimpsest's under-text and it could equally be applied to the dead in *The Two Noble Kinsmen*. Harris describes the temporalities of the palimpsest using the example of a manuscript called the Archimedes Palimpsest. It contains, among others, two works by the Greek mathematician Archimedes: a study of hydraulics, *Floating Bodies*, and a treatise on the mathematical concept of infinity, both probably dating from the late fifth century. The manuscript has been overwritten with medieval Greek Orthodox liturgical material by a monastic scribe in 1229 and painted over with faux-Byzantine images in the twentieth century.[77] As Harris writes,

> the net effect of the Archimedes Palimpsest – within which, as the manuscript's official name suggests, the [...] under-text about floating bodies buoyantly rises through and above the [...] over-text beneath which it has supposedly been submerged – is not just one of supersession. It is equally one of untimely irruption.[78]

In *The Two Noble Kinsmen*, these floating bodies "buoyantly rising through and above the over-text" are, quite literally, the unburied dead Argives or Chaucer shouting from underground. Polynices' body in *Antigone* is an even better example, because Antigone tries repeatedly to cover it with dust, push it down, but

70 Harris (2009), p.16.
71 Harris (2009), p.17.
72 Harris (2009), pp.91 ff.
73 See Harris (2009), p.15.
74 'Superseded' in the sense of Hegel's term *aufgehoben* as in G. W. F. Hegel (1807), *Phänomenologie des Geistes*. See Harris (2009), pp.29-31. 'Superseded' in this sense does not mean that the past is completely gone, though, without any traces left, but rather that the past is preserved in the present, and yet banished to the past, like the Old Testament is superseded by the New Testament in Christian belief. Harris (2009), p.15.
75 Harris (2009), p.15.
76 Harris, *ibid.*
77 Harris (2009), p.13.
78 Harris (2009), p.15.

the dust is removed and the body keeps rising to the surface. The "untimely irruption" is symbolically expressed by the Argive widows breaking in upon Theseus' wedding procession, especially in *The Knight's Tale*, where they appear like spectres and take the reins of Theseus' horse. This sounds like what Harris describes as the temporality of explosion, where "the apparition of the 'old' text shatters the integrity of the 'new' by introducing into it a radical alterity that punctures the illusion of its wholeness or finality".[79] This certainly happens in *The Knight's Tale*, where the widows destroy the celebration's "glorie and greet solempnytee" (870) when they wail about their dead husbands and disclose unasked-for details like how their bodies lie about on heaps and are eaten by dogs (944-947). Forcing him and all the people that attend the train to remember the atrocities and the victims of the war, it is impossible for Theseus to feign a happy ending by marrying Hippolyta with great splendour. They make sure that the sacrifices that were necessary for his being "swich a conquerour/ That gretter was ther noon under the sonne" (862-863) are not simply ignored or forgotten.

In *The Two Noble Kinsmen*, the widows (or the past) 'slide' into the scene rather than suddenly break in on it and then say, one after the other, "hear and respect me" (1.1.26, 28). This way, there is a stronger focus on the fact that they come from within rather than outside of the events, while, in *The Knight's Tale*, the focus is more on the force with which the past 'explodes' upon the present. In *The Two Noble Kinsmen* the existence of the past *in* the present is stressed, but still the scene is turned into its opposite by the appearance of the queens: they see to it that the triumphant mood is destroyed and the celebration is cancelled.

There are different accents or focuses, but the unrest, the unquietness of the dead is something all versions of the Thebes myth share, whether by Sophocles, Ovid, Statius, Chaucer or Shakespeare and Fletcher. And, usually, Theseus of Athens is called to impose order upon Thebes' temporal chaos. He does so by assorting some things to the past and others to the present and thus producing a story of linear progression, purpose and meaning. Lee Patterson proposes 'Boethianism' as the Other in relation to which Thebanness is defined or, rather, Thebanness is the "other that Boethianism suppresses".[80] Theban dysfunctional recursiveness ("disordered memory and fatal repetition") is the "dark mirroring of Boethian idealism".[81] In his *Consolation of Philosophy*, Boethius describes a meaningful' recursiveness, a "cosmic binding that orders the universe as a whole:"[82]

> Alle thynges seken ayen to hir propre cours [*recursus*][83], and alle thynges rejoysen hem of hir retornynge ayen to hir nature. Ne noon ordenaunce is bytaken to thynges, but

[79] Harris, *ibid.*
[80] Patterson (1991), p.75.
[81] Patterson, *ibid.*
[82] Patterson (1991), p.73.
[83] Patterson, *ibid.*

that that hath joyned the endynge to the bygynnynge, and hath maked the cours of itself stable.[84]

Here, the return to the beginning is regarded as something good, unavoidable but salutary and something that all creatures – animals, plants and even the sun, share: just as tamed lions will become wild again as soon as they taste blood, a caged bird will forever miss the woods and search for them, a bough that is bent will spring up again when it is released and the sun always returns to from where it arose.[85] Thebes' compulsive, *destructive* repetition, its "fatal doubling" of murder and incest thus appears indeed as "a dark echo of the idealistic *recursus* of Boethianism".[86] But since its "replicating history" also "preempts a linear or developmental progress",[87] it can be juxtaposed not only to Boethianism but also to 'Athenism', as it were. According to Lee Patterson, this is the case in *The Knight's Tale.* For him it is not Theseus who likes to install an Athenian ordering principle in Thebes, but the Knight who tells the story in the narrative frame of *The Canterbury Tales.* "The Knight means his narrative to record the disarming of an aboriginal Theban ferocity by Athenian civilization, the replacement of a regressive Theban repetitiveness with the purposive linearity of the Athenian *mission civilisatrice*".[88] There is no such narrator in *The Two Noble Kinsmen* and it is Theseus, the Knight's accomplice or assistant in his tale, who assumes this role in the play, i.e. tries to impose Athenian unidirectionality upon Thebes' temporal chaos. But of course his *mission civilisatrice* comes at a cost.

II.7. Theseus, Creon and the gods

The "most unbounded" Creon (1.2.63) refuses to do away with the past, to dispose of the untimely matter of the dead bodies in a city that represents inescapable fatality and a curse that is passed on forever. Theseus of Athens is called to provide remedy. He proceeds to impose his will on everyone much more brutally than his predecessor in Chaucer, as becomes clear in what remains of the "First Movere" speech. Theseus attempts to ascribe the tragic outcomes to fortune or the gods and masks his own agency in arranging the dilemmas for his subjects:[89] "Never fortune/ Did play a subtler game"; "Yet in the passage/ The gods have been most equal"; "The gods my justice/ Take from my hand and they themselves become/ The executioners"; "Oh, you heavenly charmers,/ What things you make of us!" (5.4.112-32).

---

84 Chaucer's translation of Boethius, cited from *Riverside Chaucer*: *Boece*, Book III, Metrum 2, ll. 39-46.

85 *Boece*, Book III, Metrum 2, ll. 7-39 and Patterson (1991), p.73.

86 Patterson (1991), p.77.

87 Patterson, *ibid.*

88 Patterson (1991), p.201.

89 Compare Shannon, p.108.

Creon, however, does not try to hide his agency or even the arbitrariness of his actions. Therefore he is seen as a villain, a tyrant, in *Antigone* as in *The Two Noble Kinsmen*:

A most unbounded tyrant, whose successes
Makes heaven unfeared and villainy assured
Beyond its power there's nothing; almost puts
Faith in a fever and deifies alone
Voluble Chance. (1.2.63-67)

Palamon and Arcite believe that Theseus, on the other hand, is guided by the gods before they have actually met him: Theseus, too, is preceded by the discourse around him. In that same conversation, while they are still at Thebes, Arcite says about Theseus: "But that we fear the gods in him, he brings not/ A jot of terror to us" (1.2.94-95). Just because Theseus refers to the gods often and claims that they influence events in ways "that are above our question" (5.4.136), his regulations are seen as wise and his directions are never questioned. But the play is critical of that, sometimes quite directly, as when citizens discuss the new rules Theseus arranged for the tournament:

JAILER I hope they are good.
2 FRIEND They are honourable;
How good they'll prove, I know not (4.1.30-31)

The marked distinction between "good" and "honourable" suggests that Theseus and his rules aren't both, that although he may adhere to what is formally required of a noble ruler this does not make him "good", and that at least some of the citizens perceive that not everything Theseus issues as "honourable" is "good".

At other times the critique is more subtle, for example when Theseus is deified himself the more he refers to the gods. The Argive Queens, in particular, are prone to do so when they want to persuade him to conquer Thebes: "Oh pity, Duke;/ Thou purger of the earth" (1.1.47-48), they say to him, "Oh, I hope some god,/ Some god hath put his mercy in your manhood,/ Whereto he'll infuse power" (1.1.71-73). Theseus, therefore, has to exhort them almost at regular intervals, "Pray you, kneel not" (1.1.54), "Pray, stand up" (1.1.205); "Oh, no knees, none, widow./ Unto the helmeted Bellona use them,/ And pray for me, your soldier" (1.1.74-76). Hippolyta, Emilia and Theseus' friend, Pirithous, all fall into the same pattern when they beg Theseus to spare Palamon and Arcite. Their imploration becomes a ceremonial prayer: early on, characteristics of sound and rhythm emerge that lend the plea musical quality, until it turns into an antiphon,[90] a liturgical chant dedicated to Theseus. First each of the three pleads in-

[90] See Potter, p.252.

dividually, one after the other, then the lines shorten and accelerate. Tension increases as they unite their voices toward the climax:

PIRITHOUS	By all our friendship, sir, by all our dangers, By all you love most: wars, and this sweet lady –
EMILIA	By that you would have trembled to deny A blushing maid –
HIPPOLYTA	By your own eyes, by strength, In which you swore I went beyond all women, Almost all men, and yet I yielded, Theseus –
PIRITHOUS	To crown all this, by your most noble soul, Which cannot want due mercy, I beg first –
HIPPOLYTA	Next hear my prayers –
EMILIA	Last, let me entreat, sir –
PIRITHOUS	For mercy!
HIPPOLYTA	Mercy!
EMILIA	Mercy on these princes! (3.6.202-211)

Theseus becomes sacred, godlike, especially in the last lines. The rhythm and form create a situation of worship and the vocabulary, too, consists of words from liturgical contexts, such as *crown*, *soul*, *mercy* and *prayers*. Consequently, Theseus replies, "Ye make my faith reel" (3.6.212). This refers to the constancy to his oath (of killing the kinsmen) which he feels is wavering,[91] but the choice of the word "faith" here indicates that Theseus has noticed the religious character of the plea addressed to him. His faith "reels" as he realises his subjects are putting him in the place of the god or gods to whom he usually refers as an external agency that is the cause of his actions or decrees.

II. 8. "Nat fully quyke, ne fully dede they were"

But Theseus does act as if he were an omnipotent god sometimes, just like Creon. He even gives (new) life to the kinsmen. When Palamon and Arcite appear for the first time in the play, they are at Thebes and discuss how it is equally impossible for them to leave the city as it is to stay. Theseus' attack on Thebes ends their debate. Theseus wins the battle and takes the injured and unconscious kinsmen to Athens as prisoners. Their second appearance on stage is "*on hearses*" (1.4 SD). When Theseus sees them, he asks, "What are those? [...] They are not dead?" (1.4.13-24). The herald answers "Nor in a state of life" (1.4.25). The only sign that they are not yet dead is the fact that "they breathe / And have the name of men" (1.4.27-28). Theseus immediately orders that they be "recovered," no matter at what cost:

91 *The Two Noble Kinsmen*, ed. Eugene M. Waith (Oxford: Oxford University Press, 1989, 2008), p.162.

All our surgeons
Convent in their behoof; our richest balms,
Rather than niggard, waste; their lives concern us
Much more than Thebes is worth. (1.4.30-33)

Then, as mentioned earlier, he explains that he would rather have Palamon and Arcite dead than free, but even more than that he wants them to be his prisoners. He orders that great pains be taken to restore their health, with the sole purpose of keeping them imprisoned forever, adding them to the list of people that are neither completely dead nor really alive. This means two healthy young men, not just healthy but very fit, "like to a pair of lions, [...] worth a god's view" (1.4.18-21), are almost killed, then brought back to life with huge efforts, only to be kept in an open-ended captivity, a sort of stand-by modus: not dead, but not alive either, ready to be brought back to life at any time, unlike Sophocles' Antigone, who was put in prison to die there. Palamon and Arcite are also initially imprisoned forever and Theseus likes the idea that they are his, and not death's, captives and at his disposal ("We had rather have 'em / Prisoners to us than death," 1.4.36-37), as if he were God. The kinsmen start quarrelling almost as soon as they regain consciousness, which is the story of their *Doppelgängers* Eteocles and Polynices, but told backwards: Polynices and Eteocles fight until they kill each other, while Palamon and Arcite are peacefully united until they are almost killed by Theseus' attack, then they start to fight after they rise from their "hearses". *Then* they try to kill each other, too, but Theseus doesn't let them. So while Polynices and Eteocles fight until they are dead, Palamon and Arcite are first dead (or almost), *then* start to fight. But here the stories converge again, because Polynices and Eteocles' struggle lives on after their deaths, when their cremated bodies keep up the fight or, rather, the elements (fire and smoke, a combination of fire, earth and air) continue it and thus, in Emilia's words, "effect / Rare issues by their operance" (1.3.62-63): they grant the brothers immortality and allow their strife to live on and infect Palamon and Arcite, who are brought to the brink of death before they start to fight each other, while they were, together, before their resurrection at the hands of Theseus, fighting both Theseus and Creon: Theseus in the classical sense of the word, with weapons on a battlefield and Creon morally, with their attitude, as their dialogue at Thebes shows: "'Tis in our power, / Unless we fear that apes can tutor's, to / Be masters of our manners" (1.2.42-44); "Let / The blood of mine that's sib to him be sucked/ From me with leeches, let them break and fall / Off me with that corruption" (1.2.71-74), etc.

The next scene in which Palamon and Arcite appear is not shown on stage, only described retrospectively. They are already outside Creon's city, fighting in the battle "like lions", in the prime of their life as soldiers, paragons of life, strength and energy. This is yet another example of a teichoscopy scene that illustrates the palimpsest-like character of the literary tradition. It is often used for scenes otherwise difficult to stage, like battle scenes. Here it is also used for contrastive effects: while Theseus praises the kinsmen's impressive performance in that imagined scene ("I fixed my note / Constantly on them, for they were a mark / Worth a god's view", 1.4.19-21) they are lying on stage in a completely different condition, "on hearses", unconscious, "not dead / Nor in a state of life" (1.4.24-25). This is the trigger for a series of opposites in which Theseus now characterises the kinsmen: "The very lees of such…/ Exceed the wine of others" (1.4.29-30); "Rather than niggard, waste" (1.4.32); "Rather than […]/ Sound and at liberty, I would 'em dead" (1.4.33-35); "our kind air / to them unkind" (1.4.38).

From this situation, they are transferred to the 'freedom' of imprisonment, also a (paradoxical) combination of opposites: They conceive of their captivity as (moral) freedom, a greater freedom than their former (formal) freedom at Thebes. And there the most abrupt change occurs: they switch from closest connectedness to irreconcilable enmity.

Palamon and Arcite's paradoxical situation at the beginning of the play is that if they stay at Thebes, they are sure they will get morally corrupted. But leaving their country in the hands of a tyrant, they act dishonourably as well.[92] As knights, they adhere to the chivalric code, but they get mutually exclusive instructions from it, similar to Hector's in *Troilus and Cressida*: he has to continue the war and simultaneously end it. Equally important rules of conduct are irreconcilable. Palamon and Arcite have two equally impossible options: "To be neutral to him were dishonour, / Rebellious to oppose" (1.2.100-101); "We must / Be vile or disobedient" (1.2.77-78). They are released from this dilemma by Theseus: a messenger interrupts them, informing them that they are called to war. Again, like Hector, who had come to the conclusion that the reason for the war (keeping Helen in Troy) was unjust, but that the war must be continued and Helen be kept nonetheless, they decide they must obey Creon and fight for Thebes although they cannot justify it:

ARCITE: Yet what man
Thirds his own worth (the case is each of ours)
When that his action's dregged with mind assured
'Tis bad he goes about?
PALAMON: Leave that unreasoned. (1.2.95-98)[93]

[92] Cf. Peter T. Hadorn, "*The Two Noble Kinsmen* and the Problem of Chivalry", *Studies in Medievalism*, 4 (1992), pp.45-57, p.49.

[93] Compare with Hector in *Troilus and Cressida*: "To persist/ In doing wrong extenuates not wrong,/ But makes it much more heavy. Hector's opinion/ Is this in way of truth; yet, ne'ertheless,/ […] I propend to you/ In resolution to keep Helen still" (2.2.186-191), see pp. 29-30 above.

At Thebes, contradictions are not there to be resolved. They are just there. But Theseus is coming to sort things out. He profits from Palamon and Arcite's dilemma in so far as they follow him perhaps more willingly, as Theseus seems like a solution to them when he takes them away from Thebes. His method is to bring them to the brink of death and then grant them a new life in Athens, but in a prison that he controls. Yet, as Lee Patterson puts it with regard to *The Knight's Tale*:

> the fatal quality of Thebanness [cannot] be definitively interred. [...] Unnaturally brought back to life from a Theban past Theseus is seeking to suppress, the cousins are reborn into an Athenian present they continue to disrupt; and from the Knight's perspective, they embody an irrationality that Theseus must chasten into civilization.[94]

II.9. Compulsory heterosexual marriage and linear time

II.9.1. The kinsmen in The Knight's Tale*: "Two yonge knyghtes liggynge by and by"*

The "irrationality" that Theseus strives to restrain lies, to a large degree, in the homoerotic inclinations of most of the main characters. Palamon and Arcite, for example, start to articulate their love for one another in very erotic terms as soon as they find themselves alone in prison together. In *The Knight's Tale*, the homoerotic attraction between them is hinted at even earlier, at the moment when they are first introduced. Since their first appearance in the scene at Thebes is an addition by Shakespeare and Fletcher, which does not occur in *The Knight's Tale*, Chaucer's Palamon and Arcite appear for the first time, half dead, *after* the battle between Creon and Theseus. In *The Knight's Tale*, there is no mention whether they made any impression on Theseus during the fight; instead they are selected out of the heap of bodies after the battle because of their "roial" (I 1018) armours. In *The Knight's Tale* they are perhaps even harder to distinguish than in *The Two Noble Kinsmen*;[95] they appear *united* when they are first introduced: they are "liggynge by and by, / Bothe in oon armes" (I 1011-1012), that is, wearing the same heraldic device,[96] but, given that they are found in a heap of bodies (I 1009) and that the double meaning of 'arms' is often used for (amorous) puns,[97] it does also suggest that they are lying in each other's arms. Thus the tangled bodies suggest a palimpsest themselves, as they represent both life and death, present and past at this moment: "Nat fully quyke,[98] ne fully dede they were" (I 1015).

---

94 Patterson (1991), p.200.

95 Johnston (2010b), pp.51, 58.

96 Benson, p.39.

97 In *Troilus and Cressida* and *Pericles*, too, e.g.: "dare avow her beauty and her worth/ In other arms than hers" (*Troilus and Cressida* 1.3.271-272, see p. 35 above); or "they [i.e. ladies] love men in arms as well as beds" (*Pericles* 2.3.95).

98 = 'living'. Benson, p.39.

Palamon and Arcite are thus introduced in a rather remarkable way, as part of a still life, as it were, of a heap of intertwined bodies that are neither quite dead nor fully alive. But there is an erotic touch to it as well: "Arcite and Palamon's intimacy with death is written here upon their intimacy with one another".[99] The figuration of two knights lying "'by and by' [...] evokes the intimacies of sleep as much as it does the sacrifices of the grave".[100]

The theme of funeral-marriage that pervades *The Two Noble Kinsmen* is thus invoked here, but the tone is quite gentle, as Ingham observes, in spite of "the horrifying image of these young men disguised in a heap of bloody corpses".[101] The description focuses on the tenderness of their "intimacy" with each other and leaves the horrid details of the pile of corpses out, although at other times we are not spared a gruesome description of, for example, Arcite's deadly injuries (I 2684-2699, I 2743-2760), the horror scenarios with which the temple of Mars is painted (I 1967-2050) or the effects of Saturn's influence on earth (I 2453-2469). In *The Two Noble Kinsmen*, the horrifying images appear at the wedding scene in the words of the three Queens, who interrupt the celebration to talk of their husbands lying "blistering 'fore the visitating sun" (1.1.146). The Queens start harmlessly but then change the tone abruptly when they use the image of a dove's plucked head in a context that does not prepare the listeners for such brutality:

> Speak't in a woman's key; like such a woman
> As any of us three; weep ere you fail.
> Lend us a knee;
> But touch the ground for us no longer time
> Than a dove's motion, when the head's plucked off. (1.1.94-98)

The description of a body that "i'th' blood-sized field lay swollen, / Showing the sun his teeth, grinning at the moon" (1.1.99-100) follows.

The horror scenario of the kinsmen lying entangled "in a mass of wounded flesh"[102] is used as setting for a moment of tenderness, where the tone exhibits "a fond poignancy often reserved for lovers", as Patricia Ingham notes.[103] This also appears in *The Two Noble Kinsmen*, when the friendship between Theseus and Pirithous is described as "their knot of love, / Tied, weaved, entangled" (1.3.41-42), "a phrase charged with erotic meaning".[104] During this discussion, Hippolyta also rather abruptly starts to talk of

99 Patricia Ingham, "Homosociality and Creative Masculinity in the *Knight's Tale*", in *Masculinities in Chaucer: Approaches to Maleness in* The Canterbury Tales *and* Troilus and Criseyde, ed. Peter G. Beidler (Cambridge: D.S. Brewer, 1998), pp.23-55, p.25.

100 Ingham, *ibid.*

101 Ingham, *ibid.*

102 Ingham, p.26.

103 Ingham, *ibid.*

104 Johnston (2010b), p.57.

> babes broached on the lance, or women
> That have sod their infants in (and after eat them)
> The brine they wept at killing 'em. (1.3.20-22)

In *The Knight's Tale*, the two noble kinsmen are introduced in a mass of entangled bodies, halfway between death and life and, at the same time, in erotic intimacy. Thus the moment of the kinsmen's first appearance contains both the idea of the palimpsest that Theseus tries to disentangle and the homoeroticism that Theseus tries to suppress and force into heterosexual channels in order to achieve linearity.

The idea of a funeral-marriage is there as well. In the heap of corpses Palamon and Arcite lie entangled as if after the "fight" of a wedding night. The Queens draw the comparison between deathbed and marriage bed, too, when they admonish Theseus, who is eager to proceed with the marriage: "Think / What beds our slain kings have!" (1.1.139-140).

II.9.2. The two noble kinsmen: "Ever begetting / New births of love"

In *The Two Noble Kinsmen*, the attraction between Palamon and Arcite becomes apparent a little later, when they are in prison together. Ironically, they appear quite happy in jail, as we hear in the words of the Jailer's Daughter at first:

> It seems to me they have no more sense of their captivity than I of ruling Athens. They eat well, look merrily, discourse of many things.
> (2.1.38-40)

She does of course not know about their dilemma at Thebes and therefore accredits their behaviour to their noble education, which she presumes taught them to endure hardships stoically: "I do think they have patience to make any adversity ashamed" (2.1.24-25). As a social inferior, she is duly impressed, "proud" to have them in her custody:

> The prison itself is proud of 'em and they have all the world in their chamber. [...] I marvel how they would have looked had they been victors, that with such a constant nobility enforce a freedom out of bondage, making misery their mirth and affliction a toy to jest at. (2.1.25-36)

The irony is, of course, that their good mood has little to do with their nobility and, perhaps, not even with the fact that they are now released from Creon's supposedly harmful influence (see Act I Scene 2). I suggest that "they have all the world in their chamber" because of their attraction to each other, which they are freer to express in this enclosed space. Their prison cell thus becomes a "bridal chamber, prison forever", as Antigone would say (*Antigone* 891). When the audience gets to see for themselves after the Jailer's Daughter's description, Arcite indeed cheers,

Whilst Palamon is with me, let me perish
If I think this our prison! (2.2.61-62)

Palamon agrees with him:

Certainly,
'Tis a main goodness, cousin, that our fortunes
Were twined together. (2.2.62-64)

"Twined together" echoes their first appearance in *The Knight's Tale*. There is some controversy about whether the Quarto edition's "twyn'd" is to be understood as "twinned" (Oxford) or "twined" (Arden), but both indeed concur with the image of the kinsmen lying in an entangled pile of bodies and looking identical; in fact, both are contained in the two meanings of their lying "in oon armes" in *The Knight's Tale*.
Arcite replies,

	Shall we make worthy uses of this place That all men hate so much?
PALAMON	How, gentle cousin?
ARCITE	Let's think this prison holy sanctuary To keep us from corruption of worse men. (2.2.69-72)

Palamon responds:

What had we been, old in the court of Creon,
Where sin is justice [...]? Cousin Arcite,
Had not the loving gods found this place for us,
We had died as they do, ill old men, unwept,
And had their epitaphs, the people's curses. (2.2.105-110)

It is notable that it is the idea of *growing old* in Thebes that Palamon finds so disagreeable. If Thebes stands for temporal disorder and Athens for linear chronology, being locked up forever at a young age instead of growing old outside the prison and dying as "old men" confuses this order. And yet the latter, the in-between state, appears preferable to him, more healthy (opposed to "ill" as in "ill old men") because it is connected with Athens and Theseus. Usually it is *Creon*'s rule that is stigmatised as 'unnatural' – corrupted, against the laws of god and nature, etc. But, obviously, the hegemonic discourse is so strong, at least with the kinsmen, that whatever is connected with Theseus and Athens is judged positively and, moreover, attributed to the gods, as here: it is "the loving gods" that "found this place for us" (2.2.108).

In this place that the loving gods found Palamon and Arcite glimpse Emilia through their prison window. The kinsmen's instant transformation from friend to mortal foe prefigures the later one from winner to loser, life to death and vice versa after the tournament. Here, the sudden mood swing is also meant to be comic. But before the kinsmen start to get aggressive, the atmosphere heats up in a way that accounts for the vehemence with which they react to Emilia's mere sight from afar. It becomes clear that the Jailer's Daughter's observation that "they have all the world in their chamber" (2.1.26) was quite right: the cousins picture their time in prison together not just as a couple but as a whole family:

> Here being thus together,
> We are an endless mine to one another;
> We are one another's wife, ever begetting
> New births of love; we are father, friends, acquaintance,
> We are, in one another, families;
> I am your heir and you are mine. (2.2.78-83)

Critics have, for a long time, tried to subsume this under Montaigne's friendship discourse; however, they admit that "even the intimate tone of the standard friendship rhetoric usually does not include an allusion to the two friends being 'one another's wife'".[105] "We are one another's wife, ever begetting / New births of love; we are father, friends, acquaintance" also echoes the prologue's conflation of husband, father, child and bride. In Fletcher and Beaumont's *The Maid's Tragedy*, Melantius uses a similar phrase to express his relationship to his (dying) friend Amintor: "Here was my sister, father, brother, son / All that I had" (*The Maid's Tragedy*, 5.3.266-267).[106] But the friendship is imagined only in terms of blood relations. In contrast, the two noble kinsmen's relationship also has a sexual dimension. To Arcite's "We are one another's wife, ever begetting / New births of love" (2.2.80-81), Palamon responds "like someone successfully wooed:"[107]

> You have made me –
> I thank you, cousin Arcite – almost wanton
> With my captivity. (2.2.95-97)

In the following lines they exchange promises that resemble a wedding vow: to Palamon's "I do not think it possible our friendship/ Should ever leave us", Arcite replies, "Till our deaths it cannot" (2.2.114-115), a further connection to the prologue with its postulation of "constan[cy] to eternity" (PROLOGUE 22). "An endless mine" also echoes the prologue's "an endless thing" (PROLOGUE 22). According to Richard Mallette, "holy sanctuary" (from "Let's think this prison holy sanctuary", 2.2.71) thus echoes with the suggestion of "holy matrimony".[108] Just as the prologue's commitment to faithfulness (to the literary source and to the marriage partner) serves to contrast this constancy with the changes that follow, the love, agreement and harmony expressed here sharpen the contrast to the aggression, fighting and hatred that are about to follow. However, at the same time,

---

105 Carney, p.99.

106 *English Renaissance Drama: A Norton Anthology*, ed. Bevington and others (New York: Norton, 2002), pp.1147-1214. See also Shannon, p.104.

107 Richard Mallette, "Same-Sex Erotic Friendship in *The Two Noble Kinsmen*" in *Explorations in Renaissance Drama*, ed. Mary Beth Rose (Evanston: Northwestern University Press and the Newberry Library Center for Renaissance Studies, 1997), pp.29-52, p.37.

108 Mallette, p.37.

paradoxically, they *weaken* the contrast and make both modes of expression appear as variations of the same phenomenon. Just seconds after Palamon declares, "I do not think it possible our friendship / Should ever leave us" and *while* Arcite replies, "Till our deaths it cannot", Palamon catches sight of Emilia in the garden and falls for her on the spot; Arcite has the same reaction when he sees her a moment later. They immediately start to fight. Palamon's "Is there record of any two that loved/ Better than we do, Arcite?" (2.2.111-112) now becomes, "Have I called thee friend?" (2.2.185); "Friendship, blood, / And all the ties between us, I disclaim" (2.2.174-175). Arcite shrugs, "If that will lose ye, farewell, Palamon" (2.2.179). The former promise "We shall live long and loving" (2.2.86) is now replaced by "If I hazard thee / And take thy life, I deal but truly" (2.2.205-206) or even "I shall live / To knock thy brains out with my shackles" (2.2.221-222).

It is not unusual for illicit homoerotic desire to convert into socially more acceptable homosocial aggression.[109] The promptness and intensity with which it changes its mode is surprising, though, in this example: the aggression comes in the form of an explosion, sparked by a mere glimpse of Emilia. The comical juxtaposition of the two extremes ("We shall live long and loving" versus the various ways they threaten to kill each other) highlights the absurdity of the fact that male homosocial aggression is socially permissible while male-male intimacy is not.[110] Palamon and Arcite's virtual wedding vow reflects the fluidity of the border between life and death in this play, since it exceeds the usual "till death do us part", extending beyond death: "And after death our spirits shall be led/ To those that love eternally" (2.2.116-117). Similarly, their mutual attraction does not get lost after the rupture of Emilia's appearance, but is continued with inverted parameters. Translated into a traditional heterosexual love triangle, where two men are rivals for the love of one woman, their emotions become assertions of how much they hate, and how cruelly they will kill, each other. But the more quickly such a transition can happen, the more the differences vanish, because one seems to emerge from the other. The kinsmen's enmity *explodes* upon their expressions of affection, like the past from within the present, suggesting that they formed an entity, where one contained the other.

Their mode of expression can also revert, therefore. Their tone becomes tender again, not surprisingly when Emilia is out of sight and they are alone together, this time in the forest. She still hovers over the horizon, though, because the occasion for the kinsmen's meeting is a duel to decide about who can love Emilia. While they are dressing each other for the fight, their tone is affectionate. It then adopts an increasing erotic intensity and fierceness. When Palamon asks, "How do I look?" Arcite responds, "Love has used you kindly" (3.6.66-67) and when Palamon wishes that "my embraces / Might thank ye, not my blows" (3.6.22-23), Arcite re-

[109] Mallette, pp.37-39.
[110] See Mallette, p.41.

plies, "you show / More than a mistress to me" (3.6.25-26).[111] Palamon puns on the double meaning of "arms" like Hector in *Troilus and Cressida*:[112] "I am well and lusty; choose your arms" (3.6.45). While they are putting on one another's armour, they exchange lines filled with such *double entendres*: "Do I pinch you?" (3.6.55); "I'll buckl't close. – By any means". (3.6.57-58); "Thrust the buckle / Through far enough. – I warrant you" (3.6.61-62); "I'll strike home. – Do and spare not. / I'll give you cause, sweet cousin" (3.6.69). Palamon demands, "Be rough with me" (3.1.102) and sums up the combined expression of affection and antagonism when he says, "Sir; your person / Without hypocrisy I may not wish / More than my sword's edge on't" (3.1.94-96).[113][114] In *A Midsummer Night's Dream's*, Theseus employs the same military-sexual *double entendre* when he says, "Hippolyta, I wooed thee with my sword" (*A Midsummer Night's Dream*, 1.1.16).[115]

Thus what Palamon wished during the prison scene adopts an additional meaning in retrospect:

> To be one hour at liberty and grasp
> Our good swords in our hands! I would quickly teach thee
> What 'twere to filch affection from another. (2.2.211-213)

The wish to destroy the other becomes the wish to unite with him and the supposed opposition between Palamon and Arcite once again dissolves into unity.

Before this can actually happen, Theseus interrupts the kinsmen. Angry that they have not informed him about their private activities in the woods, he commands that the duel shall take place at a later date, this time publicly and according to rules provided by him. This does not prevent what Richard Abrams calls their "simultaneous orgasm" at the tournament,[116] which refers to Theseus' own description of the combat:

> I have heard
> Two emulous Philomels beat the ear o'th' night
> With their contentious throats, now one the higher,
> Anon the other, then again the first,
> And by and by out-breasted, that the sense
> Could not judge between 'em. So it fared
> Good space between these kinsmen, till heavens did
> Make hardly one the winner. (5.3.123-130)

---

[111] See also Mallette, pp.41-42, for this scene.

[112] "Thou hast lusty arms! / Hector would have them fall upon him thus" (*Troilus and Cressida* 4.5.137-138), see above.

[113] Swords and bucklers = penises and pudends. Partridge, pp.254-255.

[114] See Mallette, p.40.

[115] Quoted from the following edition: *A Midsummer Night's Dream*, ed. Peter Holland (Oxford: Oxford University Press, 2008).

[116] Richard Abrams, "Gender Confusion and Sexual Politics in *The Two Noble Kinsmen*", in *Drama, Sex and Politics*, Themes in Drama 7, ed. James Redmond (Cambridge: Cambridge University Press, 1985), pp.69-76, p.73.

During this tournament, about which we only hear in reports from others, Emilia reflects on to whom she should compare the cousins and to her mind comes "Narcissus" (4.2.32), who fell in love with a picture of himself and "wanton Ganymede" (4.2.15), a boy desired by Jupiter. Both of them are "classical embodiments of homoerotic desire"[117] and "well-known code names for same-sex erotic types".[118]

In the light of their erotic attraction, Palamon's fantasy about Emilia seems to be, in reality, a fantasy about Arcite:

> Were I at liberty, I would do things
> Of such a virtuous greatness that this lady,
> This blushing virgin, should take manhood to her
> And seek to ravish me. (2.2.259-262)

Since the kinsmen's quarrel seems to be so much about themselves and so little about Emilia that she appears as a mere pretext for their argument, it comes as no surprise when, during their debate in the woods, Palamon and Arcite finally agree, "No mention of this woman; 'twill disturb us" (3.3.15).

II.9.3. Emilia

Emilia's, on the other hand, "stated sexual preference is for other women".[119] Recently critics observe that she "walks onstage to dramatize the most explicit case for same-sex association in the period except for Donne's 'Sapho to Philenis'".[120]

Firstly, Emilia supports and defends women's causes throughout the play. While the former Amazon Queen "is largely subdued by Theseus, her sister Emilia remains thoroughly woman-centred".[121] As "a natural sister of our sex" (1.1.125), as she calls herself, she immediately empathises with the lamenting Queens: "What woman I may stead that is distressed / Does bind me to her" (1.1.36-37). She reassures Hippolyta, "the powers of all women will be with us" (3.6.194). "Emilia invariably evaluates situations in terms that can only be described as woman centered".[122] When people praise Arcite for his "noble qualities" (2.5.10), it is Emilia who remarks, "His mother was a wondrous handsome woman; / His face, methinks, goes that way" (2.5.20-21). The already defeated Hippolyta, who is "shrunk [...] into / The bound [she] was o'erflowing" (1.1.83-84), and now usually

---

117 Johnston (2010b), p.49.

118 Mallette, p.45.

119 Abrams, p.69.

120 Shannon, p.101.

121 Alan Sinfield, "Cultural Materialism and Intertextuality: The Limits of Queer Reading in *A Midsummer Night's Dream* and *The Two Noble Kinsmen*", *Shakespeare Survey* 56 (2003), pp.67-78, p.69.

122 Shannon, p.117.

defends Theseus' 'natural' prerogatives, snaps back, "But his body / And fiery mind illustrate a brave father" (2.5.21-22). Emilia, however, continues to advocate for the independence of women. When, for example, Theseus tells her that such an admirable, indeed "perfect" (2.5.15), man as Arcite should be her master rather than her servant, she replies that she is "too wise for that" (2.5.64).

Emilia's assertion, "No knees to me. What woman I may stead that is distressed / Does bind me to her" (1.1.35-37), were "perfectly unremarkable" if made by a male knight, as Laurie Shannon points out,[123] but it is Emilia speaking. While Hippolyta, after her defeat, has embraced a position where she can only succeed with male support, Emilia resists such a passive role. Even with the Amazon Queen thus subjugated, Emilia positions herself primarily among women, both socially and affectively.[124] It has been argued, therefore, that Emilia is posited as Theseus' main counter-voice in the play and not, for example, the paradigmatic male friendship model derived from Montaigne[125] and that the play's deepest conflict is "not between the kinsmen, but between Theseus, as patriarchal ruler of Athens, and Emilia as representative of 'the powers of all women' (3.6.194)".[126] Indeed, Emilia is more persistent and successful in resisting Theseus than any of the other characters, as demonstrated on various occasions in the course of the play; but, by the end, she, too, is "conquered" and Theseus' rule prevails to create the sad scenario of the last scenes.

When the Queens ask Theseus for help, Emilia immediately encourages them, saying that

> being a natural sister of our sex
> Your sorrow beats so ardently upon me
> That it shall make a counter-reflect 'gainst
> My brother's heart and warm it to some pity,
> Though it were made of stone. (1.1.125-129)

At this point, she still trusts in her power, or the power of women united, to be capable of forming a counterforce against Theseus' absolutist reign. The ardency of their sorrow, reinforced by Emilia, will be able to melt Theseus' heart of stone. When, shortly afterwards, she acts on her promise, she does not so much "warm" Theseus "to some pity" but, rather, threatens him:

> If you grant not
> My sister her petition in that force,
> With that celerity and nature, which
> She makes it in, from henceforth I'll not dare
> To ask you anything nor be so hardy
> Ever to take a husband. (1.1.200-205)

---

[123] Shannon, p.115.
[124] Shannon, p.114.
[125] Shannon, p.121.
[126] Abrams, p.74.

This threat is effective; her request is granted.

Another occasion for her to get Theseus to change his mind occurs a little later when he, upon finding the kinsmen fighting in the woods, decides to put them to death. When Emilia asks for pity, Theseus at first resorts to sexist taunting:

> You are a right woman, sister: you have pity
> But want the understanding where to use it. (3.6.214-215)

Far from being intimidated, Emilia maintains that it is he who lacks understanding, since his decision "was rashly made and in your anger. / Your reason will not hold it" (3.6.227-228). Mallette argues that, when Theseus refuses her wish to banish the kinsmen instead of killing them "on the ground that she lacks 'understanding'",[127] Theseus fails to apprehend that "Emilia understands her difficulty more clearly than the young men understand theirs".[128] The kinsmen try to pretend that they are rivals for Emilia's love, denying their homoerotic attraction, whereas Emilia is well aware that she "shall never [...] / Love any that's called man" (1.3.84-85).

She also points out to Theseus the harmful consequences of decisions "made in passion" instead of "good heed" (3.6.232): "if such vows / Stand for express will, all the world must perish" (3.6.228-229). She goes on,

> Besides, I have another oath 'gainst yours,
> Of more authority. (3.6.230-231)

Here, again, she is successful and convinces Theseus, but it is for the last time. Before I return to Theseus' "authority" and how he applies it, I will show how Emilia is drawn not only as a feminist character but as a lesbian and that she is thus "woman-centred" in a further sense.

While Chaucer's Emelye hardly ever speaks, Fletcher and Shakespeare expand her role considerably: she has more lines than Theseus.[129] Two of her speeches are most revealing with regard to her homosexuality. In the first one, Emilia tells Hippolyta about her childhood friend, Flavina. From the beginning, Emilia's description of Flavina is erotically suggestive. She says, for example, that Flavina "made too proud the bed" (1.3.52) and refers to her as "she I sigh and spoke of" (1.3.60) or as her "play-fellow" whom she "enjoyed" (1.3.50). "Enjoy" is used in a sexual sense quite often in this play: Arcite says about Emilia, "I love her as a woman, to enjoy her" (2.2.165); the Jailer's Daughter says of Palamon, "I would fain enjoy him" (2.4.30); Theseus tells Emilia, "They cannot both enjoy you" (3.6.275); Arcite predicts, "I think / I never shall enjoy her" (3.6.267-268); The-

[127] Mallette, p.46.

[128] Mallette, *ibid.*

[129] Emilia has 11 % of the play's lines and appears in 10 scenes, Theseus has 10 % of the lines and has 9 scenes on stage (*William Shakespeare: Complete Works*, eds. Bate and Rasmussen, p.2358).

seus uses the word when he sets up the rules for the tournament with Emilia as a trophy:

Whether,
Before us that are here, can force his cousin,
By fair and knightly strength, to touch the pillar,
He shall enjoy her. (3.6.293-296)

Emilia contrasts her relationship to Flavina with Theseus' friendship with Pirithous, which suggests that her role as his 'countermodel' began even in childhood. Pirithous and Theseus' friendship, she says, is characterised by reason, "maturely seasoned" (1.3.56) and "buckled with strong judgement" (1.3.57). But there is an erotic aspect to it as well, described by Emilia perhaps with a note of irony, since it intimates that the difference between the two modes of friendship is not so great after all, except that Emilia's does not need the veneer of "judgement". "Buckled" was used by the kinsmen for their sexual puns ("I'll buckl't close"; "Thrust the buckle through" (3.6.57-62), see above); therefore "buckled with strong judgement" sounds highly ironic. Emilia continues, again, with sexual innuendo:

And their needs
The one of th'other may be said to water
Their intertangled roots of love. (1.3.57-59)

With the "intertangled roots of love", she takes up Hippolyta's description of that friendship, so that Hippolyta's words get an entirely different, very sexual, meaning. Hippolyta said about Pirithous and Theseus:

Their knot of love,
Tied, weaved, entangled, with so true, so long,
And with a finger of so deep a cunning,
May be outworn, never undone. (1.3.41-44)

"Knot" can mean "sexual congress",[130] the true and long finger a male genital, while "true" as well as "cunning" can mean "buttocks" or "anus"[131]. "Undone" is "made impotent or castrated".[132] Emilia goes on,

– but I
And she I sigh and spoke of were things innocent. (1.3.59-60)

Their innocence distinguishes their love from "Pirithous' and Theseus' love" (1.3.55), which "is more maturely seasoned" (1.3.56): "season" can mean "impregnate" and "copulate with"[133] and it is "more buckled with strong judge-

[130] Partridge, p.168.
[131] Frankie Rubinstein, *A Dictionary of Shakespeare's Sexual Puns and their Significance* (London: Macmillan, 1984, 1989), pp.65, 282.
[132] Rubinstein, p.289.
[133] Rubinstein, p.233.

ment". Emilia thus strongly suggests a sexual relationship between Theseus and Pirithous.

To the question of "which he [Theseus] loves best" (1.3.47), whether Pirithous or Hippolyta, Emilia answers Hippolyta with distinct irony:

> Doubtless,
> There is a best and reason has no manners
> To say it is not you. (1.3.47-49)

The repeated stress on the importance of "reason" and "manners" or "judgement" and even "cunning" as the deciding factors in Theseus' friendship suggests dishonesty, perhaps even hypocrisy in their supposed "love". "Reason" can also refer to the social requirement ("manners") of marrying heterosexually; Theseus, too, has to marry (Hippolyta) and claim that he loves her "best". But referred to as "cunning", "reason" is also made fun of and used equivocally ("so deep a cunning" when "cunning" means "anus"). Emilia uses Theseus and Pirithous' "mature", rational and, upon closer inspection, vulgarly sexual relation to set up her own friendship to Flavina in quite a different light: "but I / And she I sigh and spoke of were things innocent" suggests that Theseus and Pirithous are *not* and certainly not innocent in a sexual sense, as the connotations of "knot", "true", "finger", "deep cunning", "seasoned", "one the other may be said to water", etc. imply. Emilia and Flavina's friendship is based on emotion rather than "reason" or "manners" and is thus (supposedly) more authentic: we, she says,

> Loved for we did and like the elements
> That know not what nor why, yet do effect
> Rare issues by their operance; our souls
> Did so to one another. (1.3.59-64)

The reference to the elements and the souls and to the unconcious way their friendship "operated" in ignorance of rational and sexual matters stands in stark contrast to how Theseus' friendship with Pirithous is depicted. At the same time, Emilia's description of her friendship with Flavina is very intense and moving. Richard Mallette calls it "the most intensely described female erotic friendship in the Shakespearean canon".[134] When Emilia has finished speaking, Hippolyta observes, "You're out of breath!" (1.3.82). The friendship Emilia describes is presexual, but it is highly erotic, as the loss of breath indicates:

> What she liked
> Was then of me approved; what not, condemned –
> No more arraignment. The flower that I would pluck
> And put between my breasts (then but beginning
> To swell about the blossom), oh, she would long
> Till she had such another, and commit it
> To the like innocent cradle, where phoenix-like

[134] Mallette, p.32.

They died in perfume. On my head not toy
But was her pattern; her affections – pretty,
Though happily her careless wear – I followed
For my most serious decking; had mine ear
Stol'n some new air or at adventure hummed one
From musical coinage, why, it was a note
Whereon her spirits would sojourn – rather, dwell on,
And sing it in her slumbers. (1.3.64-78)

The focus is on the emotional, direct, unaffected, even unconscious or dreamlike character of their friendship ("sing it in her slumbers"), which is set in opposition to Theseus' friendship of more calculated rationality. His friendship to Pirithous is based on "reason" and "judgement", but reason and judgement are then shown to relate to deeper drives or instincts: Theseus and Pirithous' "knot of love" is "tied, weaved, entangled" (1.3.41-42), which suggests sexual embraces and entangled bodies during intercourse. The fact that their friendship is more mature or, as Emilia says, "more maturely seasoned" (1.3.56), with a pun on "season" as "copulate with", also means that they have lost their innocence ("but I and she [...] were innocent", 1.3.59-60), which is expressed in some plant imagery: Pirithous and Theseus have already grown "intertangled roots of love" (1.3.59), while Emilia and Flavina are only just blossoming, wearing "flowers", signals of maidenhead,[135] between their breasts, "then but beginning / To swell about the blossom" (1.3.66-68).

While Emilia hints at a sexual relationship between Theseus and Pirithous, she also refers to the "manners" according to which Theseus loves Hippolyta "best". "Reason has no manners / To say it is not you" (1.3.48-49), she says, employing two negatives ("no manners"; "not you") to create the positive statement that Hippolyta wants to hear. The words are put in such a way, however, that what she is saying is hardly recognisable. It is not very obvious why she refers to "manners" and "reason" here again, creating an extremely ambiguous statement. But Hippolyta is not susceptible to such subtleties; she is not "ripe for persuasion", as she puts it:

Sure, my sister,
If I were ripe for your persuasion, you
Have said enough to shake me from the arm
Of the all-noble Theseus. (1.3.90-93)

"The all-noble Theseus" sounds just as convincing as the "great assurance" she then talks of "that we, more than his Pirithous, possess / The high throne in his heart" (1.3.94-96). Emilia calls this a "faith": "I am not / Against your faith, yet I continue mine" (1.3.96-97).

Emilia and Flavina's relationship is also in some respect similar to the kinsmen's. "What she liked was then of me approved" and "she would long till she

135 Partridge, p.137. Compare 'de-flower'.

had such another" describes exactly how Arcite reacts when Palamon articulates his love to Emilia, also insisting on loving her. He also imitates the images Palamon uses to describe how he feels: "Never till now was I in prison, Arcite" (2.2.132) becomes, in Arcite's words, "now I feel my shackles" (2.2.158); he copies Palamon's words in the same way that Flavina sings Emilia's tunes.

Emilia's childhood friend, however, "took leave o'th' moon / [...] when our count / Was each eleven" (1.3.52-54). This might explain Emilia's devotion to the moon goddess Diana, also a "maid", like Flavina (1.3.84), whom Emilia addresses as "sacred silver mistress" (5.1.146). "Sacred, shadowy, cold and constant queen" (5.1.137), as she calls Diana, could also refer to her revered dead childhood friend.

Emilia finishes her speech with the conclusion "that the true love 'tween maid and maid may be / More than in sex dividual" (1.3.81-82), and when Hippolyta claims, "you shall never, like the maid Flavina, / Love any that's called man" (1.3.84-85), meaning at the same time that she shall never love a man like she loved Flavina and that Flavina, too, never loved any man, Emilia confirms decidedly: "I am sure I shall not" (1.3.85).

But this recounted childhood memory is not the only occasion where Emilia's "sapphic orientation"[136] becomes evident. Her same-sex erotic life is not superseded, restricted to the past, now overcome, but is portrayed as having "an ongoing present in the action onstage",[137] in the very scene where Palamon and Arcite see Emilia from their window and start to fight. The same scene that has been discussed so much for the (alleged) collapse of the kinsmen's friendship[138] shows Emilia flirting and finally agreeing to go to bed with her waiting woman.[139] The kinsmen observe the women but are unable to hear their conversation from the prison window – like the criticism, as Laurie Shannon notes, for it has, for a long time, tuned the women's dialogue out.[140] Their exchange runs parallel with the kinsmen's so that the audience hears two dialogues. Without the kinsmen's interspersed comments, the dialogue between Emilia and her waiting woman goes as follows:

EMILIA This garden has a world of pleasures in't.
What flower is this?
WOMAN 'Tis called narcissus, madam.
EMILIA That was a fair boy, certain, but a fool
To love himself. Were there not maids enough?

136 Abrams, p.69.

137 Mallette, p.33.

138 See Shannon, p.118.

139 See Sinfield (2003), pp.71-72; Abrams, pp.69-70; Mallette, pp.33-34; Shannon, pp.118-120; Johnston (2010b), p.54; Ute Berns, "Interioritätskonstruktionen und Freundschaftsdiskurs bei Shakespeare", *Shakespeare Jahrbuch* 144 (2008), pp.148-167, p.159.

140 See Shannon, p.118.

Or were they all hard-hearted?
WOMAN They could not be to one so fair.
EMILIA Thou wouldst not.
WOMAN I think I should not, madam.
EMILIA That's a good wench.
But take heed to your kindness, though.
WOMAN Why, madam?
EMILIA Men are mad things.
Canst not thou work such flowers in silk, wench?
WOMAN Yes.
EMILIA I'll have a gown full of 'em, and of these.
This is a pretty colour; will't not do
Rarely upon a skirt, wench?
WOMAN Dainty, madam.
EMILIA Of all flowers
Methinks a rose is best.
WOMAN Why, gentle madam?
EMILIA It is the very emblem of a maid.
For, when the west wind courts her gently,
How modestly she blows and paints the sun
With her chaste blushes! When the north comes near her,
Rude and impatient, then, like chastity,
She locks her beauties in her bud again
And leaves him to base briars.
WOMAN Yet, good madam,
Sometimes her modesty will blow so far
She falls for't. A maid,
If she have any honour, would be loath
To take example by her.
EMILIA Thou art wanton.
The sun grows high; let's walk in. Keep these flowers.
We'll see how near art can come near their colours.
I am wondrous merry-hearted; I could laugh now.
WOMAN I could lie down, I am sure.
EMILIA And take one with you?
WOMAN That's as we bargain, madam.
EMILIA Well, agree then.

Exeunt Emilia and Woman
(2.2.118-153)

"Laugh and lie down" refers to a proverb, also a card game and has sexual overtones.[141] The flirtatious tone of the whole scene and the "bargain" to which it leads suggest that the women agree to go to bed together and leave the stage to do just that.[142] Palamon and Arcite's inserted, conventional praises of her beauty

[141] Potter, p.191; Waith, p.115; Valerie Traub, *The Renaissance of Lesbianism in Early Modern England* (Cambridge: Cambridge University Press, 2002), p.173.
[142] Shannon, p.120.

obscure the fact that Emilia feels suddenly like going in after she noticed that the maid is wanton: "She is wondrous fair./ She is all the beauty extant" (2.2.148). Thereby attention is deflected "from her defiance of convention toward an endorsement of heterosexual values".[143] As Mallette points out, "[t]he flirtation between Emilia and her handmaid is more socially permissible [...] by its inclusion in a homosocial setting, an inclusion that has the effect of erasure".[144] This has obviously worked quite well, because the same-sex eroticism of this scene has received strikingly little attention in criticism until recently.[145] On the other hand, Fletcher and Shakespeare were perhaps able to depict it so openly here precisely because it is half concealed by the noise of the kinsmen's wrangling. The way the two dialogues intersect is in itself suggestive though. Not only does the way they take place almost simultaneously, with just enough distance to allow acoustic understanding (more or less; the women's dialogue obviously less), suggest a parallel between the kinsmen's homoerotic affections and Emilia's. There are also verbal echoes that connect the two dialogues in a way that makes them not seem completely separated acoustically. Emilia's "Thou art wanton" echoes Palamon's "You have made me – / I thank you, cousin Arcite – almost wanton / With my captivity" (2.2.95-97). The kinsmen discuss love ("We are [...] ever begetting / New births of love", 2.2.80-81; "Is there record of any two that loved / Better than we do", 2.2.112-113); Emilia and the Woman's conversation moves almost directly to the topic of love, in any case at the earliest opportunity: "This garden has a world of pleasures in't. / What flower is this? – 'Tis called narcissus, madam. / – That was a fair boy, certain, but a fool / To love himself". The mythical figure of Narcissus was desired by both men and women according to the *Metamorphoses*[146] (although the Arden editor leaves out the men in the note on Narcissus).[147] It was the curse of a spurned male lover that led to what he is now famous for, his falling in love with his own reflection in the mirror (*Metamorphoses* III 402-406). Emilia mentions Narcissus again later to describe Palamon; when looking at Palamon's picture she says,

> Of all this sprightly sharpness, not a smile.
> Yet these that we count errors may become him:
> Narcissus was a sad boy, but a heavenly. (4.2.30-32)

In that same scene Emilia likens Arcite to Ganymede, a boy Jupiter fell in love with (*Metamorphoses* Book X, 213-219). Instead of finding a preference for either of them, as she tried, she ends up comparing the kinsmen to classical emblems of homoeroticism. She furthermore seems to think of the scene with her maid while

---

143 Mallette, p.34.
144 Mallette, *ibid.*
145 Shannon, p.118; Mallette, p.35.
146 Book III ll.453-455.
147 Potter, p.188.

trying to choose one of the cousins for herself: "Narcissus" is an echo of that scene and so is "wanton" (Arcite is "just such another wanton Ganymede" (4.2.15), she says), echoing both her and the kinsmen's "wantonness" in the prison / garden scene ("You have made me, I thank you, cousin Arcite, wanton with my captivity" on the kinsmen's side and "Thou art wanton – Let's walk in" on hers).

The scene with her woman is the only time in the play where Emilia, who is usually rather serious, appears light-hearted and cheerful ("I could laugh now", 2.2.151) and where she employs such a light and flirtatious tone.[148] Besides, "I am wondrous merry-hearted" (2.2.151) echoes the "maiden-hearted" from her prayer to Diana,[149] where she says, "I am bride-habited, / But maiden-hearted" (5.1.150-151). As Richard Mallette points out, "maiden-hearted" has two meanings: firstly, she wishes to remain a maiden; secondly, her heart is bent towards maidens, "however she may be bride-habited toward men who are clearly more interested in one another than in her",[150] as Mallette puts it. The term "maiden-hearted" thus summarises her sexual predicament.[151] It can also refer to "the maid Flavina" (1.3.84), whose memory is obviously much alive in Emilia because she still gets out of breath when talking about her.

Then there is the fact of the location as scene-within-the-scene of Palamon and Arcite's exchange of love vows in prison. While the women's words and behaviour to a certain extent echo the kinsmen's, it is also by no means clear that Palamon and Arcite do not understand what is going on between Emilia and her woman. Even if they really are unable to hear the words, they might be able to tell what the conversation is about from facial expressions, gestures and the general atmosphere: after all, the conversation is to be acted out on stage.[152]

This seems more likely a case of conscious overlooking. The reaction of the kinsmen certainly suggests that they have noticed at least the gist of the exchange because, while they claim to fall in love with Emilia, they are in fact completely preoccupied with one another.[153] The only thing that changes in that scene is that they exchange their love vows for sexy provocations and challenges to 'fight'.

Besides, Palamon's fantasy about Emilia, if it is indeed about Emilia, and not about Arcite, suggests that he has recognised her as a queer woman, who subverts gender roles: "This lady, /This blushing virgin, should take manhood to her / And seek to ravish me" (2.2.259-262).

---

148 See Shannon, p.120.

149 Shannon, p.118.

150 Mallette, p.46.

151 Mallette, *ibid.*

152 See Johnston (2010b), p.55.

153 "Observe the total failure of either man to broach the question of Emilias wishes: she is a minor player in their game. In fact they devote far more attention to fighting each other than to wooing her". Sinfield (2003), p.72.

All in all, what happens when Emilia comes into play is "not a replacement of male bonding by heterosexual passion, but its continuation in other terms".[154] The kinsmen fight each other in equivocal terms such as "be rough with me" (3.1.102), according to the principle "Defy me in these fair terms, and you show / More than a mistress to me" (3.6.25-26), as Arcite puts it. Therefore they cannot stop fighting even when Emilia expressly asks them to (3.6.252-256), which leads to the absurd situation that, while each kinsmen claims to love her better than the other, they nonetheless ignore her desperate wish to stop the battle.[155] They sum it up themselves when they agree, "No mention of this woman; 'twill disturb us" (3.3.15), where Emilia does not even have a name anymore, but is "this woman".

II.9.4. Emilia's silencing

The way Emilia and her woman's conversation remains unheard (at least officially) prefigures the way Emilia, who appears for the first time in that scene, is silenced in the course of the play. The decisive lines at the end of the dialogue[156] are fast: "before we have a chance to take it in, they're gone".[157] Moreover, they are instantly drowned out by the noise produced by the kinsmen's quarrelling. Occasional (rather anxious) denials of homosexual implications in annotations to the play betray that these implications have been noticed, however. The Signet Classic edition of 1966, for instance, glosses "and take one with you" as "lie down with a (male) companion".[158] Even in recent editions editors find it necessary to 'clarify' the ambiguity of the dialogue. The Oxford edition informs us that when Emilia says, "agree", she means, "make your bargain",[159] as if she herself had nothing to do with it. The Arden edition at least mentions the possibility of a sexual bargain between Emilia and her handmaiden as a possible interpretation of "the first reading": "[o]n the first reading, Emilia's reply acquiesces in a sexual game; on the second, she coldly distances herself from her woman's affairs".[160] But it admits: "[s]hould well be a misreading of MS *wele* (or we'll), [...] the former interpretation would be more plausible".[161]

Similar to the editors' explanations at places where possible readings do not necessarily conform with the heterosexual norm, it is arguably precisely the noise

[154] Sinfield, p.72.
[155] Abrams, p.74.
[156] "I could lie down, I am sure. – And take one with you? – That's as we bargain, madam. – Well, agree then" (2.2.152-153).
[157] Abrams, p.70.
[158] Quoted from Abrams, p.76.
[159] Waith, p.116.
[160] Potter, p.191.
[161] Potter, *ibid.*

the two noble kinsmen produce after the Woman and Emilia have left the stage that suggests that they did hear her or, at any rate, received the general impact of their dialogue.

Their reaction, moreover, parallels the reaction to another critical moment where Emilia's words are drowned out literally by "trumpeting". In the scene where the excellence, beauty and strength of Arcite and Palamon's friends – those who have come to support them in the tournament – are described by Pirithous in great detail and obviously with great delight, Emilia manages to get in edgewise, "Must these men die too?" (4.2.113). Nobody responds to Emilia's question, but Pirithous' reaction, I think, suggests that he has heard her, for he marches on, "When he speaks, his tongue / Sounds like a trumpet" (4.2.113-114). You can hear him raising his voice when speaking these words. While the intended purpose is to drown her critical words, the trumpet flourish at the same time underlines them and gives them special emphasis. Highlighting how they are meant to erase criticism, they give the criticism more emphasis *and* draw attention to the act of silencing, just as, for example, those passages in a censored text that have been crossed out or marked black automatically attract most attention. I would argue that Pirithous' following depiction of the strength and the weapons of the knight he is describing are designed to threaten Emilia:

All his lineaments
Are as a man would wish 'em, strong and clean;
He wears a well-steeled axe, the staff of gold;
His age some five-and-twenty. (4.2.113-115)

"He wears a well-steeled axe" is threatening in itself, but it contains a sexual threat as well (referring to an erection). A few lines later, Theseus employs exactly the same metaphor to intimidate Emilia when he says to her, "You have steeled 'em with your beauty" (4.2.149). Theseus raises the spectre of 'corrective rape' in order to subdue the lesbian Emilia. Hippolyta's words show that Emilia weeps at this point: "O, my soft-hearted sister [...] / Weep not" (4.2.147-148). And, again, Hippolyta, who has already been subdued by Theseus, ostensibly comforts Emilia while assuring her that resistance is futile: "Wench, it must be" (4.2.148).

While Emelye in *The Knight's Tale* does not speak very much at all, *The Two Noble Kinsmen*'s Emilia first appears independent and self-confident and, indeed, as a figure of resistance to Theseus' tyrannical power. But she gets silenced in the course of the play. She is, however, "paradoxically, permit[ted] to comment on that act of silencing".[162] It is, therefore, an exposed, visible or rather audible silence, a lacuna, a silence that Emilia herself not only observes but also articulates when just before the tournament she asserts, "I am extinct" (5.3.20). Ironically, this

---

162 Johnston (2010b), p.52.

also shows that Theseus' programme of linear chronology and temporal determinacy does not work as supposed, for here it has produced another living dead.

Emilia may represent the concept "of individual, volitional association against the sovereign's power to reorganize one's affective arrangements",[163] which is what Theseus does when he prescribes marriage for his subjects. She also stays constant in this for a long time, very much in constrast to the kinsmen and, by the way, also to Cressida. Her "unwavering consistency" may be, as Shannon observes, "a sign of valued self-knowledge in a play (and a period) in which shifting appetites are deeply stigmatized".[164]

But, ironically, it does not help her in any way. Just as Cressida has fewer and fewer lines over the course of *Troilus and Cressida*, Emilia becomes "quieter and quieter under Theseus' ducal prerogative",[165] until at one point she gives up ("I am extinct"). Her "extinction" parallels that of homoerotics in general in the play: they are (apparently) defeated by heterosexual marriage, though this is "marked by funerals rather than celebration".[166]

Emilia's subjugation is a process that occurs by degrees and, even before she declares that she is extinct, she seems to have resigned herself to the fate that Theseus has decreed for her. She starts her prayer to her tutelary goddess Diana before the tournament with "This is my last of vestal office" (5.1.149-150). Her final resignation to, and compliance with, the story that has been written for her by others resembles Cressida's, who also from some point onwards joined the general chorus with "I will not keep my word", etc. (*Troilus and Cressida* 5.2.105). Chaucer's Emelye is still much more resolute when she prays to Diana:

I /Desire to ben a mayden al my lyf,
Ne nevere wol I be no love ne wyf.
I am, thow woost, yet of thy compaignye,
A mayde, and love huntynge and venerye,
And for to walken in the wodes wilde,
And noght to ben a wyf and be with childe.
Noght wol I knowe compaignye of man. (*The Knight's Tale*, ll. 2304-2311)

She asks the goddess, "My maydenhede thou kepe and wel conserve, / And whil I lyve, a mayde I wol thee serve" (2329-2330), an anticipation of the "maidenhead" of *The Two Noble Kinsmen*'s prologue. She asks the goddess to simply take away the kinsmen's adoration and only if that is not possible at all, "if [...] I shal nedes have oon of hem two, / As sende me hym that moost desireth me" (2323-2325). Fletcher and Shakespeare reverse this order and have Emilia pray to the goddess,

---

163 Shannon, p.101.
164 Shannon, p.112.
165 Shannon, p.121.
166 Shannon, p.102.

He of the two pretenders that best loves me
And has the truest title in't, let him
Take off my wheaten garland, or else grant
The file and quality I hold I may
Continue in thy band. (5.1.158-162)

She asks directly that the one who loves her best may win and only "else", as second option, to be able to remain unmarried, the other way round as Emelye, who, finishing the prayer, again reaffirms her conviction: "Whil I lyve, a mayde I wol thee serve" (2330).

Emilia's more humble plea reflects the fact that Fletcher and Shakespeare's Theseus is more despotic than Chaucer's. But the outcome is, in effect, very much the same. The less despotic ruler only gets more support from the gods: In *The Knight's Tale*, Diana responds with vague but hardly promising signs; Emelyes altar fire starts to "bleed":

At the brondes ende out ran anon
As it were blody dropes many oon. (2339-2340)

As if she is punished for her bolder wish, Emelye gets crueller signs from the goddess in response. Her reaction shows that she has understood the threat:

For which so soore agast was Emelye
That she was wel ny mad and gan to crye.
For she ne wiste what it signyfied,
But oonly for the feere thus hath she cried. (2341-2344)

The Knight-narrator is not necessarily to be trusted when he says that Emelye does not know what the blood might signify in relation to her maidenhood.[167]

But Fletcher and Shakespeare's Emilia's more humble and resigned wish that the one kinsman who loves her best will marry her is being granted, or so it seems: a rose tree with one rose on it appears from the altar fire. The rose then falls off. The already acquiescent Emilia gets "gracious" (5.1.173) signs from the goddess; there is no need for fear and tears for her when she interprets the prophecy:

The flower is fall'n; the tree descends. Oh, mistress,
Thou here dischargest me; I shall be gathered –
I think so – but I know not thine own will;
Unclasp thy mystery! – I hope she's pleased;
Her signs were gracious. (5.1.169-173)

Emilia's submissive wish is being granted, Emelye's is not and she has to cry as a visible sign of repentance for her self-confidence. Of course, ultimately, the effect is the same for both Emilia and Emelye: they will have to marry the knight

[167] For the role of the narrator in this scene see Andrew James Johnston, "Performing Anti-subjective Subjectivity in Late-Medieval English Literature" in Johnston (2009a), pp.91-164, especially pp.107-116.

who wins (or rather loses) the duel. Nevertheless the triumph of heterosexual marriage is undermined by Emilia's use of the term "pretenders" instead of "suitors"[168] or "claimants"[169] when she refers to the kinsmen in her prayer to Diana ("He of the two pretenders that best loves me", 5.1.158), which suggests not only that pretension is completely sufficient for a marriage but also that he who pretends best has the "truest title" in it.

Heteronormative linearity

Theseus' rule stands for linear temporality as well as for heterosexual marriage, both of which he forces upon his subjects. This puts into focus the fact that an important purpose of heterosexual marriage was social reproduction, the reproduction of a society's power structures and hierarchies by means of the production of heirs regarded as legitimate. As the story of Hippolyta, as a backdrop for this play, tells us, heterosexual coupling in marriage also concerned the hierarchy between man and woman: Hippolyta was Queen of an independent nation of women that was subdued by Theseus' army and the Queen was forced to marry him. The widows are, themselves, a group of women defined solely by the relation to their marriage partners and those partners' social status. This binary heterosexual economy, a marriage system that develops and defines family structures and organises the transmission of name and property[170] or "a deployment of alliance",[171] as Foucault calls it, regulates the reproduction of economic power structures. In early modern England, property and the authority and power it grants were thought to be legitimately held if passed from father to son through an acknowledged marriage.[172] Marriage and the production of 'legitimate' offspring also produces a teleological, hierarchizing progress narrative that creates an impression of chronological linearity, which is illustrated by the graphic depiction of genealogies in family trees.

As Kathryn Lynch has remarked, the "odd metaphor" with which *The Two Noble Kinsmen* starts, the equation of plays with maidenheads, "introduces a theme of breeding, procreation, and legitimacy that the prologue will explore in various registers".[173] These questions are not the concern of the prologue alone. When the disguised Arcite has won Athens' wrestling and running games, Theseus tries to find out who the mysterious athlete is and asks him exactly this kind of questions: where does he come from? is he of noble descent? which place

168 Waith, p.192.
169 Potter, p.298.
170 Michel Foucault, *The History of Sexuality. Volume 1: An Introduction* (New York: Vintage Books, 1990), p.106.
171 Foucault, *ibid.*
172 Sinfield (2003), p.73.
173 Lynch, p.77.

does he hold in the line for inheritance? These are all questions that relate to the identity of the 'father'. Arcite, who does not want to be recognised, gives evasive answers:

THESEUS What country bred you?
ARCITE This; but far off, Prince.
THESEUS Are you a gentleman?
ARCITE My father said so
And to those gentle uses gave me life.
THESEUS Are you his heir?
ARCITE His youngest, sir.
THESEUS Your father
Sure is a happy sire then. (2.5.5-9)

The last lines, according to the logic of patrilinearity, imply that Arcite's older brothers must be even greater.[174] Theseus' questions and Arcite's answers use the same vocabulary as when the prologue deals with questions of literary origin and 'legitimacy': "It has a noble breeder [...] / Chaucer, of all admired, the story gives" (PROLOGUE 10-13). Hippolyta also says she has "not seen so young a man so noble" (2.5.18), so a direct connection between nobility and linear time is assumed.

II. 10. Pericles*: Authorship, patriarchy, the "dynastic agenda"*[175] *and linear time*

Pericles is similarly concerned with the 'author-function' and combines the search for identifiable literary origins with the question of 'good parentage' as in *The Two Noble Kinsmen*'s prologue. Masten analyses the recognition scene between Pericles and his daughter Marina, among others,[176] looking closely at the establishment of dynastic claims to power and authority. The questions and answers that are employed to secure "Pericles's author/ity"[177] are very similar to Theseus' questions and Arcite's answers: "Report thy parentage" (*Pericles* 5.1.120), Pericles demands; "tell thy story" (5.1.125). Marina does so gradually, starting with the "patriarchal-absolutist derivation"[178] of her name: "The name / Was given me by one that had some power: / My father, and a king" (5.1.138-140). Pericles wants to know, "Where were you bred? / I'll hear you more, to th'bottom of your story" (5.1.154-155). Compare Theseus' catalogue of questions, which, without Arcite's answers, runs like this: "What country bred you?" "Are you a gentle-

174 See Potter, p.208.
175 Masten, p.82.
176 Such as the scene where Pericles himself has to explain "Of whence he is, his name and parentage" (2.3.71), or the brothel scenes. Masten, pp.80-86.
177 Masten, p.88.
178 Masten, p.87.

man?" "Are you his heir?" "What profess you?" The conclusion is: "You are perfect" (*The Two Noble Kinsmen* 2.5.5-15). In *Pericles*, 'parentage' is always connected to authorship, what Masten calls "author/ity", meaning "authority, father, instigator, ruler, writer".[179] Therefore Pericles says to Marina: "I will believe you by the syllable / Of what you shall deliver" (*Pericles* 5.1.158-159), as if she were literally giving birth to her words. Pericles is also identified by his writing: Thaisa is handed a piece of writing and asked, "Know you the character?" She replies, "It is my lord's (3.4.3-4). Thus "Pericles's character – his position as patriarchal father, his position of authority – is [...] guaranteed only by a text in his own character, of his own authority".[180]

The play also deals with the differentiation between legitimate and illegitimate derivation. Pericles, himself a prince, marries the daughter of Simonides, who is ruler of Pentapolis and so becomes its legitimate ruler. The 'healthy' parental relations of Simonides and Thaisa or Pericles and Marina are contrasted with the incestuous relationship between Antiochus and his unnamed daughter. She is not 'legitimate', not authorised and therefore has no name, unlike Marina, whose name has an enormous effect:

PERICLES Thy name, my most kind virgin?
Recount, I do beseech thee. Come sit by me.
MARINA My name is Marina.
[...]
PERICLES Thou little knowst how thou dost startle me
To call thyself Marina. (5.1.131-138)

This is not the only occasion where being able to give the right name means having one's identity acknowledged. When after long trials and tribulations, Pericles meets his wife Thaisa again, he asks her:

PERICLES Can you remember what I called the man?
I have named him oft.
THAISA 'Twas Helicanus then.
PERICLES Still confirmation. (5.3.52-55)

The importance of a 'proper' name also becomes clear for example by what Arcite states as his reason for his participation in the games. When Theseus asks, "What made you seek this place, sir?" Arcite replies, "Noble Theseus, / To purchase name" (*The Two Noble Kinsmen* 2.5.25-26), meaning, "to acquire fame",[181] but also implying that "name" can be bought, "purchased". The connection of the authority that is derived from rightful, approved parentage to the authority over a particular text is made by the repeated equation of the act of narration,

[179] Masten, p.66.
[180] Masten, p.89.
[181] Waith, p.128.

the telling of a story, to the act of giving birth. When Pericles has the physician Cerimon relate how Thaisa came back to life after a shipwreck, to confirm that it is indeed her, he says, "Will you deliver / How this dead queen relives?" (*Pericles* 5.3.63-64), suggesting that she is born, or reborn, through Cerimon's narration of the story.[182] Pericles applies this metaphor to himself, too, as he begins his own version of the story with, "I am great with woe, and shall deliver weeping" (5.1.97).[183] *The Two Noble Kinsmen*'s prologue uses the same image when he calls the play the writers' "child". Pericles's physician Cerimon revives or gives birth to Thaisa in a similar way as Theseus' surgeons bring the unconscious Palamon and Arcite back to life and, similarly, the successful operation is called the gods' working when Cerimon is declared a "man / Through whom the gods have shown their power" (*Pericles* 5.3.60-61).

The illegitimate incest relationship of Antiochus and his daughter is contrasted with these rightful and authorised familial relations and marriages just as, in *The Two Noble Kinsmen*, Theseus as ruler of Athens is contrasted with Creon of Thebes. There are no intimations that Creon is not 'legitimately' ruling Thebes; instead, the city has the incest inscribed in its founding myth, as Oedipus won the throne *because* of his marriage to his mother. Theseus is portrayed as having the gods on his side, while Creon thinks of himself as a god. Both of them write a particular kind of history. Theseus' history is arranged linearly while Creon's is disorganised, circular, palimpsest-like in the sense that the present coexists with multiple pasts, so that the old can at any time resurface and replace the new or exist alongside it, while the new, in turn, can rewrite the old, as temporal layers of all sorts coexist with no particular order.[184]

Theseus is eager to organise the palimpsested chaos he finds in Thebes, represented by the unburied bodies of the dead kings, into a linear progress narrative where death and life, past and present are clearly separated. This refers also to the dead writer (Chaucer) who continues actively to influence the metamorphoses of his own story. This could not easily happen in a world following the rules of linearity, where the past is hermetically sealed. It also concerns Theseus' own private and political life. Although his own marriage appears as an *inversion* of the funerals that surround it (of Hippolyta, the Argive Kings and other victims of the wars he has fought) he tries to put these events into a chronological, teleological order and make them a sequence of successes: firstly his victory over the Amazons, then his marriage to their Queen, then another victory over Thebes, then the burial of the Kings.

He also organises his subjects into heterosexually married couples, with the purpose, among other things, of producing 'legitimate' offspring, so that, in a

182 See Gossett, p.402.

183 See Gossett, *ibid.*

184 See Harris (2009), pp.1-25.

sense, he gives birth to people himself, while securing his authority over them. Giving birth is here, as in *Pericles*, equated with the production of text.

Pericles had to answer the same questions as Arcite himself when, at his first meeting with Thaisa, her father demanded, "tell him we desire to know / Of whence he is, his name and parentage" (*Pericles* 2.3.70-71). When Marina describes her "derivation" (5.1.81), Pericles is obviously reminded of how he once had to give account of his ancestry himself:[185] "My fortunes – parentage – good parentage – / To equal mine. Was it not thus?" (5.1.88-89).

There is no parallel in *The Two Noble Kinsmen* to the way Marina also fathers Pericles. He addresses her as "Thou that beget'st him that did thee beget" (*Pericles* 5.1.185) and, in the same vein, says to her: "Thou art a man, and I / Have suffered like a girl" (5.1.127-128). The daughter thus begets the father or the text its author,[186] in a circularity that almost surpasses the Theban warriors and their "chthonic return".[187]

Theseus, who is represented as author of a particular kind of history writing, "imposes marriage on *everyone*, as an expression of his control over them":[188] the kinsmen fight only for the right to love Emilia. Theseus turns this into the right, or rather the obligation, to marry her, although marrying Emilia is not what the kinsmen aspire to.[189]

But *The Two Noble Kinsmen* shows the futility of Theseus' regulations and highlights their cost for the characters, none of whom is able to enjoy happiness or erotic fulfilment in the play, although this is a chief promise of matrimony.[190] Marriage is forced upon them as an attempt to control their desire, but the play focuses on the resistance of desire to compulsory marriage rather than the success of Theseus' policing.[191]

Hippolyta was forced to marry Theseus to seal her subjugation. Palamon, Arcite and Emilia are represented as much more committed to their respective homosexual relations than to the heterosexual ones Theseus arranges for them, even though the kinsmen claim otherwise. The unidirectional approach that Theseus exhibits towards history is thus linked to compulsory heterosexuality, to use Adrienne Rich's formulation.[192] The way he sorts out the palimpsest into a monolithic, unambiguous and linear history is linked to the kind of linearity

---

185 See Gossett, p.378.

186 See Masten, p.89.

187 Patterson, p.75.

188 Shannon, p.111.

189 Mary Beth Rose, *The Expense of Spirit: Love and Sexuality in English Renaissance Drama* (Ithaca, NY: Cornell University Press, 1988), p.220.

190 Mallette, pp.32, 44.

191 Mallette, p.32.

192 Adrienne Rich, "Compulsory Heterosexuality and Lesbian Existence", in *Blood, Bread, and Poetry* (London: Virago Press, 1986), pp.23-75.

produced by family trees and to the logic of lineage as legitimisation of positions of power. At the end of the play, heterosexual marriage is victorious, but only institutionally, not emotionally: the cost of that victory is emotional and sexual fulfilment for the main characters, none of whom achieves happiness.[193] For Palamon, Arcite and Emilia, Theseus' marriage arrangement misses the point completely. The play highlights the pain caused by the exclusion of unacknowledged subject positions and the loss that their arbitrary confinement creates,[194] as the limits of linear history writing become the limits of linear life writing, so to speak, when Theseus turns the lives of his subjects into arbitrarily devised linear stories.

In addition to the sacrifice of the protagonists' emotional fulfilment for compulsory cross-sex marriage or for the definite allocation of present and past, Arcite loses his life in a way that emphasises the arbitrariness and the violence with which Theseus' order is purchased.[195]

Emilia, as a representative of "the powers of all women" (3.6.194), is at first installed as a counterpoise to Theseus' regime, but then she gradually disappears and the problems that arise when authority is located in one individual alone, as here in the figure of Theseus, become imminent. Theseus' autocratic rule is, perhaps, depicted as so problematic partly because the play was written in collaboration: Theseus also stands for a certain kind of writing and he 'writes' the life stories of his subjects, as if to exemplify Masten's word creation "author/ity" as a combination of both author and authority.[196] The catastrophe begins when Emilia, Theseus' counter-voice in the play, becomes silent.

Emilia does not want to marry either of the kinsmen and since she cannot be compelled to choose, a tournament is set up to enforce the decision. Everyone agrees to it, Palamon and Arcite enthusiastically, Emilia more melancholically, with resignation. Arcite wins the duel but loses his life in an equestrian accident immediately afterwards, during his triumphal procession: "His victor's wreath / Even then fell off his head" (5.4.79-80) and Palamon, at the point of being beheaded, with his head already on the block, replaces Arcite and marries Emilia. This is another hint at the arbitrariness of the rules that Theseus applies, since the rules of the tournament do not dictate that Palamon should now marry Emilia. They only said that the winner will marry Emilia and the loser will be executed: "[t]he absurdity of the situation is palpable: the winner dies, and so Emilia is betrothed to the loser".[197] According to the rules, there is no reason

193 See Mallette, p.44.
194 Cf. Judith Butler, *Bodies that Matter: On the Discursive Limits of "Sex"* (New York: Routledge, 1993), p.xiii.
195 Cf. Harris, *Shakespeare and Literary Theory* (Oxford: Oxford University Press, 2010), p.40.
196 Masten, p.66.
197 Mallette, p.36.

why the loser should be pardoned nor why Emilia, instead of being off the hook after Arcite's death, should now have to marry Palamon. It shows that the institution of marriage creates the rules rather than marriage being dictated by the rules. The rules can be interpreted very flexibly behind the veneer of a logical, fixed system, to which, in addition, the gods often grant their support.

Arcite appears one last time, on the brink of death, replacing Palamon who was there but a moment ago. He is carried on stage in a chair (5.4.85 SD), echoing his former appearance on a hearse (1.4.1 SD). Although he is fully conscious this time, he then dies and is carried off the stage dead. This is the first time that he is really separated from Palamon, who stays behind lamenting,

> Oh, cousin!
> That we should things desire, which do cost us
> The loss of our desire! That nought could buy
> Dear love, but loss of dear love! (5.4.109-112)

At this point, Palamon no longer curses Arcite, although he so often professed to wish his death. Arcite was, just a moment ago, in Palamon's position, saying almost exactly the same thing:

> Emilia,
> To buy you, I have lost what's dearest to me,
> Save what is bought. (5.3.111-113)

The sudden substitution of winner for loser and vice versa brings both kinsmen into the same situation again, as they used to be before Arcite was released from prison and exiled. They are made indistinguishable once again, just before Arcite leaves and Palamon stays: Arcite's story is cut off at this point and they are separated for good. The confusing doubling of the cousins, who seemed veritable embodiments of the early modern idealisation of likeness in friendship,[198] is finally over. But both Palamon and Arcite do not, in their turn, merely lament the loss of their closest friend: precisely because their indistinguishability is restored at this point, there is a clear sense in which Palamon mourns not just his friend when Arcite dies but himself, or his "lost self".[199] As Richard Abrams puts it: "Split by a zero-sum contest, the survivor symbolically becomes half a man, while Emilia, 'bride habited, / But maiden-hearted' is also split, condemned to wed both life and death".[200]

The emphasis on the kinsmen's sameness here stresses the unjustifiable cost of the attempt to simply cut off the past, while the way that they are exchanged from the executioner's block at the last possible moment underlines the arbi-

---

198 As in the friendship discourse around Montaigne's *Of Friendship* (1580). See Shannon, pp.92-94, 104-108, Masten, pp.32-37, and Mallette, pp.30-33.

199 Abrams, p.73.

200 Abrams, *ibid.*

trariness of the assignment to either present or past, remembrance or oblivion. But Palamon and Arcite's likeness is nothing new; all through the play both of them had referred to it:

ARCITE Am not I
Part of your blood, part of your soul? You have told me
That I was Palamon and you were Arcite.
PALAMON Yes. (2.2.187-190)

At other times, they remark that "our fortunes / Were twined together" (2.2.63-64) and call themselves twins (2.2.18). Therefore Palamon loses not only Arcite, his cousin, or his twin or "dear love" (5.4.112), but himself, too. So when Arcite says, "I have told my last hour" (5.4.92) with a pun on "tolled",[201] that toll, like the one in John Donne's *Devotions*,[202] concerns both kinsmen alike. Theseus' role in this is hinted at in the Argive Queens' ambiguous praise of Theseus: "Your fame / Knolls in the ear o'th' world" (1.1.133-134), where the word "knoll" alludes to a death knell,[203] so that Theseus' name or "fame" subtly sounds with the ominous ring of a knell.[204]

II.11. The Great Mover's *Speech – Palamon and Arcite's function for Theseus*

It is impossible to distinguish and, therefore, to judge between the kinsmen; yet this is what the tournament and Theseus' decree try to do. Before the play ends, Theseus delivers a speech in which he tries to explain what has just happened. His speech is a very abbreviated version of Theseus' final speech in *The Knight's Tale*, which is strongly influenced by Boethius and usually referred to as the "First Movere" speech, as Theseus begins with "the Firste Moevere of the cause above" (*The Knight's Tale* 2987): Jupiter, who presides over an ordered universe where all things have a particular position, duration and purpose. This purpose may sometimes be hard to discern but it can be trusted to generally serve and preserve the order of the world. The understanding of temporality that is expressed here is teleological: time occurs as a series of "self-identical moments" that are strictly separated from one another:[205]

201 Potter, p.325.

202 "Never send to know for whom the bell tolls; it tolls for thee", etc. John Donne, *Devotions Upon Emergent Occasions*, Devotion XVII. *John Donne: Complete Poetry and Selected Prose*, ed. John Hayward (New York: Random House Inc., 1949), p.538.

203 Potter, p.151.

204 It has a similar effect in Valerius' description of Theseus: "Theseus, who, where he threats, appals" (1.2.90). See Potter, *ibid.*

205 Harris (2009), p.189.

"That same Prince and that Moevere," quod he,
"Hath stablissed in this wrecched world adoun
Certeyne dayes and duracioun
To al that is engendred in this place,
Over the whiche day they may nat pace,
Al mowe they yet tho dayes wel abregge." (2994-2999)

It is better to die when one is popular than to die when one's fame has faded; therefore they can only be happy for their dead friend (3047-3056). It would be foolish to mourn since it does not help in any way (3041-3046) and Arcite cannot thank them (3064). The upcoming marriage of Palamon and Emily is praised in a way that suggests that it can somehow compensate for Arcite's death and help to forget about it. Emilia's unwillingness to marry is not mentioned further.

The narrator, the Knight who tells the story within the narrative frame of the *Canterbury Tales*, assists Theseus in his project of imposing (Athenian) progressive order on an unruly (Theban) world and endorses Theseus' attempt to give the story a definite and "truly conclusive" ending:[206] "Thus endeth Palamon and Emelye" (3107).

While this does not seem very satisfactory, in *The Two Noble Kinsmen* where such a narrator does not exist, Theseus does not even try to make the outcome appear satisfactory. Of the one hundred and six lines of the "First Movere" speech in Chaucer, twenty-six remain in Fletcher and Shakespeare's play. Before Theseus decides that it is time to stop mourning, Chaucer's Arcite has received a spectacular funeral celebration which is described in detail: the body is carried on a bier "al overspradde / With clooth of gold, the richeste that he hadde" (2871-72). Great white horses carry his weapons, the street is covered in black and Theseus himself carries gold vessels "of hony, milk, and blood" (2908). All the while, the narrator emphasises that this happens on Theseus' initiative: "Theseus hath ysent" (2871); "Theseus leet [...] brynge" (2889); "Theseus, with al his bisy cure" (2853), etc.

The contrast to Shakespeare and Fletcher's Theseus could not be greater, since all he has to say, pointing to Arcite's body, is "Bear this hence" (5.4.109). Even the relatively unimportant, anonymous Argives had a whole scene for their "funeral solemnity" (1.5 SD), with everything from "vapours" and "sighs" to "vials fill'd with tears" (1.5.2-5).[207]

---

206 Patterson (1991), p.201.

207 On the occasion of the funeral, the queens also employ some aphorisms that merge synchronic and diachronic textual references to a cross-temporal, polychronic, palimpsest-like tissue: "Heavens lend / A thousand differing ways to one sure end" (1.5.13-14) echoes *The Duchess of Malfi*'s "I know death hath ten thousand several doors / For men to take their exits" (4.2.216-217), while "This world's a city full of straying streets, / And death's the market-place where each one meets" (1.5.15-16) recalls *The Knight's Tale*'s "This world nys but a thurghfare ful of wo, / And we been pilgrymes, passynge to and fro" (2847-2848). See Potter, p.178.

After a rather hurried, superficial attempt at philosophic depth, Theseus breaks off abruptly:

> Let us be thankful
> For that which is, and with you leave dispute
> That are above our question. Let's go off
> And bear us like the time.
> *Flourish. Exeunt.* (5.4.134-137)

Thus ends the final act. Theseus' final speech in *The Knight's Tale* was well known to Shakespeare and Fletcher's audience. But, in *The Two Noble Kinsmen*, it is cut so short and ends so abruptly that, in most recent performances, something like a tableau, a procession or a repeat of the opening song has been added to round it off in some way.[208] The audience would probably also have expected a spectacular show for Arcite's funeral, which is celebrated elaborately in *The Knight's Tale*. The casting of valuable objects on the funeral pyre in the 1566 performance of *Palamon and Arcite* (a lost play based on *The Knight's Tale*) had caused a sensation.[209] The comparison with Chaucer was, after all, explicitly advocated by the prologue ("Chaucer the story gives, constant to eternity it lives"). *The Two Noble Kinsmen*'s Theseus' sole comment, "Bear this hence", thwarts these expectations cruelly.

The playwrights deliberately frustrate audience expectations here, as if to demonstrate an author's ability to play with, or even manipulate, a story: the story appears completely subject to the authors' disposal, similar to how the Gower character treats it in *Pericles*. On the other hand, as I will try to show in the rest of this chapter, they prove that there are other, more subtle, continuities operating beneath the surface and which elude the writer's influence and control: Theseus is unable to definitely separate presence and past. His inference that "The conquered triumphs; / The victor has the loss" (5.4.113-114) echoes the Bible's "The last will be first, and the first last" (Matthew 20:16) but, apart from these textual indicators of the coexistence of multiple times, there are more symbolic, visualised ones, like the horse that kills Arcite, as we will shortly see, or the kinsmen themselves.

The flexibility of time that the Gower of *Pericles* had demonstrated in his guided tour through the events of the play is noticeable at the end of *The Two Noble Kinsmen*, too, when, along with the abbreviated speech, comes a shorter mourning period of "a day or two". Where, in *The Knight's Tale*, the mourning ends "by processe and by lengthe of certeyn yeres" (2967), in *The Two Noble Kinsmen*, Theseus ordains,

> A day or two
> Let us look sadly and give grace unto

208 Potter, p.327.

209 Potter, pp.66-67, 327; Waith, p.28.

The funeral of Arcite, in whose end
The visages of bridegrooms we'll put on
And smile with Palamon. (5.4.124-128)

The dramatically shortened period of mourning shows how flexible time is even, or rather especially for Theseus, although he promotes a linear concept of temporality. He also distances himself more from the events. Chaucer's Theseus delivers his speech "with a sad visage" and "siked stille" (2985). *The Two Noble Kinsmen*'s Theseus turns this into "Let us *look* sadly" (5.4.125, emphasis mine), stressing the theatricality of emotions and the fact that they, too, need to be performed. The same goes for the celebratory mood for Palamon: Theseus proposes to put on "the visages of bridegrooms [...] and smile with Palamon" (5.4.127-128) at the end of the "day or two" of mourning, as if emotions can be changed like a mask, like the theatre masks worn by actors in ancient Greek drama. He also says of Arcite "His part is played" and that "it were too short" (5.4.102). These are self-reflexive moments that lead out of the performance towards the end of the play and when Theseus says, "He did it well" (5.4.103), the words hold the possibility that he is not talking about the character Arcite but rather about the actor's performance as Arcite. In this way, he is taking leave from the scene and from the play.

In *Romeo and Juliet,* "times of woe afford no times to woo" (3.4.8) but, here, Palamon and Emilia get married almost *while* Arcite gets buried, as Arcite says to Palamon, "Take her. I die" (5.4.95). This, too, links the play's end to its beginning with Theseus and Hippolyta's funeral-marriage.

When Palamon is released from his ordained execution, this is ascribed to the gods: "Noble Palamon, / The gods will show their glory in a life / That thou art yet to lead" (5.4.43-44). On the other hand, while the incidence with the horse that kills Arcite is officially called an accident, it is then described as if it had been effected by infernal powers: the horse is "a black one, owing / Not a hair-worth of white" (5.4.50-51), which, according to "superstition" (5.4.53), indicates its viciousness. The speaker does not *say* the horse is from hell; in fact he denies saying anything like that:

What envious flint,
Cold as old Saturn and, like him, possessed
With fire malevolent, darted a spark,
Or what fierce sulphur else, to this end made,
I comment not. (5.4.61-65)

This is familiar from *Troilus and Cressida,* where everyone calls Cressida a prostitute by quoting other sources. "I comment not" is the equivalent of "I tell you what my authors say", because, of course, the horse *is* described by the speaker as a satanic agent, with attributes like "possessed" and "fierce" and it is associated with "fire malevolent", "a spark" and even "sulphur". It is also "hot as fire" (5.4.65) and of supernatural skill and speed. Its gait looks like "dancing" (5.4.59), the horse "the calkins / Did rather tell than trample" (5.4.55-56) and it "would make his length a mile" (5.4.57).[210] In Boiardo's *Orlando Innamorato* an evil ruler gives a black horse that is faster than the wind as a present.[211] Note that the horse was given to Arcite by Emilia (2.5.42-55; 3.1.17-22), as Pirithous, who delivers the speech, does not fail to remind us here: "a steed that Emily / Did first bestow on him" (5.4.49-50).

Emilia is thus made twice responsible for Arcite's fate. First by being so beautiful that Arcite has no choice but to love her, as he says: "Ask that lady / Why she is fair, and why her eyes command me / Stay here to love her" (3.6.168-170). Hippolyta, who has already given in and married Theseus, tries in the same way to put pressure on her to choose one of the kinsmen as husband: "That face of yours / Will bear the curses else of after ages / For these lost cousins" (3.6.186-188). But Emilia refuses to be extorted like that: "In my face, dear sister, / I find no anger to 'em, nor no ruin" (3.6.188-189). This is also a cross-reference to *Pericles*' Marina, who similarly complains about unwanted suitors, "I am a maid, / My lord, that ne'er before invited eyes, / But have been gazed on like a comet" (*Pericles* 5.1.75-77). This astronomical imagery is, in turn, reflected when Theseus says to Emilia before the tournament, "You must be there: / This trial is as 'twere i'th' night, and you / The only star to shine", to which Emilia replies, "I am extinct" (5.3.18-20). Theseus, too, tries to render Emilia responsible for the kinsmen's misadventure.

Secondly, Emilia has given Arcite a horse that is possessed by Satan, as Pirithous tries to suggest.

In *The Knight's Tale* Arcite's horse is not specified, no horse given to Arcite by Emilia is mentioned and the accident is not caused by the horse's wilfulness, but by a fury sent by Pluto (at the request of Saturn). The fury startles the horse and makes it stumble (2684-2690). It is also directed by infernal powers, but these powers are located 'outside' the horse, in the fury: it is "a furie infernal" that starts "out of the ground" (2684); the devil resides underground. Interestingly, though, the fury leaves a trail that leads to Theseus, not to Emilia.

Hippolytus alias the Kinsmen

The "infernal" fury is an anachronism in the supposedly classical ancient world of *The Knight's Tale*. Shakespeare and Fletcher, too, leave the realm of ancient mythology once again when they turn to the Christian mythology of Christ and Satan that they employ for this scene. All these elements are interwoven and form an example of the polychronic compression of various moments in time.[212]

---

210 That is it is able to take mile-long paces. Potter, p.322.

211 Potter, *ibid.*

212 Harris (2007), p.471.

But the ancient layer also adds another story: in ancient mythology, Poseidon kills Theseus' son Hippolytus at Theseus' request by sending a sea monster that startles Hippolytus's horses. Hippolytus is then thrown from his chariot and killed.[213] Theseus orders this 'accident' and it is executed by a god who was known to turn into a horse himself from time to time.[214] It is, of course, an interesting twist (and another reminder of the palimpsest-like nature of time) that this ancient story takes place in the future of what is presented on stage, a future where Theseus and Hippolyta already have a grown-up son.

The parallels to Arcite's accident are obvious. In the ancient stories, a monster scares the horses whereas, in *The Two Noble Kinsmen*, the horse itself becomes a monster. Chaucer's version is, in a way, a combination of the ancient versions with Shakespeare and Fletcher's, because "a furie infernal [...] from Pluto sent" (2684-2685) frightens the horse (Pluto is the god of the underworld); the sea monster that kills Hippolytus on Theseus' behalf has changed its shape into a fury. Thus Theseus becomes connected to hell or the underworld. The story of Theseus' son continues in some versions with Hippolytus being brought back to life by Apollo's son, who restores him "with his artful remedies" (*Metamorphoses* Book XV l. 624), which is similar to how Theseus orders the kinsmen to be resurrected by "all our surgeons" (1.4.30): "for our love / And great Apollo's mercy, all our best / Their best skill tender" (1.5.45-47). Hippolytus also gets a new face and a new name and is made older (*Metamorphoses* XV 630-638). The kinsmen awake to a new life under Theseus in a different temporality. They are not related to Theseus, but to Creon, but when one looks at the story this way, reading it along with the other texts that surround it in the palimpsest, Theseus switches sides, from 'white' to 'black,' the realm of light (Athene, Jupiter) to the underworld realm of shade when he affiliates with Pluto or orders the murder of his son. Thus he becomes Creon or Creon becomes him.

A Barbary Horse:[215] *Otherness*

So, while there is a visible trail in the palimpsest of myths and stories around the Theseus figure that suggests Theseus is the originator of the equestrian accident in *The Two Noble Kinsmen*, the *horse* is made responsible for it. The horse is also furnished with all the attributes of the *Other* and it comes from Emilia. This diabolic, out-of-control horse can be read as a symbol for the dangers associated

[213] Ovid, *Metamorphoses*, Book XV, ll. 587-617; Virgil, *The Aeneid*, Book VII, ll. 765-780. Quoted from Virgil, *The Aeneid*, trans. C. Day Lewis, with intro and notes by Jasper Griffin (Oxford: Oxford University Press, 2008).

[214] *Paulys Realencyclopädie der Classischen Altertumswissenschaft*, ed. Konrat Ziegler, Dreiundvierzigster Halbband (Stuttgart: Alfred Druckenmüller Verlag, 1970), p.483.

[215] Iago calls Othello "a barbary horse" (*Othello* 1.1.119). "Barbary" refers to a region in Africa. *William Shakespeare: Complete Works*, p.2089.

with all that is *Other*, women: Emilia (who is not yet completely subdued by Theseus); homosexuality, which has to give way to heterosexual marriage in this play; 'black', the prototypical 'other' colour (the horse owns "not a hair-worth of white" (5.4.51)). Notions of Otherness can also be used to construct the Middle Ages as modernity's Other, "the dark continent of history"[216] (as I tried to show in the chapter on *Troilus and Cressida*) or to describe the temporal 'disorder' brought about by polychronicity, represented in *The Two Noble Kinsmen* by the accursed Thebes. Thebes is ruled by the "most unbounded" Creon who "makes heaven unfeared" (1.2.63-64) and is set in opposition to a concept of linear time which is connected with Athens and the god Jupiter, installed and represented by Athens' ruler Theseus.

Pirithous' description of Arcite's accident illustrates how ascriptions of Otherness work, how an Other is created in binary opposition to a less noticeable Self, how this construction is then naturalised and the Other is constructed as a danger, a threat: the horse is dangerously unrestrained, cannot be tamed and it is directed by an evil and powerful supernatural agency: it "fell to what disorder / His power could give his will" (5.4.66-67), just like Creon, who is "most unbounded" and makes "villainy assured / Beyond its power there's nothing" (1.2.63-65); Creon also "attributes / The faculties of other instruments / To his own nerves and act" and "makes heaven unfeared" (1.2.64-69). The horse, too, recognises no superior authority, but is "dancing as 'twere to th' music / His own hoofs made" (5.4.59-60). Creon "puts / Faith in a fever" (1.2.65-66), the horse is "hot, hot as fire" (5.4.65). It "forgets school-doing" (5.4.68), a simplified notion of history as a linear succession of singular events can be seen as "school-doing" and the fact that the horse does not take heed of the rules anymore is in itself threatening (supposedly).

Pirithous describes the accident as if the horse has a fit whose intensity increases until at one point Satan takes full possession of it: when it finally "bounds, comes on end" (5.4.67), it becomes a monstrous hybrid of several animals: "pig-like he whines" (5.4.69). It then "seeks all foul means" (5.4.71); "nought served" (5.4.73). Finally, the rider is in an 'unnatural' position: "Arcite's legs, being higher than his head, / Seemed with strange art to hang" (5.4.78-79). "With strange art" suggests witchcraft. The description culminates in the satanic image of a Christ figure hanging upside down, with a crown of thorns ("His victor's wreath", 5.4.79) that "even then fell off his head" (5.4.80).

Accountability for the accident is directed at the Other – Satan, blackness, disorder, the woman – and thus kept away from the Self – "the gods" or Jupiter, whiteness, maleness, order, Theseus as a representation of that. But Pirithous does not explicitly say so. He does not *say* that the fact that the horse owns "not

216 Dagenais and Greer, p.431.

a hair-worth of white" makes it suspicious, but that "some will say" so and that "many will not buy / His goodness with this note" (5.4.51-53). He calls it a mere "superstition", but a superstition that "here finds allowance" (5.4.53-54). While professing to praise the horse's impressive qualities, he insinuates that it has supernatural powers: it can "make his length a mile" and its "art" is "strange" (5.4.79). Exactly what took possession of it "with fire malevolent" (5.4.63) he does not say: "I comment not" (5.4.65), but lets the "sulphur" (5.4.64) that comes along with the "spark" (5.4.63) suggest that that fire is from hell. The horse's hoofs are also repeatedly mentioned ("His own hoofs", "his hind hoofs", 5.4.60, 5.4.76); the devil is often pictured with one or two hoofs. But Pirithous pretends that he himself has nothing to do with what he allegedly just reports. Others are responsible for his assertions: he says "some will say" (5.4.51), "many will not buy" (5.4.52), "as they say" (5.4.60) and "I comment not" (5.4.65). As was the case with Cressida's reputation, the speaker does not have to do much to create the image he is conveying. Mere hints are sufficient because the story is already written out in the discourse for him.

Theseus' 'other' side

But there are also other versions in the discourse where Theseus appears as a more negative figure and the play uses them to caution against what he stands for. The accident itself is a combination of many versions of the classical myth from different times that point to Theseus as the originator of the accident, in addition to the fact that it was him who brought Arcite into that situation in the first place by ordering the tournament. Had Arcite not died, Theseus would have killed Palamon, whose head is on the block already when the accident happens and Arcite and Palamon are exchangeable for him. He was also going to kill Palamon's three friends, whom he can now pardon as if he was being extraordinarily generous.

The story of Hippolytus was well known in the Renaissance, despite what D'Orsay Pearson calls a "critical myth" about Theseus,[217] namely that he represented the ideal Renaissance ruler and was famous for his equity in the early modern age.[218] Pearson argues that, to the contrary, Theseus' image in antiquity, the Middle Ages and the Renaissance as a perfidious and unfaithful father and lover outweighed his accomplishments such as uniting the *demes* of Athens or being an exemplary friend.[219] Theseus became the embodiment of the "ideal

---

217 D'Orsay Pearson, "'Unkinde' Theseus: A Study in Renaissance Mythography", *English Literary Renaissance*, 4:2 (1974), pp.276-298, p.276.

218 Pearson, p.276. See also Shannon, p.109.

219 Pearson, *ibid.*

ruler of both his lower nature and his subjects"[220] in 20th century criticism nonetheless, both in Shakespeare criticism and in Chaucer studies. D.W. Robertson, for example, wrote about the "noble duc Theseus" of *The Knight's Tale* that

> his reputation as the conquering hero of the Thebaid and the wise leader of a city whose 'patron saint' was Minerva,[221] the goddess of wisdom, was firmly established in the Middle Ages. [...] It would not have been easy for Chaucer to make any abrupt departure from the traditional associations of wisdom and virtue which surrounded this 'character'; and indeed, he shows no inclination to do so.[222]

Pearson argues that, instead, his reputation as an abandoner of women (Ariadne, Hippolyta) and murderer of his own son is critical to understanding *A Midsummer Night's Dream*, which thus becomes much more serious and ironic, especially if it is to be seen as a 'marriage play'.[223] And, as Shannon points out, *The Two Noble Kinsmen* to an even greater extent dramatizes a Theseus who rules irresponsibly and egotistically.[224]

Pearson also proposes that Shakespeare deliberately chose the name 'Hippolyta', rather than the 'Antiope' of other versions of the story, for the defeated Amazon Queen in *A Midsummer Night's Dream* to recall the fate of Hippolytus, the child of the marriage that play celebrates.[225] These sombre prospects of Theseus and Hippolyta's marriage add to the funereal character of the wedding in *The Two Noble Kinsmen*. Pearson points out that, while Theseus was admired for the deeds of his youth, such as the killing of the Minotaur and his political successes in Athens, the older Theseus was associated with treachery and lechery.[226] In the *Confessio Amantis*, Gower calls him "unkinde / Theseüs, which no trouthe kepte" (Liber Quintus, ll. 5424-5425) and who "Fulfild of his unkindeschipe/ Hath al foryete the goodschipe / Which Adriane him hadde do" (Liber Quintus, ll. 5427-5429). He is repeatedly referred to as "unkinde" in the following lines (ll. 5453, 5469, 5479).[227] This image of the "unkind", the ungrateful and inconstant Theseus must be recognised alongside the more positive pictures of Theseus as chivalric knight, as he appears in Boccaccio's *Teseide* or Lydgate's Siege of *Thebes*, Pearson argues.[228] But the image of the perfidious, unfaithful Theseus needs not replace that of the noble and reasonable Theseus who united the settlements of

---

220 Paul A. Olson, "*A Midsummer Night's Dream* and the Meaning of Court Marriage", *English Literary History*, 24 (1957), p.101; cited in Pearson, p.276.

221 The Roman name for Athene.

222 D.W. Robertson, *A Preface to Chaucer: Studies in Medieval Perspectives* (Princeton, NJ: 1962), pp. 260-261, cited in Pearson, pp.276-277.

223 Pearson, pp.280-281; Shannon, p.109.

224 Shannon, *ibid.*

225 Pearson, p.297.

226 Pearson, pp.286-287, 290.

227 See Pearson, pp.284-285.

228 Pearson, p.285.

Attica under Athenian rule etc.: both images can coexist. In *The Two Noble Kinsmen*, Theseus appears as a perfidious ruler who is nonetheless regarded as noble and who organises chaos into order.

When Theseus says, "The gods my justice / Take from my hand and they themselves become / The executioners" (5.4.120-122), he distracts from the fact that *he* is the "executioner". He then pardons Palamon's knights, who are presumably still waiting by the scaffold,[229] as if he was being especially merciful ("Call your lovers from the stage of death/ Whom I adopt my friends" (5.4.123-124)) when it was his idea to have the knights killed in the first place, a "sadistic adjudication" in the words of Alan Sinfield.[230]

At the same time, "call your lovers from the stage of death" (5.4.123) is part of the metatheatrical level that is opening up at the end of the play and Theseus is speaking here as it were to the playwrights. Thus when he says, "Never Fortune / Did play a subtler game" (5.4.112-113), he might be talking about himself, i.e. fortune never played more subtly than him, for example in masking his agency and ascribing evil events to external forces, or he might be talking about the playwrights, who 'play' more subtly than fortune when they dramatise the destructive effects of Theseus' rule, but also show – critically – how little effort it takes him to appear as the equitable ruler and how little his words, actions and decrees are questioned by people, because his equity is already inscribed in the discourse for him.

Ironically, while he stands for linear time and tries to press circularity into that scheme, it is repetition that ensures this power, because the power of a ruler needs to be acted out, performed and this performativity, in turn, needs reiteration in order to be effective.[231] The power of a ruler is also an effect of the sedimentation of ritually repeated words and acts, and this is what ensures that Theseus and his deeds will appear as sanctioned by the gods in (almost) any event. They are also seen in opposition to the Other, which is represented as either evil forces from hell, the tyrant Creon or temporal chaos, all of which appear on the same side here, opposed to the good, the essential, the gods. But the play also shows that Theseus' rule is no less arbitrary than Creon's and that his particular temporal order, the linear allocation of events to present and past, remembrance and oblivion respectively, is not just arbitrary, which would not be so terrible, but generates violence and suffering. The light tone of Theseus' final speech, as Shannon puts it, "belies the spiritual bruises, long faces, and blood that surround him".[232]

---

229 Potter, p.327.

230 Sinfield (2003), p.75. In *A Midsummer Night's Dream*, too, Theseus exceeds what is demanded of him when he tells Hermia that she has to die if she marries against her father's will. See Pearson, p.293.

231 See, for example, Butler (1993), pp.171-172.

232 Shannon, p.108.

Creon is denounced because he defies the gods. But Theseus, too, erodes the vow of chastity Emilia has made to the goddess Diana when he forces her to marry one of the kinsmen. Emilia is separated from her vow not by her own doing, but by Theseus' decree: even "Diana's mythic power is eclipsed by Theseus' absolute sovereignty".[233] With the support of hegemonic discourse, Theseus makes his decisions appear not only as backed up or supported by the gods, sometimes they are even carried out by the gods themselves:

> Fairest Emily,
> The gods by their divine arbitrament
> Have given you this knight. (5.3.106-108)

However, Theseus decided that Emilia has to marry the winner of the tournament. But at the same time, the play is critical of these supposedly divine decrees. The quotation above, for example, is from the short period of time in which Emilia is to marry Arcite, so it is *Arcite* Theseus refers to here, not Palamon, whom she later actually marries. The word "arbitrament" thus sounds ambivalent, because the arbitrariness of the "divine" choice of "*this* knight" is stressed. To make it even clearer, Theseus 'elaborates':

> He is a good one
> As ever struck at head. (5.3.108-109)

Again, our attention is drawn to how little he cares about either of the knights: he does not even try to give a more concrete reason. This is especially striking compared with the long and specific descriptions of the six friends of Palamon and Arcite earlier (4.2.73-143). On top of that, Theseus says almost the exact same thing a few lines later, but this time about Palamon:

> Oh, loved sister,
> He speaks now of as brave a knight as e'er
> Did spur a noble steed. (5.3.114-116)

It shows how interchangeable the kinsmen are for Theseus. He uses the same stereotypical standard activities of knights to describe both. The other knights, their friends, were described individually, with minute detail as to their bodies, features, complexion, eyes, age, voice and temperament. Palamon and Arcite are as good a knight as any or as brave a knight as ever. When Theseus saw them in the battle at Thebes, however, they did attract his attention ("I fixed my note / Constantly on them", 1.4.19-20), but as a pair: they were "like to a pair of lions", together made "lanes in troops aghast" and "they were a mark / Worth a god's view" (1.4.18-21).

Theseus seems to care little about which one of the cousins lives and which one dies. This indifference indicates the contingency of linear history writing,

233 Shannon, p.117.

but the play puts special emphasis on the price of strictly dividing time into a progressive sequence of singular units, where the past is simply cancelled and no polychronic remains, "no untimely trace or survival of the not-now" is permitted.[234] In *The Two Noble Kinsmen*, the price is expressed as compulsory heterosexual marriage and violent death, the former as concerns both kinsmen and Emilia, whose desire is erased when she is married at the end of the play, regardless of the evidence throughout the play that it is as inappropriate to her[235] as it is to Palamon, and the latter (violent death) especially as concerns Arcite, who loses his life, and all who are affected by his death, particularly Palamon. Since Theseus forces both upon his subjects, heterosexual marriage is linked to linear history writing. Thus traditional marriage's role in maintaining the social hierarchy is stressed, within marriage between the genders and within society as a whole, as concerns the distribution of status and property. At the same time, this highlights the hierarchy inherent in linear history writing, because it usually writes the story of the winners.[236] Arcite's violent death represents a past that is cancelled, cut off, "hermetically sealed from the now".[237] The relation of what is lost (delegated to the past) and what is won (kept for the present and future) is represented here as one-to-one, as exactly one half of the virtually identical "twins of honour" gets lost. It is, furthermore, suggested on several occasions during the play that Palamon also dies when Arcite dies, as would be the case the other way round.

This would, of course, also mean that Arcite remains alive as long as Palamon lives, a comforting idea but one which inevitably recalls Walter Benjamin's thought that our cultural history owes its existence to two kinds of people, to the celebrated geniuses that are remembered for creating it and to their nameless contemporaries whose drudgeries enabled these creations but who are forgotten. Therefore, according to Benjamin, every document of culture is simultaneously one of barbarism.[238] Then the buried Arcite would stand for these people's anonymous contribution, which is like an invisible shadow of our cultural achievements and the people to whom we generally ascribe it, who would be represented by Palamon, who survives. But since, technically, it is Arcite who is celebrated as victor (of the tournament), albeit very briefly, this pattern is not strictly followed. According to Walter Benjamin, conventional historicism leads to empathy with the victors and

> all rulers are the heirs of those who conquered before them. Hence, empathy with the victor invariably benefits the rulers. [...] Whoever has emerged victorious participates to

234 Harris (2009), p.29.

235 Mallette, p.36.

236 See Walter Benjamin, *Über den Begriff der Geschichte* [*On the Concept of History*], VII (Berlin: Suhrkamp, 2010), pp.96-97.

237 Harris (2007), p.471.

238 Benjamin, p.97.

this day in the triumphal procession in which the present rulers step over those who are lying prostrate.[239]

Now Arcite rides in this triumphal procession and is then, himself, trampled underfoot. Thus, in *The Two Noble Kinsmen*, the focus is above all on the arbitrariness of the decision of what is kept for the present and what is dismissed to the past, since the kinsmen are drawn so much alike and this is not a case of for example the kinsmen (lying prostrate) versus Theseus (stepping over them), the Amazons versus Theseus or the Thebans versus the Athenians, etc. The focus is thus slightly different from Benjamin's idea. Theseus appears as the one who directs the triumphal procession but does not care about who is in it: his own position is not affected by it.

Thus, each of the indistinguishable kinsmen has the opportunity to hold a goodbye speech to the other, since both are winners at one point. Their "title is [...] momentary" (5.4.17), as Palamon's friends declare just before the accident happens. The friends thus join in the hegemonic discourse and contribute to the impression that everything is determined by fate and that they lose their lives because life is transitory, even if they are victims of Theseus' rule and are at the point of losing their lives as they speak. The knights who accept their 'fate' so patiently summarise the arguments in their brief farewell speeches: that the victor's title is momentary, that fortune "at her certain'st reels" (5.4.21) and that only "death is certain" (5.4.18). This occludes the fact that these particular deaths at this particular time are Theseus' work. The knights think (or claim to think) that, with their patience, they "anger tottering Fortune" (5.4.20), while in fact they help Theseus.

As if finally becoming aware of the illusion, Palamon asks at the end of the play: "What / Hath waked us from our dream?" (5.4.47-48). This can refer to the theatrical situation, the play is about to end, to the masking of Theseus' agency which he may finally have realised or to Arcite and his strange in-between state since Theseus took control of them when he revived them after the battle to finally sort them out, one to the present, the other to the past. "What / Hath waked us from our dream?" also draws a link to *A Midsummer Night's Dream* and shows that *The Two Noble Kinsmen* really is a darker version of *A Midsummer Night's Dream* or even "*A Midsummer Night's Dream, Part II*", as one critic calls it.[240]

Really the best answer to the question of whether Athens or Thebes, linear chronology or recursive antisequentiality are given the preference here is exactly this: in *A Midsummer Night's Dream*, there is another Theseus and another mar-

---

239 Benjamin, *Über den Begriff der Geschichte* VII, trans. Harry Zohn in Walter Benjamin, *Illuminations*, ed. Hannah Arendt (New York: Schocken, 2007), p.256.

240 Glynne Wickham, "*The Two Noble Kinsmen* or *A Midsummer Night's Dream, Part II*?" in *The Elizabethan Theater*, VII (1980), pp.167-196, cited in Abrams, pp. 69, 75, and Sinfield (2003), p.68.

riage with another defeated Amazon Queen Hippolyta. Since *A Midsummer Night's Dream* is the earlier play, *The Two Noble Kinsmen* is in fact a repetition of it (a varied citation). Theseus exists, in fact, in innumerable incarnations. Besides the ones in *The Two Noble Kinsmen* and *A Midsummer Night's Dream*, there are versions of Theseus in Chaucer's *The Knight's Tale* and *Anelida and Arcite*, in Spenser's *Faerie Queene*, where the story of Hippolytus, his death and Theseus' role in it is also told (Book I Canto V), in Lydgate's *Siege of Thebes*, Boccaccio's *Teseida*, Statius' *Thebaid*, Plutarch's *Parallel Lives*, Ovid's *Metamorphoses* and *Heroides*, Virgil's *Aeneid*, in several dramas by Euripides and Sophocles and in many other works, including many, especially by the ancient Greek dramatists, that are now lost. The very existence of this assemblage of Theseus characters refutes the logics of linearity and shows that a notion of time that is based purely on teleological seriality is not an adequate way of thinking the past and that iteration and the re-emergence of past events and their simultaneous existence in a palimpsest that is rewritten and re-rewritten somehow prevails.

II.12. Structural repetition

This is also indicated by the fact that "the play closes on the note it began, with a funeral-marriage",[241] not only because Arcite is getting buried and Palamon getting married almost simultaneously, but also because *The Two Noble Kinsmen* at the end constructs a marriage-union of two characters who are both more attached to their same-sex dead friends than they are to one another, since the play fails to construct the union between Palamon and Arcite or Emilia and Flavina:[242] "What remains is an empty hull of public married respectability".[243] Emilia, the character who used to contradict Theseus openly and who constituted a counterbalance against his absolutist rule for some time ("I have another oath 'gainst yours, / Of more authority", 3.6.230-231), is subdued in the course of the play. She has fewer and fewer lines and finally becomes an empty hull herself: "I am extinct" (5.3.20). Her gradual defeat by Theseus, completed in the last act, also repeats her sister Hippolyta's earlier subjugation, which was about to be celebrated in the first scene of Act I. Since there are numerous ways in which the play ends in the same way it began, even the repetition is reiterated. Thus it is made clear in more than one way that a neat distinction between discrete temporal units arranged in a progressive temporal order does ultimately not work. To pick out some things from the palimpsest that are to be current – symbolised by Palamon, the winner – and sweep others under the rug or shovel them under the earth, like Arcite, and thus to create a linear, teleological pro-

[241] Mallette, p.47.
[242] Mallette, *ibid.*
[243] Mallette, *ibid.*

gress narrative is not very convincing when the hidden layers of the palimpsest keep resurfacing, like the sand that does not stick to Polynices's body in *Antigone*. The multiple traces of the past in the present are, for example, represented in this play by the figure of Chaucer, who cries out from under the ground in the prologue, demands an active role in the present and shows how the past residing in the present could be imagined. The resurgence of the past(s) is also embodied by the Argive Queens who interrupt the wedding or, perhaps most forcefully, by the unruly black horse, a symbol not only for the invincible past but also for many things that are suppressed and *Other*, which bolts, and finally throws off the rider. In this way, the past will break through to explode upon the present. The horse with all its Christian, or rather the opposite, satanic imagery written into a scene that is supposed to take place in an ancient, pre-Christian past is itself an example for palimpsested time, for traces of the future in the past. The fiery, "hot" (5.4.65), "dancing" (5.4.59) horse is also a reminder that "the past is always potentially alive",[244] even though Arcite is at this moment being sent into the realm of the dead. Theseus, the leading figure in the project of imposing a linear order upon disorganised time, is himself only one in a large number of reincarnations of Theseus from different moments in literary history, one member of a "polychronic assemblage"[245] of Athenian rulers that set out to conquer Thebes, the city of circular time, over and over again. Thus multitemporality, different organisations of time, is articulated: recursive time and progressive, linear time but, ultimately, to borrow Theseus' own words, "The conquered triumphs; / The victor has the loss" (5.4.113-114), the conquered Thebes' polychronicity, the simultaneousness of different moments in time, proves more durable.

244 Harris (2009), p.25.
245 Harris (2009), p.17.

Conclusion

Palimpsested time, a temporality "that is not one",[1] challenges the idea of unilinear temporality, of time as a chronological, teleological sequence of events. Just as the past is not cancelled by the present but is contained in it, history is not divisible into clearly distinct epochs that replace one another successively. Rather, multiple temporal layers that are interwoven in the manner of a palimpsest transform and rewrite each other constantly. Analysis of two of Shakespeare's plays, *Troilus and Cressida* and *The Two Noble Kinsmen*, written in cooperation with John Fletcher, has shown that the self-identical moment, or the self-identical period, does not exist.

These plays ultimately derive from classical ancient sources (the *Iliad*, the *Aeneid* and others) that had been rewritten multiple times by the time the early modern authors adapted them. Comparing them especially with Chaucer's adaptations (*Troilus and Criseyde* and *The Knight's Tale*) and also with the ancient texts (especially Homer's *Iliad*, Ovid's *Metamorphoses*, Statius' *Thebaid* and Sophocles' *Antigone*) this study has shown how earlier temporal layers shine through in the early modern plays. These texts challenge simple systems of periodization by being of several times. Palimpsested time makes it possible that even works like *Antigone*, which, to our knowledge, neither Chaucer nor Shakespeare knew directly, could have reached them via later works that contained them. Echoes of *Antigone* are recognisable, for instance, in the motif of the 'floating' bodies that rise through and above the surface of the earth (like earlier textual layers of a palimpsest rise through the over-text) or in the motif of the "buried life" in captivity, in between death and life, past and present. In a palimpsest, the past is always potentially alive[2] and therefore able to speak, intervene in the present, interrupt or even "shatter" it,[3] as the Argive widows do when they interrupt Theseus' marriage in *The Two Noble Kinsmen*, exemplifying what Gil Harris calls the "temporality of explosion".[4] The Argives introduce the motif of a marriage-funeral, the "anachronistic proximity of supposedly distant and disparate moments",[5] which also echoes *Antigone*, where grave and marriage bed are conflated, in turn, indicating the future fate of Hippolyta, whom Theseus marries after defeating her in war. After the wedding, the legendary Amazon queen no longer has a literary life of her own, so that with the marriage she indeed enters, in Antigone's words, a "tomb, bridal chamber, prison forever" (*Antigone* l. 891).

---

1 Harris (2009), p.24.
2 See Harris (2009), p.25.
3 Harris, (2009), p.143.
4 Harris, (2009), p.16.
5 Harris (2009), p.169.

Resisting linear chronology, these texts exhibit a temporality "that is not one", where the past is contained in the present similarly to the way that earlier textual layers of a palimpsest are contained in later inscriptions. The metaphor of the palimpsest is a more adequate way of imagining time than seeing the past as entirely different from the present. To assume an *a priori* break between *then* and *now* is too restrictive and has, especially in the case of the Middle Ages, which are often seen as modernity's exact opposite, its binary Other, led to a very limited picture of the past. *Troilus and Cressida* reconstructs and, at the same time, collapses the border that separates the Middle Ages from modernity. The two parties, Trojan and Greek, are drawn as dichotomised opposites, illustrating that the process of Othering, usually related to areas of geographical distance, can also create temporal Otherness. Following Eric Mallin I argued that Troy is drawn as a medieval world, while the Greeks represent early modernity in ways that are often diametrically opposed to the Trojans. While the Trojans are, for example, associated with values like honesty and humility, and the literary form of poetry, the Greeks are associated with dissimulation, over-estimation and drama. The Greeks are in a crisis but it is Troy that is destroyed in the end, although Troy's end happens only symbolically in this play. It is prefigured by the way Achilles kills Hector in their final fight. These two heroes are very much representative of their respective parties. Just before the fight they become almost indistinguishable in their opposition. Then the boundaries are conflated and they merge, illustrating how the Other is a part of the Self and thus inseparable from it. In their final dialogue, the play gestures towards the sonnet tradition, creating a poetological palimpsest as well. This is because, on a larger scale, poetry and drama are roughly associated with the Middle Ages and early modernity respectively, and, on a smaller scale, the intense popularity of sonnets was already over by the time Shakespeare wrote *Troilus and Cressida*. In Achilles and Hector's 'sonnet' (among other scenes in the play), one genre shines through the other, so they are inseparably interwoven.

The way that protagonists from the Middle Ages (both Troilus and Cressida/Chryseis are mere names in the classical source) are placed in an ancient setting, on the early modern stage, for this play shows how multiple temporal layers can be interconnected. Moreover, Cressida's behaviour in the present is especially influenced by not only her past but also her future history. Cressida appears as the embodiment of the performativity of history itself and the reiteration that performativity demands. Her character is denied subjectivity, the alleged new achievement of modernity, in a way that draws attention to the fact. A lacuna is exhibited in the place where her subjectivity should be. Discourse and repetition as the origins of social reality appear completely undisguised here and in precisely the character that has the reputation of being deceitful.

In *The Two Noble Kinsmen*, the stage itself becomes a palimpsest. If the stage were a manuscript, the bodies of the characters moving vertically below and above the stage ground would be the various textual layers. Whether dead or alive, the bodies are always in motion and are characteristically not in the 'right' place, the place where Theseus tries to put them. This goes especially for the protagonists, the two noble kinsmen. Theseus stands for a linear understanding of time. In a similar way as, in *Troilus and Cressida*, Troy and Greece represent the Middle Ages and modernity, respectively, and the relationship between them, time is mapped out spatially in *The Two Noble Kinsmen*. But here, different conceptions of time and temporality rather than different periods are represented by places, but these also concern the relationship of present and past. Following Lee Patterson's description of *Thebanness* in Chaucer, I argued that, in *The Two Noble Kinsmen*, too, Thebes and its ruler Creon stand for recursive time, while Athens, ruled by Theseus, represents linearity. Just as Cressida does not really belong to either party and moves from Troy to the Greek camp in *Troilus and Cressida*, the kinsmen, too, belong simultaneously to both sides and to neither. Theseus, on his mission of establishing linear order, transports them from Thebes to Athens. There, their transitional status is maintained for some time when they are 'buried' alive. Then the line between present and past is drawn right between the kinsmen. Although the tournament that is to decide which kinsman is allocated where is set up according to rules that are carefully described, the final decision is made without these rules. One kinsman is left alive and given to marriage and procreation (assorted with the present and future) while the other one dies (is assorted with the past). At the last moment, the kinsmen are exchanged in a way that highlights the arbitrariness of the decision of what is forgotten and what is remembered.

In the same way that he installs linear order, Theseus is also preoccupied with arranging heterosexual marriages, both for himself (with Hippolyta) and for the kinsmen and Emilia. But all of these marriages are inappropriate in one way or the other. He marries Hippolyta after he has defeated her in war ("I wooed thee with my sword", as the *Midsummer Night's Dream*'s Theseus says, 1.1.16), and, I argue, the desire of the kinsmen and of Emilia is presented as homosexual rather than heterosexual. In Emilia and the kinsmen's case heteronormativity is therefore linked to linear time and the arbitrary exclusion and oblivion that both demand is stressed. Both are 'successfully' installed at the end but at a terrible cost.

What Theseus presents as a series of successes, a chronological progress narrative, has cost too many victims to appear convincing. Besides, the concept of unidirectional, linear time is subverted throughout the play as the past keeps on reappearing, especially when the play ends with another funeral-marriage (Arcite's burial, Emilia and Palamon's wedding) that links the end to the beginning, suggesting "Theban" circularity. There are further reiterations, such as Emilia's slow subjugation during the play, which repeats Hippolyta's earlier one, or Theseus' recurring military campaigns. Linear time is articulated in this play but because the past keeps returning and working on the present, it is made clear that there is no definite partition between *then* and *now*. And, if time cannot be divided and arranged in progressive sequence, then the self-identical moment, just like the self-identical period, does not exist and premodernity is a part of modernity rather than its opposite.

Bibliography

PRIMARY SOURCES

Beaumont, Francis and John Fletcher, *The Maid's Tragedy*, in *English Renaissance Drama: A Norton Anthology*, ed. by David Bevington and others (New York: W. W. Norton & Company, 2002), pp.1147-1214.

Caxton, William, *The Recuyell of the Historyes of Troye*, ed. by H. Oskar Sommer (New York: AMS Press, 1973).

Chapman's Homer: The Iliad, ed. by Allardyce Nicoll (Princeton: Princeton University Press, 1998).

Fletcher, John and William Shakespeare, *The Two Noble Kinsmen*, ed. by Lois Potter, Arden Shakespeare, Third Series (London: Thomson Learning, 1997).

–, *The Two Noble Kinsmen*, ed. by Eugene M. Waith, The Oxford Shakespeare (Oxford: Oxford University Press, 1989, 2008).

Geoffrey Chaucer: Troilus and Criseyde *with facing-page* Il Filostrato, ed. by Stephen A. Barney (New York: W. W. Norton & Company, 2006).

Gower, John, *Confessio Amantis*, ed. by Russell A. Peck (New York: Holt, Rinehart & Winston, 1968).

John Donne: Complete Poetry and Selected Prose, ed. by John Hayward (New York: Random House Inc., 1949).

The Holy Bible, Revised Standard Version: Containing the Old and New Testaments Translated from the Original Tongues, being the Version set forth A.D. 1611, revised A.D. 1881-1885 and A.D. 1901, Compared with the most Ancient Authorities and Revised A.D. 1946-1952 (New York: Meridian, 1974).

Homer, *The Iliad*, trans. and with an introduction by Richmond Lattimore (Chicago: University of Chicago Press, 1951).

–, *The Odyssey*, trans. and with an introduction by Richmond Lattimore (New York: Harper, 1965, 2007).

Horace, *Ars Poetica*, ed. with notes by Augustus S. Wilkins (London: Macmillan, 1939).

Lydgate, John, *Troy Book*, ed. by Henry Bergen (London: Kegan Paul, Trench, Trübner, 1906-1935).

Ovid, *Metamorphoses*, ed. and trans. by Charles Martin (New York, London: W.W. Norton & Company, 2010).

Ovidius Naso, Publius, *Metamorphoseon libri quindecim. Lateinisch/ Deutsch*, ed. and trans. by Michael von Albrecht (Stuttgart: Philipp Reclam, 1994, 2003).

Ovid's Metamorphoses: The Arthur Golding Translation 1567, ed. by John Frederick Nims (New York: Macmillan, 1965).

The Riverside Chaucer, ed. by Larry D. Benson, 3rd edn (Oxford: Oxford University Press, 1987).

Shakespeare, William, *A Midsummer Night's Dream*, ed. by Peter Holland, The Oxford Shakespeare (Oxford: Oxford University Press, 1994, 2008).

–, *Julius Caesar*, ed. by David Daniell, The Arden Shakespeare, Third Series (London: Methuen, 1998).

–, *Pericles*, ed. by Suzanne Gossett, The Arden Shakespeare, Third Series (London: Thomson Learning, 2004).

–, *Romeo and Juliet*, ed. by Jill L. Levenson, The Oxford Shakespeare (Oxford: Oxford University Press, 2000).

–, *Troilus and Cressida*, ed. by David Bevington, The Arden Shakespeare, Third Series (London: Thomson Learning, 1998, 2006).

Sophocles, *Antigone*, in *Sophocles I: Oedipus the King, Oedipus at Colonus, Antigone*, ed. by David Grene and Richmond Lattimore (Chicago: The University of Chicago Press, 1991), pp.159-212.

Statius, Publius Papinius, *The Thebaid: Seven Against Thebes*, trans. and with an introduction by Charles Stanley Ross (Baltimore: The Johns Hopkins University Press, 2004).

Virgil, *The Aeneid*, trans. by C. Day Lewis, with an introduction and notes by Jasper Griffin (Oxford: Oxford University Press, 2008).

Webster, John, *The Duchess of Malfi*, in *English Renaissance Drama: A Norton Anthology*, ed. by David Bevington and others (New York: W.W. Norton & Company, 2002), pp. 1749-1832.

William Shakespeare: Complete Works, ed. by Jonathan Bate and Eric Rasmussen, The RSC Shakespeare (London: Macmillan, 2007).

William Shakespeare: The Complete Works, ed. by Stanley Wells and others, The Oxford Shakespeare, 2nd edn (Oxford: Clarendon Press, 2005).

SECONDARY SOURCES

Abrams, Richard, "Gender Confusion and Sexual Politics in *The Two Noble Kinsmen*", in *Drama, Sex and Politics*, Themes in Drama 7, ed. by James Redmond (Cambridge: Cambridge University Press, 1985), pp.69-76.

Aers, David, "A Whisper in the Ear of Early Modernists; or, Reflections on Literary Critics Writing the 'History of the Subject'", in *Culture and History 1350-1600: Essays on English Communities, Identities and Writing*, ed. by David Aers (New York: Harvester Wheatsheaf, 1992), pp.177-202.

Ashcroft, Bill, Gareth Griffiths and Helen Tiffin, *Key Concepts in Post-Colonial Studies* (New York, London: Routledge, 1998).

Barr, Helen, "'Wrinkled deep in time': Emily and Arcite in *A Midsummer Night's Dream*", in *Transporting Chaucer* (Manchester: Manchester University Press, 2014), 140-165.

Baudelaire, Charles, *Artificial Paradises*, trans. by Stacy Diamond (New York: Citadel Press, 1996).

Benjamin, Walter, *Illuminations*, trans. by Harry Zohn, ed. and with an introduction by Hannah Arendt (New York: Schocken Books, 2007).

–, *Über den Begriff der Geschichte*, ed. by Gérard Raulet (Berlin: Suhrkamp, 2010).

Berns, Ute, "Interioritätskonstruktionen und Freundschaftsdiskurs bei Shakespeare", *Shakespeare Jahrbuch* 144 (2008), pp. 148-167.

Bethke, Kathrin, *"Nothings monstered": Economies of Pride in 'Coriolanus' and 'Troilus and Cressida'*, unpublished paper held at the Shakespeare Association of America's 40th Annual Convention, Boston, 6 April 2012.

Bhabha, Homi K., "DissemiNation: Time, Narrative, and the Margins of the Modern Nation", in Bhabha, *The Location of Culture* (New York, London: Routledge, 1994), pp.199-244.

Biddick, Kathleen, *The Typological Imaginary: History, Technology, Circumcision* (Philadelphia: University of Pennsylvania Press, 2003).

Bradbrook, M.C., "What Shakespeare Did to Chaucer's *Troilus and Criseyde*", *Shakespeare Quarterly*, 9:3 (1958), pp.311-319.

Braden, Gordon, "Shakespeare's Roman Tragedies", in *A Companion to Shakespeare's Works, Volume I: The Tragedies*, ed. by Richard Dutton and Jean E. Howard (Oxford: Blackwell, 2003, 2006), pp.199-218.

Briggs, Julia Ruth, "'Chaucer ... the Story Gives:' *Troilus and Cressida* and *The Two Noble Kinsmen*", in: *Shakespeare and the Middle Ages: Essays on the Performance and Adaptation of the Plays with Medieval Sources or Settings*, ed. by Martha W. Driver and Sid Ray (Jefferson, N.C.: McFarland & Company, 2009), pp.161-177.

Burckhardt, Jacob, *The Civilization of the Renaissance in Italy*, trans. by S.G.C. Middlemore, Introduction by Benjamin Nelson and Charles Trinkaus (New York: Harper, 1958).

Butler, Judith, *Bodies that Matter: On the Discursive Limits of "Sex"* (New York, London: Routledge, 1993).

–, *Excitable Speech: A Politics of the Performative* (New York, London: Routledge, 1997).

Cantor, Norman F., *The Last Knight: The Twilight of the Middle Ages and the Birth of the Modern Era* (New York: Free Press, 2004).

Carney, Jo Eldridge, "The Ambiguities of Love and War in *The Two Noble Kinsmen*", in *Sexuality and Politics in Renaissance Drama*. Studies in Renaissance Literature Vol. 10, ed. by Carole Levin and Karen Robertson (Lewiston, N.Y.: Edwin Mellen Press, 1991), pp.95-111.

Caxton's Trace: Studies in the History of English Printing, ed. by William Kuskin (Notre Dame, Ind.: University of Notre Dame Press, 2006).

Certeau, Michel de, *Heterologies: Discourse on the Other,* trans. by Brian Massumi, foreword by Wlad Godzich (Minneapolis: University of Minnesota Press, 1986, 1995).

–, *The Writing of History*, trans. by Tom Conley (New York: Columbia University Press, 1988).

The Challenge of Periodization: Old Paradigms and New Perspectives, ed. by Lawrence Besserman (New York: Garland, 1996).

Cheney, Patrick, *Shakespeare's Literary Authorship* (Cambridge: Cambridge University Press, 2008).

Cohen, Jeffrey Jerome, "Introduction: Midcolonial", in *The Postcolonial Middle Ages*, ed. by Jeffrey Jerome Cohen (London: Macmillan Press, 2000), pp.1-17.

–, *Medieval Identity Machines*. Medieval Cultures 35 (Minneapolis/ London: University of Minnesota Press, 2003).

Cook, Carol, "Unbodied Figures of Desire", *Theatre Journal* 38:1: *Dramatic Narration, Theatrical Disruption* (1986), 34-52.

Cooper, Helen, *The English Romance in Time: Transforming Motifs from Geoffrey of Monmouth to the Death of Shakespeare* (Oxford: Oxford University Press, 2004).

Crocker, Holly, "'As False as Cressid': Virtue Trouble from Chaucer to Shakespeare", *Journal of Medieval and Early Modern Studies*, 43:2 (2013), 303-334.

Cultural Reformations: Medieval and Renaissance in Literary History, ed. by James Simpson and Brian Cummings (Oxford: Oxford University Press, 2010).

Dagenais, John and Margaret R. Greer, "Decolonizing the Middle Ages: Introduction", *Journal of Medieval and Early Modern Studies*, 30:3 (2000), 431-448.

Davis, Alex, "Living in the Past: Thebes, Periodization, and *The Two Noble Kinsmen*", *Journal of Medieval and Early Modern Studies*, 40:1 (2010), 173-195.

Davis, Kathleen, "National Writing in the Ninth Century: A Reminder for Postcolonial Thinking about the Nation", *Journal of Medieval and Early Modern Studies*, 28:3 (1998), 611-637.

–, *Periodization and Sovereignty: How Ideas of Feudalism and Secularization Govern the Politics of Time* (Philadelphia: University of Pennsylvania Press, 2008).

Dinshaw, Carolyn, *Chaucer's Sexual Poetics* (Madison: University of Wisconsin Press, 1989).

Donaldson, Ethelbert Talbot, *The Swan at the Well: Shakespeare Reading Chaucer* (New Haven, Ct.: Yale University Press, 1985).

Driver, Martha W. and Sid Ray, *Shakespeare and the Middle Ages: Essays on the Performance and Adaptation of the Plays with Medieval Sources or Settings* (Jefferson, NC: McFarland & Company, 2009).

Elton, William R., *Shakespeare's 'Troilus and Cressida' and the Inns of Court Revels* (Aldershot: Ashgate, 2000).

Ferguson, Margaret W., "Feathers and Flies: Aphra Behn and the Seventeenth-Century Trade in Exotica", in *Subject and Object in Renaissance Culture*, ed. by Margreta de Grazia, Maureen Quilligan and Peter Stallybrass (Cambridge: Cambridge University Press, 1996), pp.235-259.

Ferguson, Wallace K., *The Renaissance in Historical Thought. Five Centuries of Interpretation* (Boston: Houghton Mifflin, 1948).

Foucault, Michel, *The Archaeology of Knowledge* (New York: Vintage Books, 1972, 2010).

–, *The History of Sexuality, Vol. 1: An Introduction* (New York: Vintage Books, 1978, 1990).

Fumerton, Patricia, "Introduction: A New New Historicism", in *Renaissance Culture and the Everyday*, ed. by Patricia Fumerton and Simon Hunt (Philadelphia: University of Pennsylvania Press, 1999), pp.1-17.

The Future of the Middle Ages and the Renaissance: Problems, Trends, and Opportunities for Research, ed. by Roger Dahood (Turnhout: Brepols, 1998).

Ganim, John M., *Medievalism and Orientalism: Three Essays on Literature, Architecture and Cultural Identity* (New York: Palgrave Macmillan, 2005).

Geertz, Clifford, *The Interpretation of Cultures* (New York: Basic Books, 1973).

Genette, Gérard, *Palimpsests: Literature in the Second Degree* (Lincoln, Nebr.: University of Nebraska Press, 1997).

de Grazia, Margreta, "The Modern Divide: From Either Side", *Journal of Medieval and Early Modern Studies*, 37:3 (2007), 453-467.

Greene, Jody, "*The Two Noble Kinsmen*: Philadelphia, or, War", in *Shakesqueer: A Queer Companion to the Complete Works of Shakespeare*, ed. by Madhavi Menon (Durham and London: Duke University Press, 2011), pp.404-413.

Hadorn, Peter T., "*The Two Noble Kinsmen* and the Problem of Chivalry", *Studies in Medievalism*, 4 (1992), 45-57.

Harris, Jonathan Gil, "The Smell of Macbeth", *Shakespeare Quarterly*, 58:4 (2007), 465-486.

–, *Untimely Matter in the Time of Shakespeare* (Philadelphia: University of Pennsylvania Press, 2009).

–, *Shakespeare and Literary Theory* (Oxford: Oxford University Press, 2010).

Heng, Geraldine, *Empire of Magic: Medieval Romance and the Politics of Cultural Fantasy* (New York: Columbia University Press, 2003).

Howard, Jean Elizabeth, "The New Historicism in Renaissance Studies", *English Literary Renaissance*, 16:1 (1986), 13-43.

–and Paul Strohm, "The Imaginary 'Commons'", *Journal of Medieval and Early Modern Studies*, 37:3 (2007), 550-577.

Ingham, Patricia Clare, "Homosociality and Creative Masculinity in the *Knight's Tale*", in *Masculinities in Chaucer: Approaches to Maleness in the 'Canterbury Tales' and 'Troilus and Criseyde'*, ed. by Peter G. Beidler (Cambridge: D.S. Brewer, 1998), pp.23-55.

James, Heather, *Shakespeare's Troy: Drama, Politics, and the Translation of Empire* (Cambridge: Cambridge University Press, 1997).

Jameson, Fredric, *The Political Unconscious: Narrative as a Socially Symbolic Act* (New York: Methuen, 1981).

–, *Postmodernism, or, The Cultural Logic of Late Capitalism* (Durham: Duke University Press, 1991).

–, *A Singular Modernity: Essay on the Ontology of the Present* (London, New York: Verso, 2002).

John Lydgate: Poetry, Culture, and Lancastrian England, ed. by Larry Scanlon and James Simpson (Notre Dame, Ind.: University of Notre Dame Press, 2006).

Johnston, Andrew James, "Wrestling with Ganymede: Chaucer's *Knight's Tale* and the Homoerotics of Epic History", *Germanisch-Romanische Monatsschrift*, 50 (2000), 21-43.

–, *Performing the Middle Ages from 'Beowulf' to 'Othello'* (Turnhout: Brepols, 2009).

–, "Sailing the Seas of Literary History: Gower, Chaucer, and the Problem of Incest in Shakespeare's *Pericles*", *Poetica* 41:3/4 (2009), 381-407.

–, "Geschlechter-Lektüren: Emotion und Intimität in Chaucers *Troilus and Criseyde*", in *Machtvolle Gefühle*, ed. by Ingrid Kasten (Berlin: de Gruyter, 2010), pp.246-259.

–, "Subjectivity and the Ekphrastic Prerogative: Emilia's Soliloquy in *The Two Noble Kinsmen*", in *Solo Performances: Staging the Early Modern Self in England*, ed. by Ute Berns (Amsterdam: Rodopi, 2010), pp.49-65.

Jones, Ann Rosalind and Peter Stallybrass, *Renaissance Clothing and the Materials of Memory* (Cambridge: Cambridge University Press, 2000).

Keller, Wolfram, "Passionate Authorial Performances: From Chaucer's Criseyde to Shakespeare's Cressida", unpublished paper presented at the conference *Performing the Poetics of Passion: Chaucer's 'Troilus and Criseyde' and Shakespeare's 'Troilus and Cressida'*, Free University of Berlin, 13-15 May 2010.

Kindlers Neues Literaturlexikon, ed. by Jens Walter and others, 22 vols (Munich: Kindler, 1988-1998).

Kopytoff, Igor, "The Cultural Biography of Things: Commoditization as Process", in *The Social Life of Things: Commodities in Cultural Perspective*, ed. by Arjun Appadurai (Cambridge: Cambridge University Press, 1986), pp.64-91.

Kuskin, William, "Recursive Origins: Print History and Shakespeare's *2 Henry VI*" in *Shakespeare and the Middle Ages*, ed. by Curtis Perry and John Watkins (Oxford: Oxford University Press, 2009), pp.126-150.

Lacan, Jacques, "Some Reflections on the Ego", *International Journal of Psychoanalysis*, 34:1 (1953), 11-17.

Lerer, Seth, *Chaucer and His Readers: Imagining the Author in Late-Medieval England* (Princeton, NJ: Princeton University Press, 1993).

Lewis, Sarah, "Shakespeare, Time, Theory", *Literature Compass*, 11:4 (2014), 246-257.

Loomba, Ania, "Periodization, Race, and Global Contact", *Journal of Medieval and Early Modern Studies*, 37:3 (2007), 595-620.

Lynch, Kathryn L., "The Three Noble Kinsmen: Chaucer, Shakespeare, Fletcher", in *Images of Matter: Essays on British Literature of the Middle Ages and Renaissance. Proceedings of the Eighth Citadel Conference on Literature, Charleston, South Carolina, 2002*, ed. by Yvonne Bruce (Newark: University of Delaware Press, 2005), pp.72-91.

Mallette, Richard, "Same-Sex Erotic Friendship in *The Two Noble Kinsmen*", in *Explorations in Renaissance Drama*, ed. by Mary Beth Rose (Evanston: Northwestern University Press and the Newberry Library Center for Renaissance Studies, 1997), p.29-52.

Mallin, Eric Scott, "Emulous Factions and the Collapse of Chivalry: *Troilus and Cressida*", in *Inscribing the Time: Shakespeare and the End of Elizabethan England*, (Berkeley: University of California Press, 1995), pp.25-61.

Margherita, Gayle, "Historicity, Femininity, and Chaucer's Troilus", *Exemplaria* 6 (1995), pp.243-269.

Masten, Jeffrey, *Textual Intercourse: Collaboration, Authorship, and Sexualities in Renaissance Drama* (Cambridge: Cambridge University Press, 1997).

McDonald, Russ, *The Bedford Companion to Shakespeare: An Introduction with Documents* (Boston: Bedford/St. Martin's, 2001).

*Medievalism in the Modern World: Essays in Honour of Leslie Workma*n, ed. by Richard Utz and Tom Shippey (Turnhout: Brepols, 1998).

Montrose, Louis Adrian, *The Purpose of Playing: Shakespeare and the Cultural Politics of the Elizabethan Theatre* (Chicago: University of Chicago Press, 1996).

Muscatine, Charles, *Chaucer and the French Tradition: A Study in Style and Meaning* (Berkeley: University of California Press, 1957).

Orgel, Stephen, *The Illusion of Power: Political Theater in the English Renaissance* (Berkeley: University of California Press, 1975, 1991).

Parker, Patricia, *Shakespeare from the Margins: Language, Culture, Context* (Chicago: The University of Chicago Press, 1996).

Partridge, Eric, *Shakespeare's Bawdy* (New York, London: Routledge, 1947, 1968).

The Past and Future of Medieval Studies, ed. by John Van Engen (Notre Dame: The University of Notre Dame Press, 1994).

Patterson, Lee, *Negotiating the Past: The Historical Understanding of Medieval Literature* (Madison: The University of Wisconsin Press, 1987).

–, "On the Margin: Postmodernism, Ironic History, and Medieval Studies", *Speculum*, 65 (1990), 87-108.

–, *Chaucer and the Subject of History* (Madison: University of Wisconsin Press, 1991).

–, "The Return to Philology", in *The Past and Future of Medieval Studies*, ed. by John Van Engen (Notre Dame: The University of Notre Dame Press, 1994), pp.231-244.

Paulys Realencyclopädie der Classischen Altertumswissenschaft: Neue Bearbeitung begonnen von Georg Wissowa, fortgeführt von Wilhelm Kroll und Karl Mittelhaus. Dreiundvierzigster Halbband, Pontarches bis Praefectianus, ed. by Konrat Ziegler (Stuttgart: Alfred Druckenmüller Verlag, 1953, 1970).

Pearsall, Derek, *The Life of Geoffrey Chaucer: A Critical Biography* (Oxford: Blackwell, 1992).

Pearson, D'Orsay W., "'Unkinde' Theseus: A Study in Renaissance Mythography", *English Literary Renaissance*, 4:2 (1974), 276-298.

Potter, A. M., "'Troilus and Cressida': Deconstructing the Middle Ages?" *Theoria*, 72 (1988), 23-35.

Reading the Medieval in Early Modern England, ed. by Gordon McMullan and David Matthews (Cambridge: Cambridge University Press, 2007).

Renaissance Medievalisms, ed. by Konrad Eisenbichler (Toronto: CRRS Publications, 2009).

Rich, Adrienne, "Compulsory Heterosexuality and Lesbian Existence", in *Blood, Bread, and Poetry: Selected Prose 1979-1985* (London: Virago Press, 1980, 1986), pp. 23-75.

Rogers, Jami, "Cressida in Twenty-First Century Performance", *Shakespeare*, 10:1 (2014), 56-71.

Rose, Mary Beth, *The Expense of Spirit: Love and Sexuality in English Renaissance Drama* (Ithaca: Cornell University Press, 1988).

Rubinstein, Frankie, *A Dictionary of Shakespeare's Sexual Puns and their Significance* (London: Macmillan, 1984, 1989).

Rust, Martha Dana, "'Le Vostre C': Letters and Love in Bodleian Library MS Arch. Selden. B. 24", in *New Perspectives on Criseyde*, ed. by Cindy L. Vitto and Marcia Smith Marzec (Asheville: Pegasus, 2004), pp.111-138.

Sanders, Julie, "Mixed Messages: The Aesthetics of *The Two Noble Kinsmen*", in *A Companion to Shakespeare's Works, Volume IV: The Poems, Problem Comedies, Late Plays*, ed. by Richard Dutton and Jean E. Howard (Oxford: Blackwell, 2003), pp.445-461.

Sanok, Catherine, "Criseyde, Cassandre, and the *Thebaid*: Women and the Theban Subtext of Chaucer's *Troilus and Criseyde*, *Studies in the Age of Chaucer*, 20 (1998), pp. 41-71.

Sexuality and Politics in Renaissance Drama, ed. by Carol Levin and Karen Robertson (Lewiston, NY: Edwin Mellen Press, 1991).

Shakespeare and the Middle Ages, ed. by Curtis Perry and John Watkins (Oxford: Oxford University Press, 2009).

Shannon, Laurie, "Professing Friendship: Erotic Prerogatives and 'Human Title' in *The Two Noble Kinsmen*", in *Sovereign Amity: Figures of Friendship in Shakespearean Contexts* (Chicago: University of Chicago Press, 2002), pp.90-122.

Simpson, James, *Reform and Cultural Revolution: The Oxford English Literary History, Volume 2. 1350-1547* (Oxford: Oxford University Press, 2002).

Sinfield, Alan, "Cultural Materialism and Intertextuality: The Limits of Queer Reading in *A Midsummer Night's Dream* and *The Two Noble Kinsmen*", *Shakespeare Survey*, 56 (2003), 67-78.

–, "The Leather Men and the Lovely Boy: Reading Positions in *Troilus and Cressida*", in *Shakesqueer: A Queer Companion to the Complete Works of Shakespeare*, ed. by Madhavi Menon (Durham, N.C. and London: Duke University Press, 2011), pp.376-384.

Spivak, Gayatri Chakravorty, "The Rani of Sirmur", in *Europe and its Others, Vol. 1: Proceedings of the Essex Conference on the Sociology of Literature, July 1984*, ed. by Francis Barker and others (Colchester: University of Essex, 1985), pp.128-151.

Stallybrass, Peter, "Worn Worlds: Clothes and Identity on the Renaissance Stage", in *Subject and Object in Renaissance Culture*, ed. by Margreta de Grazia, Maureen Quilligan and Peter Stallybrass (Cambridge: Cambridge University Press, 1996), pp.289-320.

Stock, Brian, "The Middle Ages as Subject and Object: Romantic Attitudes and Academic Medievalism", *New Literary History*, 5 (1974), 527-547.

Stretter, Robert, "Flowers of Friendship: Amity and Tragic Desire in *The Two Noble Kinsmen*", *English Literary Renaissance*, 47:2, (2017), 270-300.

Strohm, Paul, "Storie, Spelle, Geste, Romaunce, Tragedie: Generic Distinctions in the Middle English Troy Narratives", in *Speculum*, 46 (1971), 348-359.

–, *Theory and the Premodern Text* (Minneapolis: University of Minnesota Press, 2000).

Strong, Roy, *The Cult of Elizabeth: Elizabethan Portraiture and Pageantry* (London: Thames and Hudson, 1987).

Summit, Jennifer and David Wallace, "Rethinking Periodization", *Journal of Medieval and Early Modern Studies*, 37:3 (2007), 447-451.

Summit, Jennifer, *Memory's Library: Medieval Books in Early Modern England* (Chicago: University of Chicago Press, 2008).

Theatre and Religion: Lancastrian Shakespeare, ed. by Richard Dutton (Manchester: Manchester University Press, 2003).

Thompson, Anne, *Shakespeare's Chaucer: A Study in Literary Origins* (Liverpool: Liverpool University Press, 1978).

Traub, Valerie, *The Renaissance of Lesbianism in Early Modern England* (Cambridge: Cambridge University Press, 2002).

Wagoner, Michael M., "The Dramaturgical Space of Solo Scenes in Fletcher and Shakespeare, or a Study of the Jailer's Daughter", *Shakespeare Bulletin*, 35:1 (2017), 97-118.

White, Hayden V., *Tropics of Discourse: Essays in Cultural Criticism* (Baltimore: Johns Hopkins University Press, 1978).

Yachnin, Paul, "Shakespeare's Problem Plays and the Drama of His Time: *Troilus and Cressida, All's Well That Ends Well, Measure for Measure*", in *A Companion to Shakespeare's Works, Volume IV: The Poems, Problem Comedies, Late Plays*, ed. by Richard Dutton and Jean E. Howard (Oxford: Blackwell, 2003, 2006), pp.46-68.